TEACHING
FROM
THE
H·E·A·R·T

TEACHING FROM THE H·E·A·R·T

Theology and Educational Method

Mary Elizabeth Mullino Moore

Trinity Press International
Harrisburg, Pennsylvania

TEACHING FROM THE HEART
Theology and Educational Method

Trinity Press International is a Continuum imprint.

Scripture quotations unless otherwise noted are from the Revised Standard
Version of the Bible, copyright © 1946, 1952, and 1971 by the Division of
Christian Education of the National Council of Churches.

Cover design by Corey Kent.

Library of Congress Cataloging-in-Publication Data

Moore, Mary Elizabeth, 1945–
    Teaching from the heart : theology and educational method / Mary
Elizabeth Mullino Moore.
        p.   cm.
    Includes bibliographical references and index.
√ ISBN 1-56338-253-9 (alk. paper)
    1. Process theology. 2. Education—Methodology. I. Title.
BT83.6.M66   1998
230'.071—dc21   98-35795
                                                                    CIP

Printed in the United States of America

03   04   05   06   07   10   9   8   7   6   5   4   3   2

to
Allen Joe Moore
Life Companion and Colleague

CONTENTS

ACKNOWLEDGMENTS

"If Pigs Could Fly…." Copyright © Julie Roberts-Front. Used by permission.

Excerpts from *The Aims of Education and Other Essays* by Alfred North Whitehead. Copyright © 1929 by Macmillan Publishing Company, renewed 1957 by Evelyn Whitehead. Reprinted by permission of Simon & Schuster.

Excerpts from *Process and Reality: An Essay in Cosmology* by Alfred North Whitehead. Copyright © 1929 Macmillan Publishing Company, renewed 1957 by Evelyn Whitehead. Reprinted by permission of Simon & Schuster.

Excerpts from "Those Who Saw the Star" in *Threatened with Resurrection: Prayers and Poems from an Exiled Guatemalan* by Julia Esquivel. Copyright © 1982 Brethren Press, Elgin, IL 60120. Reprinted by permission.

Excerpts from *Concept of Nature* by Alfred North Whitehead. Copyright © 1971 Cambridge University Press. Reprinted by permission.

Excerpt from *Zorba the Greek* by Nilos Kazantzakia. Copyright © 1952 Simon & Schuster, renewed 1981. Reprinted by permission of Simon & Schuster.

Excerpts from *Science and the Modern World* by Alfred North Whitehead. Copyright © 1925 Macmillan Publishing Company, renewed 1953 by Evelyn Whitehead. Reprinted by permission of Simon & Schuster.

Excerpt from *To Know As We Are Known: A Spirituality of Education* by Parker J. Palmer. Copyright © 1983. Reprinted by permission of HarperCollins, Publishers, Inc.

PREFACE TO THE NEW EDITION

The heart of this book is teaching from the heart—a dream that points to the *quality* of teaching. The dream is one in which teachers are called to in-spire, breathing spirit into all that they do and sharing spirit with all whom they teach. Teachers are called to receive and give, receive and give, receive and give the Spirit of Life.

Since I first completed this book, I have had the privilege of talking with religious teachers, faculty in university departments of religion, faculty in professional schools, and religious educators in many settings about the heart of this book. My greatest delights have come in conversations where people have shared their own delight in a book that encourages teaching from the heart and integrates across disciplines. A group of professors of nursing saw the book as speaking to the kind of education they most want to practice and the kind of nursing practice they want to encourage in their students. One person stopped me at a large meeting where she had read my nametag and said, "Your book has become the bridge that has allowed my colleagues and I to talk across our various religious disciplines and to work together in planning and teaching." Others have shared with me that they use the book in interdisciplinary courses because it is a truly interdisciplinary book. Teachers of religious education have largely used the book to focus on qualities and approaches in teaching.

TEACHING FROM THE HEART—REVISITED

My excitement for this subject continues to grow. I am especially hopeful that the Hebrew understanding of heart, amplified by the metaphorical understanding of the heartbeat at the center of the human body, will suggest the importance of re-envisioning teaching as a dynamic center of religious life. I am more convinced than ever that teaching from the heart has to do with re-vering the Spirit of life and all of God's creation. Thus, the quest for organic theology and organic educational practice continues. To that end, I delight in this opportunity to revisit the themes of the last chapter, adding some poetic and narrative reflections to the proposals offered in that chapter for educational practice.

Re-vering the Spirit of Life

The ground of teaching is re-vering the Spirit and Source of life—a reverence expressed in the poem "Spirit."

Spirit—
I know the touch of wind
   blowing over the mountains;
Spirit—
I know the chill of crisp
   breezes in Autumn;
Spirit—
I know the refreshing calm of air
   moving on a hot day;
Spirit—
I know the wonder of love
   that is larger than those who love;
Spirit—
I know the power of grace
   moving in anger and in sadness;
Spirit, spirit—
I know your movements,
   but I will never KNOW you;
You are SPIRIT!

Re-vering the Other

Re-vering the other can be done in simple ways. Once, I spoke in a conference where I knew very few people. Entering the conference room on the first day, I saw an old friend; she was greeting everyone in sight. After we chatted a bit, I asked my friend if I could sit with her during the first session. She said, "Of course; if you stick with me, you will meet everyone here before this meeting is over." As the session closed, my friend leaned over and said to me, "For the rest of the time, wherever I go, you may go." My friend was teaching from the heart, extending hospitality in such a way that she was re-vering me and welcoming me into her community.

Such re-vering of the other can be difficult if the other is different from ourselves, whether in race, gender, social class, religion, or sexual orientation. To re-vere others is to respect and appreciate differences, to celebrate uniqueness, as expressed in "Clouds":

Watching the clouds of the sky,
They look ever so much like yesterday's clouds,
But they are not the same;
They move gently or swirl wildly,
They turn from white to gray to black and back again,
Sometimes they even disappear from sight.
Broadly speaking, you can identify different kinds of clouds—
Cumulus, cirrus, stratus, altostratus—
Categories of clouds for scientific purposes;
But oh how little do those categories tell you
About the clouds that pass today.
Categories are great deceivers—
Good for simple teaching and communication,
But ever so deceptive when it comes to knowing clouds.

Re-vering Oneself

Re-vering oneself is also important to teaching from the heart. The being of the teacher is part of what we teach. Consider "I, the Teacher":

I have wanted all of my life to be a teacher;
Yet here I am teaching and fretting
That I am not up to the task—
Not smart enough,
Not charismatic enough,

Not articulate enough,
Not at all wise.

And yet, I have to teach—
You and I have experiences of God that are meant to be shared;
I know ideas and practices that I want you to know,
And visions of hope that I want you to see;
I can glimpse gifts in you that I want to encourage,
And sense the deep inner knowing that is yours to explore;
I know the possibility that we can face the world together,
   Know it together,
      Act in it for better,
         And celebrate the wisdom of ages past
            And ages to come!

Re-vering Relationships

Re-vering relationships can be pleasant or painful. It has to do with building community, reconciling hurts, celebrating joys, and responding to movements deep within relationships, even those that are barely visible on the surface. Consider "My Body Fills with Tears":

My body fills with tears
And they will not overflow;
They pour into my body—
   through the veins
   that carry salty tears to my heart;
My heart receives them
And sends the tears
   to every cell of my crying body.

My body fills with tears
But no moment opens
   to let them flow;
No one is present with me
   to receive them,
And I hurt too much to cry.

My body fills with tears
And I walk and talk

And teach and lead
   with tears living within me.
They will not flow
   because no one can understand:
No one can see what I see
   or touch what I touch;
I am alone—
But so many are standing around
   that I cannot cry.
My body fills with tears!

Re-vering relationships has to do with discerning and respecting the internal cries of others. Such re-vering is not motivated by curiosity or pity, nor by naive expectations that we can remove others' pain or take care of their problems. Such re-vering is, rather, to honor every aspect of relationships, nourishing the strength in these relationships so they can contribute to the wellbeing of the people involved and the larger community.

Re-vering the Process of Education

A few weeks ago, my class was to discuss a book that we had collectively moved to a new place on the printed syllabus. I had announced it twice so that the class members would remember to read the correct book. On the day of the seminar, only half of the class had read the book; this became obvious as the discussion began. After a short time, one class member (Jane) said that she had a problem. She had forgotten to read the book, and she was completely unprepared. At this moment, I had a fresh reminder that what we say in teaching has minimal influence; the decision to shift class assignments was not remembered. I responded to Jane: "Well, you have been prepared for every class all semester, and everyone is entitled to mistakes; you can depend on others to help you understand the book." Then, I checked with others in the class and discovered who had read the book and who had not. Because of plans for the following week, we could not delay the discussion; I encouraged the class to depend on those who had read the book to help everyone else understand. We had a good discussion, after all.

   The story continues. Later in the semester, I had a problem. I planned to return papers to the class on a particular day, but I had numerous

extra meetings at the school and three unexpected writing deadlines, which led me to work night and day to the point of exhaustion. I did not have the papers graded, and I apologized to the class. One of the students said: "I remember a few weeks ago when Jane did not have her reading done; you told her that she was always prepared for class, and everyone is entitled to make a mistake. We should tell you the same—you are always prepared for class, and we can live without our papers." At that moment, Jane also spoke up, "Grace! You can't beat it!" This simple story leads into the heart of re-vering the education process—Grace! You can't beat it!

Re-vering the Ordinary

The ordinary is embodied in every moment. In one such moment, I was aware of how easily ordinary moments are passed by and ignored. Consider "Passing by the Sea":

They stepped up and looked—
How calm the sea!
Yet only a moment before
The water hurled against the rocks
And washed the stones with fury.
They walked on
And never knew.

A similar theme arises in "Something to See." I wrote both of these poems when visiting Lobos Point in Northern California. The poems were stirred by my sadness that people (myself included) rarely pause to honor the ordinary, even when on holiday.

She called to her family,
"Hurry! Let's go see the sea lions;
There is nothing here to see.
Come on!
Aren't you coming?"
Reluctantly her children leave the rocks
    by the sea.
They are off to the next stop.
I wonder if she will find anything there to see.

Another poem was stirred by a very different moment, one in which my husband and I visited some elderly friends. A perfectly ordinary visit with them moved us to gratitude for life, expressed in "Souls Soar."

Souls soar in the presence of beauty,
And in the soaring,
They meet and touch
Until even the hues of beauty deepen.

Souls soar in the presence of humor,
For humor wrestles with demons
And blesses the tragic and trivial
With the spirit of laughter.

Souls soar in the presence of compassion,
For being together in passion
Is being together in suffering and joy—
Being together in the fullness of time.

Our souls soar in moments with you—
Moments of stunning beauty
And quiet humor
And com-passion for LIFE!

I wish for the readers of this book many moments of knowing the extraordinary power of the ordinary. Teaching from the heart is teaching that savors and honors those moments, allowing them to reveal Love and Truth, Justice and Beauty.

REFLECTIONS AND RESPONSES

In some ways, the first edition of this book was ahead of its time; certainly, the discourse on educational method has escalated since I first completed the book in 1991. Discussions of university teaching and religious education have converged more than ever, and a new journal, *Teaching Theology and Religion,* has emerged. Furthermore, the search for creative approaches to teaching has led to educational experiments in religious communities, public schools, and colleges and universities. My only disappointments in reading responses to my book have been moments when readers seem to have missed the heart. Perhaps I can remedy that by urging readers to pay particular attention to the last chapter and the last two sections of Chapters 2 through 6. I urge this because the value of the book lies in the fruits of dialogue between educational method and theology.

Some reviewers thought that my choice of only one theological perspective, process theology, was unfortunate. To this critique, I would like to respond. The dream of this book is to engage people in significant conversation at the intersection of theology and educational method and to emerge from those conversations with a transformed view of both. The purpose is not to convert people to one method or one theological framework, but to tap the rich resources of methods that presently exist, bringing them together in one place, and to propose reformulations of theology and educational method into even greater fullness.

Ironically, people in the process theological community have not given this book a great deal of attention because I interact with diverse worldviews and I address a "low-class," practical discipline of education. People in the educational community value education but would have had me choose five theological perspectives, or at least, a perspective that is more socially acceptable within Christian religious communities. In truth, the choice of five educational methods does introduce diverse theologies. Some of these methods are linked explicitly with particular perspectives, such as existential theologies (in the case of incarnational teaching and phenomenological method) or liberation theologies (in the case of liberative teaching and conscientization). Likewise, feminist-womanist-mujerista theologies provide threads that weave many chapters and ideas together.

In light of my responses, then, what are the issues? I suspect that one is process theology itself, a theology that is difficult to understand and is often dismissed with misunderstandings, as well as with honest disagreements. I suspect a more fundamental issue is at stake, however, namely the dialogical method of the book itself. Theology is engaged here, but not simply as content to be taught or foundations for practice. It is a *partner* in dialogue. Some other books are very helpful in presenting theological perspectives as content or foundations for education; however, this is a different sort of book. *Teaching from the Heart* is intended to probe the depths of one perspective for its potential; it is also intended to wrestle with questions and possibilities that arise at the convergence of perspectives. It is not an either/or book, urging a choice among perspectives. The intent is to engage readers in a quest for fresh insights, emerging where diverse theologies and methods meet.

My greatest hope does not lie in abstract theological and educational formulations. My hope is that this book will make a difference in our ways of teaching in the church and other religious and educational institutions. Educational practice is important because it has potential to connect people more deeply with God, the human community, and the natural world. What is particularly hopeful is that these relationships will contribute to the justice, peace, and wellbeing of God's creation. If this book makes a small contribution to that hope, it has been worthwhile.

I look forward to the dialogue that follows re-publication of this book; I expect to learn much. Even more important, however, is the possibility that the dialogues that arise will empower all of us to engage more fully in teaching from the heart, thus, to participate more fully in the heart of God.

Mary Elizabeth Mullino Moore
Claremont, California
April 1998

PREFACE

Day by day I know more of the dangers of being a multidisciplinary person in academia. For one thing I have more than one discipline in which to read and stay abreast. I have more than one set of colleagues. And I have more than one set of expectations placed on me. I fit in many places, but I do not fully fit in any one place.

I began my higher education studies in psychology with a B.A. and M.A. This discipline stays with me as I teach psychology of religion and as I do everything else that I do. I then lived and worked in the church for a number of years. This, too, stays with me as I continue to participate in the life of the church, as I teach ministry studies, and as I do everything else that I do. In the next season of my life I studied systematic theology and education, and these stay with me as I teach in both areas and as I do everything else that I do.

But the multidisciplinary background is not so clearly an advantage as it may seem. I am sometimes viewed with disdain by theologians who see me as "just a religious educator." I am sometimes viewed with suspicion by educators who think I am too theological. Faculty colleagues advise me to write in theology to enhance my status in academia. At the same time church folk and education professionals advise me to write practical education tracts. I stand in the middle, wondering what my contribution should be.

To these confessions, I want to add that I write as a woman in what is still largely a male academic profession, and yet I am a woman in religious education, a field viewed even by many women in the academic and church professions as a stereotyped, second-class woman's field. I write as a woman who fills female quotas on church and professional boards. I write as a woman who is angry about androcentric biases in religious and educational institutions. I write as a woman who loves to teach and to be friend and colleague with other faculty and students. I write as a woman who enjoys the companionship of marriage and the joys and responsibilities of parenthood and grandparenthood. I write as a woman who, as inheritor of the supermom expectations, is overly conscientious in everything I do; thus, I always have more than enough to do.

Having made these confessions, I am not surprised that I am in the process of writing three different book manuscripts. But what I really want to confess is why I have chosen to complete this one first. I think that will help explain why I think this book is important. I complete it partly as a rebellion against those who advise me to write in theology for the sake of status, and also partly as a rebellion against those who advise me to write an educational tract for the sake of popularity. I write this book because *I think it needs to be written*.

One of the advantages of being a woman who has come into teaching through a long, circuitous route is that hopes for status and popularity have never flown high in my life world. My hopes have been gradually replaced by disillusionment and, finally, by some degree of freedom from the boundaries of such hopes. I like that freedom.

Another advantage of being a woman who was taught by my family and culture to live in close personal relationships is that I enjoy rich primary relationships with family and friends. However much these have been pushed and reshaped by movements toward liberation, these relationships nourish me and give me some degree of courage. I like that courage.

With the measure of freedom and courage I enjoy, I launch into writing a book that is itself multidisciplinary, like me. It probably will fit in many places of dialogue, but like me it probably will not fit clearly in any one place. My hope is that it will be a contribution to people who work in theology, in education, and in both. My hope is that the book itself will contribute to multidisciplinary dialogue. My hope is that others will experience it as a book that needed to be written and will share some of the vitality that I have experienced in writing it.

My thanks go to Martin Seeley and Robert Rebur, the director and former director of the Thompson Center, and to Richard Tombaugh, formerly director of the Educational Center. These two St. Louis institutions cosponsored a seminar in Process Theology and Education in January 1986. This book began as lectures I prepared for that seminar, and it was informed by dialogue with seminar participants and the other seminar leader, Schubert Ogden. I am most grateful to all of these people for the opportunity to put these thoughts together and for the discussions that have reformed the original presentations.

One of my earliest dilemmas in writing this manuscript was communicating the importance to others. Four people were especially important to me as I struggled with that question. Sharon Parks encouraged me when I most needed a mentor. Conversations with Marjorie Suchocki about process theology, the church, and theological education have deepened and enlivened my work. To James Wall I posed the question, "How can I convince people that this work is important?" His reply to me was, "What are you mad about?" I have worked on that question ever since. The fourth person was Jack Verheyden. Though standing outside of both process and feminist theology, he understood what I was doing; from the beginning, he expressed conviction about the importance of this work. In the last rounds of revision, he asked me another critical question, "What do you stand against; what do you want to change?" He called forth convictions from deep inside me so I could be more explicit about how I want to change the world. And I *do* want this book to make a difference!

I owe a hearty thanks to the Center for Process Studies at the School of Theology at Claremont. The center sponsored a conference to discuss an earlier draft of this book, and I received enormous help from the multiple responses offered in the dialogue. The responses were illuminating, and the book is much stronger as a result. Special thanks go to Nancy Howell, David Griffin, and John Cobb for planning the conference and responding extensively to the manuscript, and thanks to other formal respondents: Randy Litchfield, Kathi Breazeale, Philip Bashor, William Beardslee, Jack Verheyden, Frank Rogers, and John Sweeney. Thanks also to Christelle Estrada who responded helpfully to chapter 5 in another center-sponsored dialogue.

In a more general way I owe thanks to the communities who raise the questions that I address in this book. In hundreds of conversations with teachers and religious educators, I have heard recurring pleas: What can we do within existing institutions to humanize and communicate the holy through our work? How can we effect change in the church and in the world? How can we teach more effectively?

What difference does our teaching make? I am grateful for these questions and for the wrestling that we together have done. I have learned much, and these conversations have shaped the book.

Another arena for important wrestling has been the proliferation of work in feminist theology and methodology over the past decade. The feminist and womanist movements have unearthed major biases in theology and education that must be taken seriously. Through many conversations, books, and formal lectures and seminars, I have met sisters who share my concerns, who see the same biases, and who offer provocative analyses. These conversations have made me all the more aware of my anger and my hopes for theology and education.

One other arena for wrestling has been the Association of Process Philosophers of Education, who have provided a forum for probing the possibilities in process philosophy for education. Robert Brumbaugh has carried on a lively conversation with me via the mails, and I have benefited much from conversations with Grace Evans, Malcolm Evans, and Philip Bashor.

Very specifically, I could not have conceivably completed this book without considerable technical assistance from research assistants John Sweeney, Vernon Jahnke, and Kathi Breazeale, and without the secretarial and computer assistance of Virginia Hodges, Candace Lansberry, Stephanie Graham, Linda Hipskind, and Randy Litchfield. I am also very grateful for the fine work Kim Rogers and Terri Reynolds Litchfield did on the index. Michael West and Lois Torvik of Fortress Press have been unusually encouraging and helpful at every turn of this manuscript, and I am very grateful.

One person has pushed me to the limits of my ability and to a refinement of my ideas that even I did not think possible. John Cobb has been mentor-colleague-friend. He has read more than one draft of most chapters and has taken my work very seriously. He has responded honestly, critically, and appreciatively.

Thanks also to my mother, Elizabeth Heaton Mullino, who has always lived full-heartedly and passed that legacy to me.

And to my children I owe much of my passion for theology and education. I have lived with Cliff and Rebecca through their struggles and victories, and I have marveled at their capacity to learn and to teach me. I have also learned much from Glenda, Joyce, and Nan as they engage in the education of their own children.

Finally, my husband, Allen J. Moore, has been colleague and companion *par excellence*. He has discussed the issues and the book with me for the five years of its birthing. He has wrestled with me, evoked ideas, debated, and encouraged. To him, with much appreciation, I dedicate this book.

To all of my immediate and extended family members, friends, and communities, I owe much of my passion for a world made new—a world in which theology fosters life and teaching is from the heart.

—*Mary Elizabeth Mullino Moore*

1
PASSION ABOUT METHODOLOGY

T his book is an invitation to passion—*passion about theology and educational method*. The passion is for theology and education to stand in relationship, to speak to one another, and to be re-formed by one another.

Of course, the relationship should be obvious. At least within religious communities, no one would dare to say that theology and education are independent of one another. But the relationship that seems so obvious to some is often deeply buried, masked, or ignored so that theologians and educators act as if the relationship were not even there. What a pity! We lose interesting topics of conversation; but even worse, theology remains little affected by educational practice, and educational practice is little affected by theological reflection.

Surely systematic theologians care deeply about how their reflections on faith interact with people's lives in the learning community and how they fit, or do not fit, with what people do when they gather in those communities. Surely educators with religious sensitivities care deeply about how their practice draws from theology and how seriously their experiences in communities of learning are taken by people engaged in theological reflection. If theologians and educators did not care about such things, then theologians would not become so angry about the lack of theological seriousness in educational practice, and educators would not become so angry about the lack of theological interest in the issues of their work.

Despite the overlapping concerns between systematic theologians and educators, the disciplinary boundaries are still felt. Specializing tendencies keep people on their own side of those boundaries. Both in academia and in religious communities, people expect different kinds of contributions from people on the different sides of the divide. Educators are expected to be concerned with growth and formation; theologians, with truth and dogma. Ironically, the theological statements of religious communities have often emerged for the sake of teaching. The Torah, Didache, and Apostles' Creed were all modes of communicating faith in order to teach.

The second passion of this book is a *passion for organic teaching and organic theology*. One dream is for the art of teaching to be practiced in such an organic way that people are connected with themselves, with one another, with social systems, with the earth, and with transcendent reality. The other dream is for the art of theology to be practiced in such an organic way that theological reflection touches and connects all dimensions of life. No metaphor is fully adequate in itself, but the metaphor of organism promises a connective vision of teaching and theology that calls attention to the reality of relationships; thus, it encourages the nurture of healthy relationships and the disruption of sick, abusive, and oppressive relationships.

The very word *organic* connotes the natural world in which everything is related to everything else. Human beings are part of that world; we exist in a web of relationships. Cultural symbols, social structures, the geography of the land, and close personal relationships all influence who we are. The word *organic* suggests various metaphors from the natural world, such as the metaphor of a body or an ecological system. These metaphors are very promising for education. They offer a much-needed alternative to the mechanistic metaphors that have dominated in the last two decades, such as the technological metaphors that give rise to stress on input-output and on goals and objectives.[1]

The yearning for organic teaching seems unrealistic when stated so boldly. Yet the passion is very real; it is often expressed by persons

---

[1] I am joined by many others in seeking alternatives for mechanistic images of teaching. See particularly the reconceptualists' writing in William Pinar, ed., *Heightened Consciousness, Cultural Revolution, and Curriculum Theory* (Berkeley: McCutchan, 1974); Pinar, ed., *Curriculum Theorizing* (Berkeley: McCutchan, 1975).

who teach or guide the educational life of schools and religious communities. It is expressed by women who experience alienation in the often male-formed systems of education; these women insist on more respect for human agency and meaning and more appreciation for resistance in educational systems.[2] It is expressed by cultural groups for whom organic living is natural, and compartmentalized education seems unnatural.[3] It is expressed in charters for universities, in Protestant denominational statements about Christian education, in the Vatican II documents regarding Roman Catholic education, and in charters for Jewish schools and universities. The yearning is actually expressed more broadly than this, though with variations on the theme. In public schools in the United States, for example, the hope for more organic education is often expressed in public documents and in the pleas of teachers, principals, and superintendents. The language of theology is not used directly in public education, but educators express concern about the worldview underlying educational practice and about the holistic growth of students.

The yearning for organic teaching is so broadly expressed, but it is so rarely practiced! Why? In part, organic teaching means different things to different people. The history of the word *organic* has sometimes included more hegemonic visions of communal relationship (in which one group or view dominates), and sometimes more conflictual visions (in which different groups or views live together in tension). The use of organic here does include cooperation and unity within the organic system, but it also includes conflict and disruption.[4] The unity of the organism is not based in uniformity. It includes working together as a unified community and also heeding the lone voice that cries out in pain or anger, even when the lone voice disrupts the sense of unity and movement. Both kinds of movement are part of organic systems, and both are important in the educational process.

---

[2]Weiler has reviewed studies of gender and class issues in teaching. She also points to race as a major factor in raising questions of power and social change. See Kathleen Weiler, *Women Teaching for Change: Gender, Class and Power* (South Hadley, Mass.: Bergin & Garvey, 1988).

[3]See, for example, All Africa Conference of Churches, "The Village Vision: A Vision for Christian Education in Africa," Church Related Institutions, Dossier V, Paper 2; *Harvard Educational Review*, Special Issue: Community-Based Education, vol. 60, no. 1 (February 1990).

[4]Weiler, *Women Teaching*, 52–55. Weiler points out, for example, that feminist teaching highlights conflictual dynamics, including both resistance and counter-hegemony.

Decisions must be made about what dynamics of relationship are especially important in a particular situation. These are made in light of the total complex of relationships and the context in which teaching takes place. These decisions must not be made by the power elite alone because the elite will almost always be willing to sacrifice minority and less powerful voices. The many voices of students, teachers, administrators, pastors, and the broad community need to be heard; organic relationships need to be nurtured and re-formed and revolutionized accordingly.

Another passion of this book is a *passion for educational theory and practice to stand in relationship.* Surely they already do, for every educational theory that exists has been informed by the theorist's educational experience and every theory has implications for practice. Also, every educational practice has theoretical assumptions underlying it, whether or not these are ever expressed. When the theory-practice connections are ignored, educational method is reduced to a bag of techniques, and theory becomes so abstract as to be irrelevant to teaching. The passion of this book is to name the interconnections so that self-conscious conversation can follow, and transformation of theory and practice can follow.

The bifurcation of theory and practice in education is ironic, given the obvious connections. The fact remains, however, that practitioners do not trust theorists, and theorists do not trust practitioners. The communication gap among those who focus more on one or the other is so large that it is often expressed as disdain. In such a situation, practioners are not sharing their practical wisdom with theorists; nor are theorists sharing their theoretical wisdom with practitioners. The further irony, of course, is that no one is ever a pure practitioner or theorist. Unfortunately, the communication gap can even exist within a person. Very often, people practice the art of teaching without any regard to their own theories of education, or they spin educational theories without drawing any insight from their teaching.

Still another passion that stirs in this book is a *passion for connections in the educational enterprise,* connections among public school educators, community educators, and religious educators, and among people in children's education, higher education, and continuing education. The many and various educators share the common vocation of humanization—the vocation of supporting human life and the quality of that life. Unfortunately, the common calling is often pushed into the background or ignored, subordinated to the particular purposes in a particular educational setting. Of course, these particular purposes are vital, but the common vocation of humanization is also vital to the future of the world. The vocation requires that we share our wisdom and concerns across educational settings.

As might be expected, no book born of passion can be without hope. This book is written on the bridge between the lands of educational method and theology, and hope seems to flow from both lands. The lands are really parts of one whole, artificially divided by a culture that puts everything in categories and an academic structure that reinforces the categories. Standing on the bridge, I can become very angry about the separations that make the bridge necessary. After all, the waters beneath the bridge and the land beneath the waters already connect the two lands. But standing on the bridge, I can also become hopeful about the interchanges made possible by having a bridge to travel. The bridge connects the parts so that they can function as an organic whole. The bridge itself does not resolve the splits among academic disciplines and among communities of educators and theologians. It is simply a pathway for communication and for greater recognition of the connections that already exist. Perhaps people will use this bridge to travel from one land to the other and back home again. Perhaps they will discover parts of themselves already shaped in each land and even on the bridge. Perhaps they will be different after they make the journey, and their work will be reshaped.

PASSIONS TURN TO HOPES

The dream of this book, then, is for a more holistic vision of education. The hope is to put forth new visions of educational method enriched and enlarged by theology. The hope, too, is to put forth new visions of theology enriched and enlarged by educational theory and practice. Issues arise in both arenas, and the dialogue between education and theology can offer much-needed insight for both.

Because of wide interest in organic teaching, and because these interests are often connected with theological or spiritual questions, I have chosen to engage in this search with a broad audience of conversation partners in mind. The search can bear much fruit, the seeds of which can grow in almost any educational setting. Some will

grow most easily in religious communities, and some will grow, even more specifically, in Christian religious communities. My hope in writing the book, however, is that the insights will grow in many places, according to what is fitting in each place. Further, my hope is that the insights will be more than new answers to educational and theological questions. My hope is that new questions will result and new searchers will join the quest for organic teaching and organic theology.

In some ways this book is a new venture, but in other ways people have been on this quest for a long time. For this reason, the book itself is a dialogue with persons who have been engaged in shaping organic approaches to theology and teaching. The book draws particularly on movements within process theology, a self-consciously organic view of theology, and on educational methods that have forged new possibilities in organic teaching.

Where the book is, indeed, a new venture is in its attempt to bring these theories and practices together. In so doing, it is a work in practical theology, an attempt to bring the theory and practice of theology into dialogue with the theory and practice of education. This book will be an adventure into new ways of reflecting on theology and education, and both enterprises will be richer as a result.

Process theology and the five selected educational methods are not the only dialogue partners that could be chosen, but these are significant ones. The five methods are themselves attempts to practice education organically. Process theology is chosen because it is organic through and through; in fact, it could easily be designated as organic theology rather than process theology.

The educational methods studied in this book are case study, gestalt, phenomenology, narrative, and conscientization. Each in its own way attempts to make organic connections among different dimensions of life. Case study focuses on the connections between practice and theory. Gestalt focuses on the way in which people organize a variety of elements into a whole, such as the way they make sense of seemingly disparate beliefs or images. Phenomenological method attempts to help people make connections with the empirical realities around them and with their internal meanings. Narrative connects people with the experiences of others through their stories. Stories themselves weave life experience into an organic whole that connects past, present, and future and connects characters and life events.

Finally, conscientization focuses on the influence of social structures and the ways by which people become conscious of those structures and instrumental in revolutionizing them.

The hopes in exploring these methods are filled with challenge. Among those challenges are to articulate the methods so that they might be chosen and followed more self-consciously, and to revise them in light of an organic view of the world so that they might be even more helpful in the practice of organic teaching. The methods are in some ways compatible with one another and with process theology; in other ways, they stand in dramatic tension. The purpose of this book is not to resolve all of the tensions but to promote a dialogue that stirs mutual critique and reform.

Challenges also exist for process, or organic, theology. Process theology is often criticized as being too abstract and remote from everyday problems. This is an ironic criticism to address to a philosophical system intended to be concrete and practical, but the complex technical language used by Alfred North Whitehead, the "father" of process thought, has been part of the heritage of process theology. This language often seems far removed from everyday, conversational English.

The language gap may represent a dilemma larger than the words themselves, however. One reason for the technical language is that ordinary English (Whitehead's native language) expresses a particular view of reality. The view is a picture of the world made up of unchanging and separable substances. Whitehead and others after him propose a different view, and they cannot express that view without some changes in ordinary language. Inevitably, what does not fit easily into common words and habits of thought will seem abstract, even if the process thinkers claim to be concrete. The problem of language, then, is also a problem of ideas, and process ideas fit strangely with many assumed patterns of thought about God and the world.

Whatever justification may be given for the apparent abstractness of process theology, another serious limitation is lurking. Process theologians have focused on theory rather than on practice. They have approached practice from theory rather than theory from practice. This is no more true of process theologians than of many others in intellectual discourse, but their approach is subject to criticism from those who would emphasize the importance of seeking knowledge from practice. Bernard Lonergan and David Tracy have proposed theological methods of drawing knowledge from practice, and black, feminist, and Latin American liberation theologians have shown the powerful effects of that kind of work. Such work offers a significant challenge to process theologians because it calls for a shift in method within process theology itself.

Process theologians have continued to build from the metaphysics of Alfred North Whitehead and Charles Hartshorne, applying process ideas to various fields of thought and practice. The challenge now is for these theologians to reflect on human experience and practice, and to create a dialogue in which both process theory and existing practices will be informed and transformed.

THE TASK LOOMS LARGE

The task outlined here is considerable because it is not the easiest or most typical way to proceed. The more common approaches to relate theological systems and education are (1) to recognize theology as the content to be taught, having little or no influence on educational method; (2) to base an educational program on what theologians have said about educational practice with little regard to their larger systems of thought; and (3) to derive a few basic principles from a theological system that are then applied to the educational enterprise. Each of these has merit, but none is sufficient in itself. All of these approaches have been used to relate process theory to education, and the resulting work has been important to the field of education, particularly religious education.

One of the principal ways process theology has been related to education is as *content to be taught*. Gloria Durka and Joanmarie Smith have introduced very clearly the strength of the view of God in process theology. In *Modeling God* they present some specific ideas about God offered in a process view, and they point to some of the reasons why proposing these ideas in teaching can enhance human growth.[5]

Others have emphasized content as well, especially Randolph Crump Miller. He has done interpretive work to make content more

---

[5]Gloria Durka and Joanmarie Smith, *Modeling God: Religious Education for Tomorrow* (New York: Paulist Press, 1976).

accessible and understandable to educators and other persons who have no previous study in process thought.[6] The work of the Center for Process Studies associated with the School of Theology at Claremont (California) has been similarly oriented in its Faith and Process program to providing clear and accessible content to be used in teaching and other areas of ministry.

The advantages of offering such content are obvious to those who see promise in the process vision of reality. Particularly compelling are the idea that God participates in every moment of reality, luring every event to God's purposes; the idea that all of reality is in process so that nothing is fixed and unchanging; and the idea that all of reality is interconnected so that nothing can be viewed as separate from the whole. These ideas will be discussed further in later chapters, but the hope here is to communicate the vitality of these attempts to offer process theology as content for teaching. The adequacy of the educational enterprise is certainly affected greatly by the formal content that is communicated.

The second major way process thought has been related to education is especially common in general education. Attention has been given to *Whitehead's own philosophy of education in relation to educational practice*. Whitehead wrote several essays on the subject, and his major collection, *The Aims of Education*, is the basic text for this approach. Certain generative themes can be derived from this book and other writings, and these have proved fruitful for educational theory.[7] Some of the leaders of this enterprise have been Robert Brumbaugh, Joe Burnett, Harold Dunkel, Brian Hendley, and Nathaniel Lawrence.[8]

---

[6]Works that have been particularly oriented to offering study materials for broad audiences are Randolph Crump Miller, *The American Spirit in Theology* (Philadelphia: United Church Press, 1974); Miller, *The Language Gap and God* (Philadelphia: Pilgrim Press, 1970); Miller, *The Theory of Christian Education Practice* (Birmingham, Ala.: Religious Education Press, 1980). Miller does not limit himself to theology as content, particularly in *Theory of Christian Education*, but content does receive his primary attention. He notes ways in which content itself begins to offer some clues for educational emphases and practices.

[7]See Alfred North Whitehead, *The Aims of Education* (New York: Free Press, [1929] 1957); Whitehead, *The Organisation of Thought: Educational and Scientific* (Westport, Conn.: Greenwood Press, [London: 1917] 1975); Whitehead, *Science and the Modern World* (New York: [Macmillan, 1925] Free Press, 1967), esp. 193–208.

[8]See, for example, Robert S. Brumbaugh, *Whitehead, Process Philosophy, and Education* (Albany: State University of New York Press, 1982); Brumbaugh, "Whitehead's Educational Theory: Williams & Northgate, Two Supplementary Notes to the Aims of Education," *Educational Theory* 16 (July 1966): 215; Joe R. Burnett, "The Educational Phi-

One central theme in *Aims of Education* is Whitehead's concept of
the rhythm of education. Reflecting on British education in the early
1900s, Whitehead noted certain rhythmic patterns to learning: people
pass cyclically through three stages in learning a new subject matter.[9]
The basic idea is that people learn best when they begin a study in
a stage of romance, intrigued with novel facts and ideas. Many people
can remember, for example, their initial interest (even enthusiasm) in
being introduced to the times tables in mathematics. The next stage
is precision, in which learners focus on analyzing facts. This includes
the more disciplined process of memorizing the times tables and analyzing the different patterns of numbers. The third stage is generalization, in which learners synthesize the facts and ideas, generalizing
the knowledge to various situations. In this stage a person might
begin to use the times tables in concrete problem solving or in complex
multiplication problems.

The third way for relating process theology to education is to *derive
some basic principles from a theological system and apply them to the educational enterprise.* This has been done less extensively than the first
two, but one notable example was a 1973 symposium of articles in
Religious Education. Norman Pittenger, for example, derived certain
basic theological constructs about the dynamic quality of God, the
relational and organismic quality of the universe, the persuasive (rather than coercive) power of God, and the freedom of all creation. He
related these ideas to the practice of education.[10]

Joining in this enterprise are such theologians as Bernard Meland,
Schubert Ogden, and John Cobb who have been influenced by Whitehead and Hartshorne and who have lectured or written on the subject

---

losophy of Alfred North Whitehead" (Ann Arbor, Mich.: University Microfilms, 1958), Ph.D.
dissertation, New York University; Harold B. Dunkel, *Whitehead on Education* (Columbus:
Ohio State University Press, 1965); Brian P. Hendley, Dewey, Russell, *Whitehead: Philosophers as Educators* (Carbondale: Southern Illinois University Press, 1986); Nathaniel
Lawrence, *Alfred North Whitehead: A Primer of His Philosophy* (New York: Twayne, 1974);
Lawrence, "Nature and the Educable Self in Whitehead," *Educational Theory* 15 (July
1965): 205–16.

[9]Whitehead, "The Rhythm of Education," *The Aims of Education*, 15–28.

[10]Norman Pittenger, "Process Theology and Christian Education," *Religious Education*
68 (May–June 1973): 307–14. Other contributors to the symposium followed a similar
pattern of identifying features of process theology and applying them to religious
education. Included in the same issue were contributions from Randolph C. Miller,
"Whitehead and Religious Education," 315–22; Eugene Fontinell, "Pragmatism, Process
and Religious Education," 322–31; and Ewert H. Cousins, "Teilhard, Process Thought
and Religious Education," 331–38. Part of the same symposium was another article
published later: Terry Hokenson, "A Process Pedagogy for Christian Education," *Religious Education* 68 (Sept.–Oct. 1973): 595–607.

of education. Bernard Meland has addressed the area of higher education and framed the educational task in terms of forming appreciative consciousness, or a creative openness to the world of past, present, and future. The educational goal for Meland is grounded in assumptions about the power of human consciousness and the wholeness of time. In addition, Meland believes that education needs to proceed holistically, bringing together the critical and imaginative capacities, and the analytic and feeling dimensions of human life.[11] Schubert Ogden has described the educative task in terms of serving the purpose of creation and helping people enter into the creative process.[12] John Cobb, writing on theological education with Joseph Hough, accents the unification of Christian theological curriculum around Christian identity and the relation of the church to the world.[13] Cobb and Hough discuss connections among disciplines, between the church and world, and between theory and practice. Cobb writes from a process perspective, and Hough describes his perspective as Barthian in influence. These brief comments on a few theologians already suggest that a process theological analysis can cut many ways and can find common concerns with people in other theological perspectives.

These works taken together offer rich resources for education in many of its forms—general and religious, early and advanced. They form a background for the present work, but this work moves in a new direction. The purpose here is threefold: to focus on forms of educational method as they are currently understood and practiced, to focus on process theology as a theological system, and to begin a dialogue between educational method and theology that might transform both.

This venture will take current educational theory and practice more seriously than many others have done. Likewise, it will focus more broadly on process theology than many works based in Whitehead's educational philosophy. Finally, it will be based in an interactive approach to the material in which educational method will be subjected

---

[11]Bernard E. Meland, *Higher Education and the Human Spirit* (Chicago: University of Chicago Press, 1953).

[12]Schubert Ogden, "Christian Theology and the Task of Education" (Lecture presented at the Seminar in Process Theology and Education, the Thompson Center and the Educational Center, St. Louis, January 1986).

[13]Joseph C. Hough, Jr., and John B. Cobb, Jr., *Christian Identity and Theological Education* (Chico, Calif.: Scholars Press, 1985).

to the scrutiny of process theology and vice versa. It will not be a one-way application of process thought to education.

WHY PROCESS THEOLOGY?

This is a good question, and one answer has already been given: process theology is an organic theology. Another answer, undoubtedly, is my own appreciation for this perspective on God and God's relation to the world. On the other hand, the question is important also for those who do not share this appreciation or, perhaps, have not encountered process theology at all. Because process theology does offer a radically different perspective on the nature of God and the world and their interconnections, it has potential for offering new perspectives on education.

Alfred North Whitehead actually put forth a cosmology, a theory or story of the universe. From his work have come philosophers and theologians who have been labeled as process thinkers because of their assertions about the ongoing process of reality, over against commonly held views of the static or substantive nature of reality. This book will concentrate on the aspects of a process cosmology concerned with God and the world. The focus, however, will include broad aspects of Whitehead's philosophy, recognizing that process theology has philosophical roots and assertions. Because of the breadth of the system and its focus on relationships, growth, and change, process theology promises fruitful constructs to education.

Because Whitehead viewed God and the world as inseparable, the sacred and secular realms become difficult or impossible to separate within process thinking. For the purposes of this discussion, both general and religious education will be considered, with no attempt to make an emphatic distinction. The distinction can be made for other purposes, but the attention here is on education broadly conceived. The value in this is the recognition that discussions of God are relevant to general education and discussions of the world are relevant to religious education.

Whitehead's own attention was drawn into educational questions, and his work in this area was most provocative. As mentioned earlier, this book is not focused solely on Whitehead's explicit educational philosophy, but the fact that he had educational interests is interesting in itself. Some preliminary attention will be given here to Whitehead's educational philosophy to stir curiosity and introduce his educational thinking. Whitehead is often known by his quotable quotes, as the following discussion indicates.

On the question of relationships across time, Whitehead speaks of the unity of past, present, and future. The knowledge of the past is relevant to the present because it is contained in the present: "The only use of a knowledge of the past is to equip us for the present. . . . The present contains all that there is. It is holy ground: for it is the past, and it is the future."[14]

On the question of relationships among ideas, Whitehead offers a similar notion that ideas are not important in themselves, but only in relation to other ideas and human responses: "Ideas which are not utilised are positively harmful. By utilising an idea, I mean relating it to that stream, compounded of sense perceptions, feelings, hopes, desires, and of mental activities adjusting thought to thought, which forms our life."[15] This statement implies that the disconnectedness among ideas and disciplines—so typical of most education systems— is deadly. The organic hopes for education are undercut by such divisions.[16]

Another major theme in Whitehead's philosophy of education is the recognition of the individual learner as one who initiates learning and whose growth is at the center of the learning process. Some critique and enlargement of this idea will be offered later in this book from the perspective of the larger organic theological system of White- head and others, but one of Whitehead's famous epithets does com- municate his own valuing of each individual learner: "Valuable in- tellectual development is self-development."[17] This self-development idea highlights the initiative that comes from within the individual learner. Already in Whitehead's educational philosophy, however, is the recognition that education has to do with the individual's rela- tionship with the whole: "Education is the guidance of the individual towards a comprehension of the art of life: and by the art of life I mean the most complete achievement of varied activity expressing

---

[14]Whitehead, *The Aims of Education,* 3.
[15]Ibid.
[16]Ibid., 6–7.
[17]Ibid., 1.

the potentialities of that living creature in the face of its actual environment."[18]

This concern for the individual in relation to the whole leads naturally to another Whiteheadian theme, which is the importance of interest for effective education. Teachers who are not concerned with the interest of their students are offering a barren landscape with little promise for learning. Whitehead expresses this as follows: "There can be no mental development without interest. Interest is the *sine qua non* for attention and apprehension. You may endeavor to excite interest by means of birch rods, or you may coax it by the incitement of pleasurable activity. But without interest there will be no progress."[19]

The importance of interest does not mean for Whitehead that education will always be a frolic. In fact, education involves point and counterpoint, fitting to the rhythmic character of learning. Whitehead also describes the point and counterpoint in terms of freedom and discipline, each of which is necessary for the other: "The only avenue towards wisdom is by freedom in the presence of knowledge. But the only avenue towards knowledge is by discipline in the acquirement of ordered fact. Freedom and discipline are the two essentials of education. . . ."[20]

This journey through Whiteheadian epithets would not be complete without some recognition of how Whitehead was moving against the educational values of his day. In many ways Whitehead assumes in his writing the ideal of liberal education that characterized European education in the early twentieth century: "In its essence a liberal education is an education for thought and for aesthetic appreciation. . . . The Platonic ideal has rendered imperishable services to European civilisation. . . ."[21] On the other hand, Whitehead critiques this Platonic ideal in terms of its disconnectedness from human practice. He states with considerable power his critique of this form of education and its underlying assumptions:

> An evil side of the Platonic culture has been its total neglect of technical education as an ingredient in the complete development of ideal human beings. This neglect has arisen from two disastrous antitheses, namely,

---

[18]Ibid., 39.
[19]Ibid., 31.
[20]Ibid., 30.
[21]Ibid., 46.

that between mind and body, and that between thought and action. . . .
I am well aware that the Greeks highly valued physical beauty and
physical activity. They had, however, that perverted sense of values
which is the nemesis of slave-owning.[22]

Though Whitehead had no exposure to late-twentieth-century critical theory, his awareness of the connections between theory and
practice and between ideas and social activity does point in the direction of an education for all of life, including human action in the
world. It points also in the direction of critiquing social practices and
the educational systems that foster deleterious practices. His work is
not itself focused on social critique, but an encounter with social-
critical methods of education will be discussed later in this book. This
will be important to the critique and enlargement of Whitehead's own
theory.

One final theme emerges from this walk through Whiteheadian
sayings. It is the theme of the religious nature of education. This, for
Whitehead, is a way of discussing the way people respond to what
is and what could be in the world. He does not elaborate on this
theme, but he is often quoted as saying:

The essence of education is that it be religious. . . . A religious education
is an education which inculcates duty and reverence. Duty arises from
our potential control over the course of events. Where attainable knowledge could have changed the issue, ignorance has the guilt of vice. And
the foundation of reverence is this perception, that the present holds
within itself the complete sum of existence, backwards and forwards,
that whole amplitude of time, which is eternity.[23]

Because Whitehead refers to this kind of responsiveness as the religious essence of education, we see how inseparable would be theological and philosophical constructs for him.

So we are left with many answers to the question of why process
theology. The most compelling answer is that a process vision of reality
is organic. It has to do with the art of life—with relating the parts of
life into wholes; it is promising to any effort to reflect organically on
theology and education.

---

[22]Ibid., 50.
[23]Ibid., 14.

As I described earlier, this is a book written on a bridge. The book provides a walkway between one set of theological assumptions and educational practice. The hope is that other authors will examine other assumptions, thus widening the bridge and constructing others. The hope, too, is that this book will encourage the kinds of teaching and theological reflection that help us all move across bridges and enlarge and critique our visions of God and the world. At the very least, our teaching and theological reflection can engage us with one another in dialogue, significant action, and mutual understanding and critique.

The bridge that links education with theology is important because even the most disembodied theological system affects and is affected by educational practice. Theology and education are not really two separate worlds, and the act of bridging can bring to view the relationships between these artificially separated disciplines. A belief that truth lies only in the biblical canon, for example, leads to a religious education system that centers on the canon and includes only that which is directly derivative from biblical study. On the other hand, an educational practice in which the school's curriculum is ordered in a fixed pattern of disciplines for everyone to study contributes to a belief that a certain core of truth exists that is naturally compartmentalized into discrete disciplines. This book attempts to bridge certain educational methods with theological constructs in order to invite a critique both ways. The hope is that educators will be more conscious of their theological assumptions, and theologians, of their educational assumptions.

From a process perspective, writing on the bridge between disciplines is probably necessary because of a belief in the inherent relatedness among disciplines. What is hoped from the analysis offered in this book is that many readers will become more aware that they are already doing their own work on bridges, that they are already deeply formed by theological and educational insights. What is further hoped is that others will be attracted onto the bridge for a look around. I do not wish at the end of this book to be standing alone on this bridge waving at everyone else from afar.

WHY EDUCATIONAL METHOD?

This is another good question, and it will be considered here in relation to education in general and then in relation to educational method in particular. Education is a field that everyone knows something about because everyone has experienced some forms of formal and informal education. This makes knowledge about education readily accessible insofar as we have learned from our own experience. But our understandings of education are also more obscure because our judgments and descriptive categories are preformed, and we can easily allow our biases to preclude new insight. The challenge is to seek new possibilities for education and to discern what educators have to offer theologians.

Possibilities for Education

Even the focus and definition of education undergo radical shifts when viewed with organic concerns and revised through process thought. Bernard Meland, for example, urges that the central focus of higher education be shifted from rational or moral consciousness to appreciative consciousness.[24] Each of these three forms of consciousness is an organizing principle around which educational decisions are made. Each is based on different assumptions about reality, according to Meland, and leads to different modes of education. Rational consciousness (based in Aristotle) presumes an order to the universe accessible through rational thought. Moral consciousness (based in Immanuel Kant) presumes an order to the universe not empirically accessible but postulated through human reason. Human reason has access to universal ethical principles that can guide human decisions and action. Appreciative consciousness does not presume a fixed order to the universe, but one that is changing. All of reality is understood to be in process; therefore, education is oriented to helping persons appreciate and participate in the universe as it changes through time.

The focus of education is shifted when viewed through process thought; likewise, the definition of education is transformed. To educate, according to a definition shortened and paraphrased from the dictionary, is to develop persons by fostering growth of knowledge, wisdom, and desirable qualities.[25] Already from what has been said

---

[24]Meland, *Higher Education,* 48–49.

[25]*Webster's Third New International Dictionary,* 1968, s.v. "educate." The fuller definitions are "**1** *obs* : to bring up (as a child or animal): REAR **2** : to develop (as a person) by fostering to varying degrees the growth or expansion of knowledge, wisdom, desirable qualities of mind or character, physical health, or general competence esp. by a course of formal study or instruction. . . ."

of process thought and education we could modify this definition. To educate would be *to foster the self-development of persons in knowledge, wisdom, and qualities that are suited to the potentiality and environment of those persons.* This definition highlights the role of individuals in their own education as well as the relation of learning to each person's own gifts and possibilities and to the total environmental context.

The root of the word *educate* is the Latin *educare,* meaning "to rear" or "to bring up." The root can also be traced to *educere,* meaning "to lead out." The latter puts the accent on drawing out truth from within persons and from the environment. Therefore, we can speak of education as *leading people into growth (self-development) by drawing out truth wherever it is to be found.* For example, we reach into ourselves and draw out the truths that are there, or we reach into historical events or an ancient text and draw out the truths that are there. The accent in this definition is on leading people and drawing truth from many sources. The accent, further, is on dynamic movement. People themselves are moving, and truth is moving.

Truth in this definition has distinctive qualities. Truth is not a universal and static reality to be applied in various situations. Rather, it is to be discovered in the midst of the world of actualities, and truths about ever-changing actualities will themselves be changing. The truth, drawn from its actual source, will always be an abstraction from the source, never exactly corresponding with empirical reality. The truth may be quite useful, however.

These qualities of truth apply equally to truth drawn out of a life situation or out of a written, historical text. The interpretation of a literary or biblical text is an abstraction from the text and does not take the place of the text. Yet it may be a useful truth for understanding the world and God. Drawing truth out of a life situation or written text is like pulling on an elastic band. We reach into the text and pull out a truth, as we would pull on one end of an elastic band while the other end remains anchored in the text. We may examine the truth carefully and be guided by it in some very important ways. But when we finish defining and analyzing the truth, we release it back into the text. The next time we reach into that same text, we may be in a very different life situation, or we may use different exegetical tools; thus, we may discover a different truth.

The chapters that follow build on the definition of education as leading people into growth by drawing out truth wherever it is found.

The five educational methods that will be studied can actually be described in those terms. *Case method* is reaching into the particular case and drawing out a cluster of truths. *Gestalt method* is reaching out to many different facts and ideas and drawing out their unity. *Phenomenology* is reaching into ourselves and others to draw the meanings from within. *Narrative method* is reaching across boundaries of time and space and drawing out the stories that help people to understand and relate. And *conscientization* is reaching into the social structure and leading out to reform. The promise in these various methods will be explored in chapters 2 through 6.

Problem of Methodology

The question of why explore educational method raises the problem of methodology in general. This book is a work in methodology, or a study of methods. The entire venture suggests possibilities for rethinking educational methods from a theological perspective and rethinking theological methods from an educational perspective.

Methodology is what Sandra Harding describes as a theory or analysis of methods, or what Campbell Wyckoff calls "wisdom about method."[26] Methodology is not self-evident as a matter for concern. Educators often concern themselves first with clarifying the subject matter, assuming that methodology will naturally follow. When this is done, methodology is seen as a secondary concern oriented to the most effective communication of the prescribed subject matter. The position in this book moves in quite a different direction.

The assumption here is that methodological considerations come before, during, and after the identification of subject matter. In fact, what subject matter we choose is actually shaped by our method and by our theory or wisdom about method. If we intend to educate for

---

[26]Harding is dealing primarily with questions of research methodology in the social sciences. She distinguishes between method as the technique for gathering evidence and methodology as the "theory and analysis of how research does or should proceed." See Sandra Harding, *Feminism and Methodology: Social Science Issues* (Bloomington: Indiana University Press, 1987), 2–3. Her distinction is relevant here, though I make a further distinction between method and technique. She is making a point that harmonizes with Wyckoff's insistence that methodology is a reflection on method. See Campbell Wyckoff, interview conducted January 1985, Oral History Project of the Department of Religious Education, School of Theology at Claremont, California.

social transformation through conscientization, then our subject matter will be social structures and patterns of oppression. If we intend to educate for a breadth of human knowledge by teaching the classical knowledge of civilization, then our subject matter will be the historical and literary classics of the world. Clearly, method and subject matter are interrelated and need to be considered together in making educational decisions. This book will give attention, long overdue, to the methods of education, not as mere technique to communicate something else, but as a basic foundation to the educational enterprise.

Some brief definitions may clarify the language of this book. _Method is a systematic approach for reaching a goal or doing inquiry into an area of study_. It includes techniques and rules but these are not themselves the method. _Techniques are particular practices that people use to carry out a method_. According to Webster, a technique is a way to deal with technical details or use them to accomplish a goal.[27] Techniques are essential to method, but they can become disembodied from method and employed in scattered fashion with little or no system or coherence. They can also be put together in new patterns, giving birth to new methods.

One method will likely embrace many different techniques; likewise, one technique will often be relevant and useful to more than one method. Equating the two destroys this interchange and fluidity and contributes to the rigid use or rejection of one technique. One of the more vivid examples of this is the technique of lecture that is so widely used and so widely denounced. Many of those who denounce lecture as one-way, didactic communication are surprised to learn that Paulo Freire, the originator of conscientization method and critic of information-giving approaches to education, does sometimes lecture himself. For him, lecture can actually be a means toward conscientization.

Methodology is broader still; _it is theoretical reflection on method, the means by which we seek wisdom about method_. Methodology involves analyzing, evaluating, and theorizing about method in order to make decisions concerning which methods to use and how to shape and reshape them. As noted above, methods are too often ignored in

---

[27]_Webster's Third_, s.v. "technique." Technique is described as "the way in which technical details are treated" or "a technical method of accomplishing a desired aim."

educational inquiry to the detriment of wisdom about method. Furthermore, they are often ignored in process philosophy and theology, and this may well be sufficient reason for a dialogue between educational methods and process theology.

The sad state of affairs is regretted by persons speaking from within the theological and educational communities alike. Fred Craddock has expressed dismay that methodological questions are given second-class status in theological inquiry. He sees this as ignoring the Kierkegaardian question of *how*—how we are to live and communicate faith.[28] Paulo Freire points to the insidious dangers in traditional methods. The lack of self-critical analysis of methods leads educators to repeat the conserving patterns of education that make the educational system a tool of oppression.[29]

Craddock and Freire are minority voices, however, and their voices do not harmonize with most voices in the theological and educational communities. In fact, when I shared with one colleague in religious education that I planned to write a book drawing from process theology and educational method, he asked, "How can that be erudite; what does educational method have to do with process theology?" Indeed, as noted above, much work correlating process theology with education has focused on teaching the process ideas, and only brief reference has been given to methodological questions.

One of the clearest and fullest articulations of this method problem has been offered by Joseph Schwab. He notes that the formulation of educational method is as important as the material studied; our choice and understanding of method affect what we study, what aspects we consider as data, and how we interpret.[30] This means that discerning and formulating the problem are a critical part of learning that is often overlooked. He bemoans that students, even at the doctoral level, are often given a small piece of the professor's research to develop into a dissertation, rather than being given support for discerning and formulating a problem of their own concern.[31]

---

[28]Fred B. Craddock, *Overhearing the Gospel* (Nashville: Abingdon Press, 1978), particularly 9–22.
[29]Paulo Freire, *Pedagogy of the Oppressed*, trans. Myra Bergman Ramos (New York: Herder & Herder Press, 1970), particularly 57–74.
[30]Joseph J. Schwab, "Freedom and Complacence in Education" (Paper presented at the Conference on Whitehead and Education, Center for Process Studies, Claremont, Calif., October 9–11, 1980), 2.
[31]Ibid., 3.

The lack of attention to method leads to an unfortunate distortion of truth and our approach to it. Schwab speaks to this distortion out of his own experience as a graduate student: "It was in the Spring of my last year of doctoral training as a geneticist that a Visiting Fellow first said and then demonstrated to me that the gene, far from being a known bead on a string called the chromosome, was a highly useful invention by which to encompass a vast amount of data. It was a traumatic experience, and a salutary one."[32] Truth is distorted when we fail to recognize the limitations of what we know. The distortion is a consequence of not being self-critical of our own methods and the truths we identify by those methods.

Schwab goes one step further in his analysis. He identifies two results of this failure to criticize our methods. The first result, prominent in some areas of study, is that researchers use only one or two methods when a variety could generate fresh insight. For example, in some types of literary criticism the methodological emphasis is placed on asking questions about the author or about the times in which a piece was written. A method that raises other kinds of questions could lead to new understanding of the literature and its context. A second result of uncritical methods is prominent in many other fields; this is the tendency to use widely divergent methods and put together the conclusions without regard to the possible lack of fit. This is particularly true in the behavioral sciences such as personality study, where depth analysis, questionnaires, interviews, and other methods are used to get results that are difficult to compare and critique due to the largely divergent methods. The first of these approaches uses limited methods, thereby limiting access to truth. The second merges many methods uncritically and generates confusion and contradiction. Schwab's recommendation is simply to be self-critical, that is, to trace different conclusions back to the different methods used and consider the unique facts highlighted by each.[33]

Schwab's analysis has bearing on many areas of study. It is particularly illuminating in relation to theological studies, where the so-called classical disciplines have more often been guilty of the first error and the so-called practical disciplines, of the second. Ironically, for the sake of gaining clarity and credibility from theologians in the

---

[32]Ibid., 2.
[33]Ibid., 3–9.

classical disciplines, theologians of the practical disciplines often discuss how to move over into the first error by seeking agreement on one or two common methods. But Schwab's analysis suggests that neither classical nor practical theologians should emulate the other. All theologians, rather, should be self-critical about their own methods and their conclusions in relation to their methods.

The answer to the question of why study educational method is multiform, but it is full of promise. We are promised a reorientation in the focus and definition of education—an orientation that is more organic. The dangers are that method will be confused with technique or ignored or used noncritically, any of which can deprive education of its effectiveness. In addressing these dangers, we can also hope for a renewal of methodology and revitalization of the practice of education.

From an educational perspective this book promises to challenge educators to be more cognizant of their own expertise in method, and to use that expertise to critique their own work and that of theologians and philosophers. Wisdom about method is subject matter that educators can contribute to cross-disciplinary dialogues, not only for the sake of teaching people how to communicate the knowledge of their own disciplines, but also for the sake of informing people in other disciplines about methodological options for study within their disciplines.

The educator, too, needs to be standing on the bridge between disciplines. Too often educators have chosen, or been asked, to stand along the shoreline where they can receive boatloads of cargo from the islands of theology, philosophy, literature, or other classical disciplines. This style deprives educators of full contact with other disciplines and deprives the other disciplines of the wisdom educators have to offer.

VIEW FROM THE BRIDGE

And so with this recurring invitation to stand with me on a bridge between process theology and education, we can now look downriver at the chain of bridges that constitute this book. In the next five chapters, attention will be given to five selected methods that represent organic perspectives on the world. They are chosen partly because they are organic, dealing significantly with relationships, and partly because they represent a cross section of educational methods.

These methods are also chosen because they are significant; they offer much promise for education. They are born of extensive reflection on human beings and the world; therefore, each is grounded in methodological reflection and associated with concrete and useful techniques. Some theory and practical technique are presented in each chapter to offer readers a full view and a practical guide to teaching. Each of these methods will be presented in dialogue with process theology. The reform of both educational methods and theology will be offered as an outgrowth of the dialogue.

This book is written largely for those who have some educational and theological background, but the descriptions of educational methods and process theology will be elaborated as clearly as possible for the sake of the reader who does not have technical knowledge in one or the other. A brief look at the methods to be considered in the next five chapters may give the reader some further rationale for the choices and anticipation of the results.

Case study method, long popular in law and business schools, is beginning to have much broader application. It involves seeking truths in particular cases, and it corresponds with some basic ideas in process theology: that every empirical actuality is valuable, that each one is related to all others, and that each has something to teach about the world. Chapter 2 is a study of this method and its possibilities for teaching.

Gestalt method has two basic educational elements—experiencing many parts of knowledge and seeking unity. The gestalt teacher offers some variety of materials, facts, and ideas and then leads students toward unifying or harmonizing the many diverse elements. Interestingly, Alfred North Whitehead describes the basic process of life in terms of the many becoming one: "The many become one, and are increased by one."[34] In Whitehead's description, the objective past comes together with the novelty of the present and is brought into unity by the experiencing subject. Thus, individuals, at any moment, receive all of the influences from their past and pull them together

---

[34]Alfred North Whitehead, *Process and Reality: An Essay in Cosmology*, ed. David R. Griffin and Donald W. Sherburne (New York: [Macmillan, 1929] Free Press, 1978), 21.

into a new whole. This will be elaborated in chapter 3 as a mode of integrative teaching.

Phenomenological method will be considered in chapter 4 as a form of incarnational teaching. Two elements of teaching in this method are observing/listening and dialogue. The heart of the method is to observe and listen to oneself and others and to share with one another. This is the method of intersubjectivity, or seeking meaning in human life. It is important from an organic perspective, and it intersects with the Whiteheadian idea of internal relations, meaning that God and the world are incarnate in everything and everyone.

Narrative method taps imagination and describes relationships across time and space. A narrative is an organic description of the world, and storytelling helps to relate persons to the story that is told. As a nonlinear, indirect form of communication, narrative has power to form and transform its listeners. It also has power to communicate the organic relationships in reality. Narrative methodology is discussed in chapter 5 as relational teaching.

Conscientization method names and reforms the social reality, particularly oppressive social structures. Conscientization relates to the basic process ideas of freedom and change. Every emerging entity or society has the freedom to become something new. Conscientization is promising as an organic method because it promises to move education beyond individualism and beyond simply conserving the status quo. Conscientization is the subject of chapter 6; it offers hope for liberative teaching.

READING THIS BOOK

The reader of this book is encouraged to play and explore. Some readers will be more interested in the practical outcomes, looking for recommendations for educational practice: a section of each chapter deals with the educational method re-formed by process theology. Other readers may be more interested in the whole picture, including the educational and theological analyses. They are invited to read straight through. Still others will be more interested in the challenges for the revision of process theology; these are found in each chapter in the section on process theology re-formed by the method.

2
MIDWIFE TEACHING

Case Study Method

I come to case study method with a passion for particularity. I worry when theories are initiated with only bare contact with selected particularities, or when education focuses so heavily on theories that the particularities of life are ignored or devalued. The danger is that theories become isolated from many realities of the world, and this leads to oppression. Some people and parts of the earth are better represented in the theories than others. Some are given credibility, and others are ignored.

One of the most provocative insights in feminist theology is the importance given to women's experience in shaping theological constructions and, then, the importance of testing theological constructs by their effects on women's experience. Even feminist theology, however, is so rooted in academia that it is often formed in relation to particular communities of women, mostly educated and, until recently, mostly white and middle-class women. Some refreshing exceptions to this tendency are found in recent works in feminist theology in which women from different parts of the world tell their stories and theological reflection builds on those stories.[1]

---

[1]See particularly Letty Russell, Pui Lan Kwok, Ada Maria Isasi-Diaz, and Katie Geneva Cannon, *Inheriting Our Mothers' Gardens* (Philadelphia: Westminster Press, 1988); Ada Maria Isasi-Diaz and Yolanda Tarango, *Hispanic Women: Prophetic Voice in the Church* (San Francisco: Harper & Row, 1988). The first book is written by highly educated women, but their stories of their mothers in different parts of the world are rich and varied. The second book includes voices of many women who were interviewed in their different social circumstances.

What would happen to theology if women's experience, indeed if everyone's experience, were taken as a source of theological reflection? What would happen to theology if the particular experiences of persons and all elements of the earth were studied for theological insight? What would happen to education if these particular experiences were taken seriously and every unique culture and event were seen to be a revelation of truth? At the very least, our theological theories might be more deeply rooted in the experiences of the world and might be better tested and re-formed by those experiences. At the very least, the teachers and learners involved in the educational process might be more reverent of the particularities of the world, more appreciative of the value in their own experiences, and more aware of the wealth of experience and knowledge that goes beyond any theory.

CASE STUDY METHOD

Case study method is increasingly used in professional and moral education. The case study approach is basically an attempt to learn from a particular, concrete slice of reality. It generally takes the form of presenting a description of a particular situation. Students are then asked to reflect on the situation presented, to interpret, and to come to some judgment or decision regarding action. Most often the case has an open ending, and students are asked a question such as "What would you do?" Or the case may have sufficient ambiguity so that students are asked, "What do you think is going on here, or what should the persons have done?" In short, case study method involves reaching into a particular case and drawing out truths. The purpose is to learn to see more in the particular—to draw out multiple insights from a particular case viewed from several perspectives.

The teaching act in case methods is an act of midwifery, assisting the student to draw insight from a case, or to give birth to new ideas. When students are building and writing cases, they learn to observe and describe; they learn to attend to their world. When they are interpreting cases from their own or others' experiences, they learn to discern and analyze and draw conclusions from a concrete situation. In either case, the teacher is present in an assisting role, as a midwife is present for a birth. Also as a midwife, the teacher will work with the natural processes of the learner and will assist more or less actively as needed.

My first experience with case method was in training sessions for a group of college students who were preparing to live and study in England with the Experiment in International Living. Our group received some basic instructions about how to live internationally, and we were especially urged to be flexible in whatever we did. We then spent most of our preparation time reading and discussing brief case studies, incidents that had happened to other experimenters in various places around the world. Each case was incomplete, and we were to discuss what the experimenter should have done in that particular situation. This was a fascinating process, and even in my shyness, I entered into it eagerly. When we finished the training period, we not only felt that we had some understanding of what was expected of us and some confidence in our ability to make good decisions, but also we knew one another much better. The goals of the leaders seemed well realized.

As our plane left the ground in New York or, rather, as it did not leave and we sat on the ground for four hours, we began to discover that we indeed could be flexible. We could even laugh. Then, as we were greeted by our host families in England, we again felt the adventure of entering into another culture (albeit an English-speaking one). Two weeks later I had come to know and care for my English family very much.

One evening we sat down to watch television, as we often did in the evenings. This night the program was a documentary on medical insurance in the United States. The documentary was very critical of U.S. practices, and so was my family. They had criticized aspects of the United States before, and I had always smiled or laughed. But this time I did not agree on the issue and they had the documentary for support. This time their criticisms were unusually strong and my body was unusually tired. I left the room in tears, feeling very lonely.

When I reached my room, I cried some more, but this time my tears had nothing to do with medical insurance in the United States. This time my tears were full of shame, for I realized that I had failed to live up to the expectations my college colleagues and I had set for ourselves in discussing the case studies. I had experienced a moment much like one of the cases, and I had made a grand mess of it.

I pondered that case and my mess through much of the night, and then the next morning I experienced something that went beyond the borders of the case. My family reached out to me in a grand way and asked how I was feeling. When I apologized a hundred times, they said that they hoped I would not think any more about the incident. They, too, felt bad and were sorry that I had been hurt.

I share this story as a reminder that a case has boundaries. It cannot describe all of reality, or even all of one particular incident in reality. A case describes a segment of reality, and much will not be captured within its bounds. What it does offer, however, can be larger than what appears in the case on paper. The case, when discussed with others, becomes a part of the community life, even building the community and its shared values. The case becomes a guide to future action and a judgment on that action. The case, then, is not a mere exercise but a document that takes on meaning within the community's discourse.

Robert Evans and Thomas Parker define a case as "a focused segment of actual human experience that does not have a predetermined conclusion or 'solution.' "[2] This definition indicates the common uses of cases in education. Most often they are used to introduce typical problem situations or to give practice in resolving those problems. The uses are more broad than this, however, and the varieties of case study method merit attention.

The more particular uses of case study method can be seen by looking at areas of study where this method has been common. The earliest uses of case studies were to gather data in order to build theory; now they are commonly used also to present concrete examples in order to apply theory. In both approaches, case method is designed to facilitate the integration of theory and practice.

Historical Developments

The case study approach has been widely used in medical studies and also in specialty areas of medicine such as psychiatry. In these

---

[2]Robert A. Evans and Thomas D. Parker, eds., *Christian Theology: A Case Study Approach* (San Francisco: Harper & Row, 1976), 264.

disciplines the cases are often used to build up a body of data about a particular phenomenon until researchers have enough particulars to draw out some generalized principles. The cases are data from which theory is drawn. They are also used to illustrate the practice of medicine historically in relation to personality development, the academic study of medicine, finance, and administration.[3]

The case study approach was introduced into the law profession in 1871, but it was only gradually accepted. In law, cases are seen as a way to learn the application of principles and doctrines of law.[4] The cases exemplify legal principles, so they help students see how the principles are applied.

The Harvard Graduate School of Business Administration adopted case study method in 1908, and the school has become the model for a much wider use of case studies in education. Harvard Business School uses the cases to exemplify common business situations and to give students experience in problem solving.

Except for Clinical Pastoral Education, case studies were not introduced formally into theological education until the 1960s. They were first used in training students for ministerial practice, and not until 1967 were they introduced by Robert Evans as an approach for studying the classical disciplines of Bible, church history, and theology.[5] The approach taken by Robert Evans and Thomas Parker has been to collect data and build the findings into a focused case. Students then are asked to reflect theologically on the case and make theological judgments regarding the facts of the case. Parker and Evans see this as a way to teach the skill of discernment and to bridge the gap between theory and practice. Their book *Christian Theology: A Case Study Approach* presents case studies as an approach to doctrinal issues, organizing around the Apostles' Creed.[6] Robert and Alice Evans have

---

[3]Gert H. Brieger, "The History of Health and Disease for Health Professionals: The Case Study Approach," in *Teaching the History of Medicine at a Medical Center*, Jerome J. Bylebyl, ed. (Baltimore: Johns Hopkins University Press, 1982), 13–23.

[4]Evans and Parker, *Christian Theology*, xi–xii.

[5]Ibid., xi–xiii. Evans refers to his 1967 presentation at the Episcopal Theological School in Cambridge as the first time case study method had been proposed for study in the classical theological disciplines. He and Parker credit Wesner Fallow with introducing the method into ministerial studies. See Wesner Fallow, *The Case Method in Pastoral and Lay Education* (Philadelphia: Westminster Press, 1963).

[6]Evans and Parker, *Christian Theology*, 4, 17.

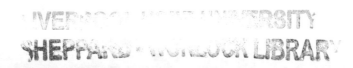

now extended this work to reflect on various action strategies for human rights and educational models for social transformation.[7]

Purposes of Case Studies

The primary purposes for doing case studies vary, so different approaches are needed. Five purposes are particularly common, and these indicate the possibilities of the method. The first purpose is *to investigate and teach about human physiology or behavior*. The investigators in anatomy describe and analyze a series of dissections of a plant or animal in order to form a comprehensive description of physical structures. In physiology, investigation builds on a series of observations leading to a description of the vital processes of living organisms. In psychoanalysis, the investigative process builds on clinical case studies drawn largely from psychotherapeutic situations. The cases are used to form and re-form psychoanalytic theory and also to teach and illustrate the theory. Very commonly in the biological and psychological sciences, then, a series of case studies or empirical observations are used simultaneously for investigation and teaching.

A second purpose is *to show how principles are applied in a particular area of study, such as business or law*. Principles of common-law marriage and related legal issues are described, for example, by offering a series of cases that illustrate various instances of this relationship.

Another common purpose of case methodology is *to evaluate a particular person or group*. This is often done through case histories, and these are used in many arenas. Case histories are often used to describe and evaluate a person's personality prior to psychotherapy or admission to an institution. Case histories may be used to evaluate a person for a job assignment or even to determine whether the person is a good credit risk. An institution may be evaluated to determine its suitability for a new program. A family may be evaluated through a case history prior to receiving a foster or adoptive child. In these instances, case methodology seems more investigative than educational, but the same kinds of evaluation are often included in the educational process to introduce students to the dynamics of human

[7]Robert A. Evans and Alice Frazer Evans, *Human Rights: A Dialogue Between the First and Third Worlds* (Maryknoll, N.Y.: Orbis Books, 1983); Alice F. Evans, Robert A. Evans, and William B. Kennedy, *Pedagogy for the Non-Poor* (Maryknoll, N.Y.: Orbis Books, 1987).

personality or group interaction. They are also used to prepare students to carry out the evaluative process in various professional settings, such as social work or business.

A fourth purpose of case studies is *to give students an opportunity to practice decision making, as when cases are used in moral or theological reflection*. This approach was brought to the forefront by Lawrence Kohlberg, who studied moral development by analyzing how people reason about particular moral dilemmas. In his writing, he advocates an approach to moral education in which students reflect together on hypothetical moral dilemmas, discussing what the characters in the dilemma should do and why. He argues that this approach stimulates moral reasoning and facilitates the movement to higher stages of moral thinking. And because Kohlberg has found a correlation between moral reasoning and moral behavior, he asserts that development in moral thinking is development toward more adequate reasoning capacities that will also affect moral behavior.[8]

A similar decision-making style is used by Evans and Parker, who ask people to reflect theologically on cases for the sake of making theological judgments. They write their cases with a focus "on specific issues or problems that require a response or decision on the part of one or more participants in the case."[9] Students are asked to reflect on the issues and to judge what would be a good decision by the participants and why. In this way Parker and Evans expect to facilitate the use of cases for making theological decisions. In their written work, they actually offer case reflections by various theologians and educators, as well as case materials for reflection by the readers.

The fifth major purpose for case study is *to help students gain insight into a life situation by identifying with a person or persons in the case*. Intercultural education sometimes uses case study as a way of communicating across cultural boundaries. This approach is used in preparing people to enter another culture or to work with others in a different culture, as in the training of the college students described

---

[8]Kohlberg does not claim that knowing what is right action will lead to right behavior, but that more adequate reasoning regarding justice does influence behavior. He says that "true knowledge, knowledge of principles of justice, does predict virtuous behavior." See Lawrence Kohlberg, *The Philosophy of Moral Development* (San Francisco: Harper & Row, 1981), 44; cf. 183–89, 121–22.

[9]Evans and Parker, *Christian Theology*, 3.

earlier. Case study is also common in anthropology, where broad insights about culture and ritual are derived from particular cases.

All of these purposes point to the possibilities in case method to help learners discern aspects of a particular situation and to broaden their understanding of human life. The potential in the method has only begun to be seen and used.

Benefits

The benefits of case study method are many. The most obvious benefit is that *a case helps bridge the gap between theory and practice*. Theoretical constructs can be exemplified by a case, and they can also be drawn out of concrete case descriptions. A concrete case can yield multiple theoretical constructs, defying simple identification between one general truth and one concrete situation. Thus, theory and practice are visibly related in case study, but not in a simplistic way. In-depth case reflection reveals theory already inherent in practice, and practice actively shaping theory. Theorizing itself comes to be seen as a form of practice, so dichotomies between theory and practice begin to fall away.

A second benefit of case study is that *a case helps persons develop skills of discernment and decision making*. Students become more astute in identifying the dynamics and issues in a situation, and they become more experienced in making decisions in ambiguous situations. This was the hoped-for benefit of the case studies my college group discussed in preparation for our English sojourn. In fact, the cases did not guarantee my making good decisions when I was actually living with a family in England, but they did guide my actions and my later reflections on actions already taken and regretted.

Another obvious advantage is that *a case introduces "real life" into academic settings by presenting real situations that defy oversimplification or overgeneralization*. Cases actually heighten the paradox between particular realities and generalizations so that each can challenge the other. In this way, cases can contribute to forming and re-forming generalizations; they also offer persistent reminders that the generalizations are never final or complete. Cases also invite us to learn about ourselves by analogy.[10] We can often see ourselves or our own

---

[10]Harriet Ronken Lynton and Rolf P. Lynton, "The Case Method," in *Training for Development*, Rolf P. Lynton and Udoi Pareek, eds. (Homewood, Ill.: Dorsey Press, 1967), 164–67.

situations in the lives of others; we learn something about ourselves as we learn about them.

Another important advantage is the way *a case can help persons see a large, complex picture, without artificially extracting particular elements.* Often academic theorizing is done by abstracting a few elements from the complexities of concrete situations. This is done legitimately for the sake of theory building, but the unfortunate consequence is that learners sometimes have difficulty relating those theories back to the complexities of life without dismissing the theory or ignoring important aspects of the life situation. Case studies provide a bridge back into the complexities, where every element is related to every other element. Case studies themselves are inevitably selective and partial, but they preserve the complexity more than most methods.

A further advantage is that *a case can be used to study the dynamics of change.* This is especially true when a case focuses on a person or group over time. Anthropologists will frequently return to a particular community to study it several years after their first study. This often gives a picture of what changes have taken place and how they have been effected.

A final benefit is a practical one, namely, *a case can be used to predict how a person or community may act in the future.* Cases are often used to study patterns of interaction and change in order to project future interactions and changes. Long-range forecasting is done this way in business; some observers have proposed that education can only be viable if projections of the future are allowed to guide educational planning. James Botkin, Mahdi Elmandjra, and Mircea Malitza have been notably outspoken about the importance of innovative learning guided by anticipation of the future. For them, maintenance learning, which is based on the patterns of the past and present, is not adequate for preparing people to live in a rapidly changing world.[11] Case method can provide a helpful approach to projecting the future. If education is to prepare students to anticipate the future, this use of case method may be critical to the educational enterprise.

Disadvantages

Case studies are not being offered here as the remedy for all educational ills. To have a full picture, some of the disadvantages need to

---

[11]James W. Botkin, Mahdi Elmandjra, and Mircea Malitza, *No Limits to Learning* (New York: Pergamon, 1979), 17–29.

be presented. The first, and most serious, disadvantage is *the difficulty of generalizing from one case to others.* A case study is itself a particular picture of a particular situation; therefore, any generalization has to be seen as tentative and partial. The method is abused if the findings from one case are applied in several others without reference to the particularities of the other cases.

A related disadvantage is *the amount of time required to learn by the case method.* Some students will experience frustrations in studying case after case with no final solution that can be generalized across all cases. Some will be frustrated by the slow process of learning through cases. By contrast, learning through formulas and prescribed answers is much faster.

Another disadvantage is *the possibility of distortions in the case material.* Jacqueline Wiseman and Marcia Aron point out how distortions can be introduced into the case material through the researcher's selective perception or memory or through the distorted views of the persons and documents from which the case is built.[12] Selective perceptions do not destroy the educative value of the case material, but they are reminders of the limits of any case and the inevitable interaction between the events of a case and the perceptions of a case writer.

Another disadvantage is a practical one. The researcher has *no clear limits on data gathering or on writing so that the development of a case can be a limitless task,* demanding much time and judgment on the part of the researcher as to where to place the limits.[13]

As these disadvantages indicate, a sense of limitations is called for in approaching both case material and its interpretation. Even so, case study can be a rich source of insight in the educational process. In fact, the limitations can even remind learners of the partiality and tentativeness of all theoretical constructs.

Data Gathering and Analysis

The process of data gathering and analysis is well established, but not fixed, in case method. Many variations are found in the procedures. The most common sources of data are in-depth interviews,

---

[12]Jacqueline P. Wiseman and Marcia S. Aron, *Field Projects in Sociology* (London: Transworld Student Library Books, 1972), 101–2.

[13]Gert Brieger, for example, discusses this problem in relation to medical cases, recognizing that a case requires a minimum of two hundred hours to prepare properly for a class to study. See Brieger, *Teaching the History of Medicine,* 18.

literary documents (such as letters, formal agreements, census reports), and oral and printed records of the chronological sequence of events. These data sources are usually approached with a principle of selectivity in mind, such as a particular incident or issue that the researcher or students want to study.

Three kinds of questions are most common in analyzing cases. *Action questions* are especially common: What should this character do, or what should the character have done, or what would I do? *Theory questions* are also frequently used to reflect on the case in light of a particular theoretical framework. Sigmund Freud and his followers used theory questions to interpret cases through a psychoanalytic frame. This is also the approach taken by Evans and Parker, who asked the theologians participating in their case studies to reflect on the cases from their own points of view. In teaching, an instructor may use theory questions to engage students in reflecting on cases from their own or another's point of view. A third approach to analysis can be through *description questions*. The interpreter seeks what the case teaches about a particular phenomenon or principle, such as a particular illness or a legal principle. These questions are used to draw descriptive data from the case that can be added to other descriptions in an attempt to create a body of data on the phenomenon or principle.

A new method for gathering and analyzing data is worth considering alongside these more established methods. This is the ethogenic method of Rom Harré. Harré, a philosopher of the social sciences at Oxford University in England, has worked collaboratively with P. F. Secord in the United States and J. P. DeWaele in Belgium. Their ethogenic method is put forth as a way of doing research in the social sciences.[14] However, it leads also to a comprehensive case history that has value in inductive learning, or learning from a person or group that may represent a more generalized population.

---

[14]J. P. DeWaele and Rom Harré, "The Personality of Individuals," in *Personality*, Rom Harré, ed. (Oxford: Basil Blackwell & Mott, 1976), 189–242. DeWaele and Harré recognize some of the benefits and limitations discussed in this chapter. The case-by-case idiographic methods escape the triviality of hasty generalizations and "inter-individual trans-specific laws," but these methods are also more difficult and time consuming, sometimes even disappointing for those looking for general laws. On the other hand, even modern physics has turned to idiographic studies because of the broad deviations that have been found among gases. (See p. 225.)

The ethogenic method is a study of the mechanisms that generate behavior.[15] It is based on two assumptions. The first is that an understanding of human beings is accessible through language. This, of course, implies that the study of what people say is a good way to learn about them. A second assumption is that all accounts of an event reveal meaning, even if they may differ; each account is true in the sense of offering someone's or some group's perspective.[16] Harré and his associates focus more on studying accounts of people's perceptions than on the correspondence of those perceptions to some "objective" or "external" reality. They emphasize the problems in talking of objective truth because reality is always accessed through people's perceptual accounts. Whether or not we agree fully with these assumptions regarding truth and correspondence, their point is clear. No *one* account can embrace the complexity and fullness of a situation. For this reason, a case needs to be built on different accounts, and different interpretations need to be heeded in the analysis.

Five steps are used in the ethogenic method for the study of human personality, and each of these adds to the case material and interpretations. One step is autobiography, in which the person being studied puts forth an account of his or her own life. Another step is to engage in direct observation of the subject's action patterns in various social settings. A third step is social inquiry, in which the researchers interview people who have known the subject in different situations. Fourth is observing the subject in contrived problem or conflict situations, like role plays. In a final step, the various parts of the data are brought together to create a coherent account.[17]

The ethogenic method not only offers additional forms of data gathering but also uses all three kinds of interpretive questions in

[15]R. Harré and P. F. Secord, *The Explanation of Social Behaviour* (Oxford: Basil Blackwell & Mott, 1972), 9.

[16]Ibid., esp. 101–23, 128–29, 134–35. See also DeWaele and Harré, "The Personality of Individuals." This particular chapter offers a good summary of the ethogenic method, which includes three basic procedures: (1) analysis of action, by looking at how various persons perceive and interpret the actions and environmental conditions; (2) analysis of persons, by looking for the source of power in their natures; and (3) accounting, by analyzing the speech that accompanies and justifies action. These three procedures indicate that attention is given to the perceptions and interpretations of various persons, to what is reported from within persons as well as from without, and to the human speech by which people constitute themselves. (See particularly p. 192 in DeWaele and Harré.)

[17]Ibid., 228–29.

analysis. Action questions are asked in terms of what action is going on and, in some cases, what action should be taken now. Theory questions are asked in terms of what different points of view are offered on the person or group being studied. Description questions—particularly prominent in the ethogenic method—are asked in terms of what the case teaches about the particular person or group and, then, about other persons or groups. We have in this method a very promising approach to building and analyzing cases. The ethogenic method does not take the place of other methods of data gathering and interpretation, but it does complement what already exists by pulling together several different approaches into one comprehensive method.

With this background on some of the available approaches to case studies, we are ready to reflect on case method from the perspective of process theology. This will lead to re-formation of case methodology and also of process theology.

PROCESS THEOLOGY AND CASE METHOD

Some compatibility between case method and process theology was assumed in selecting case study as one of the methods to be considered here. Now, the more challenging task will be addressed, that is, to reflect on case method from the point of view of process theology. This will be done by examining some relevant metaphysical concepts emerging from a process perspective, and then by exploring some basic assumptions of a process-case method.

Process Metaphysical Concepts

Several metaphysical concepts from process theology are relevant to case study method, but three will be examined here as key concepts for the analysis of the method. These concepts form a background against which further reflections can proceed.

First is the idea that *everything actual is in process*. This suggests that to know the world, or to be in harmony with reality, is to enter into the process rather than to escape from it into some ideal realm.[18] With

---

[18]According to John Cobb and David Griffin, "The bare assertion that the actual is

this premise in mind, any educational method that offers a slice of reality can be fruitful in helping us know the world and enter into the process of reality. On the other hand, a case must be viewed as just that, a slice of reality. By being written or expressed in some medium, it is offered as an unmoving piece of reality. It is thus abstracted from the process of which it is part, and this caution needs to be kept in mind as we interpret it.

For example, in the experience I had in England as a college student, I came to know that the case was only part of the reality of getting along with my new family. Other aspects of their relating with me and my relating with them interacted with the incident about medical insurance. That incident was part of a much larger dynamic situation, and my dealing with it as if it were a static case was not adequate. It was not exactly like the case we had studied in our training period; neither was it an isolated incident.

No case will ever be exactly like another case if we take seriously the processive view of reality. As Alfred North Whitehead describes the process: "The ancient doctrine that 'no one crosses the same river twice' is extended. No thinker thinks twice, and, to put the matter more generally, no subject experiences twice."[19] Every case is unique and unrepeatable. It is an event abstracted from the process of reality for study. To understand the event and to allow it to help us understand other events require that we realize how the event is part of a dynamic, ever-changing process.

A second key metaphysical concept is that *everything is internally related with everything else.* That is to say, people and things actually enter into the experience of one another. We not only talk to one another and relate as two separate beings (external relations), but also we carry the influences of one another within ourselves (internal relations). Other persons and the world enter into each of us so fully that we live in an interlocking web of reality. No piece can be separated

---

processive has religious significance even by itself. . . . The contrary notion that what is actual or fully real is beyond change leads to a devaluation of life in the world. Since our basic religious drive is to be in harmony with the fully real, belief that the fully real is beyond process encourages one or another form of escape from full participation in the world. But to understand that the process is the reality directs the drive to be 'with it' into immersion in the process." John B. Cobb, Jr., and David R. Griffin, *Process Theology: An Introductory Exposition* (Philadelphia: Westminster Press, 1976), 14.

[19]Alfred North Whitehead, *Process and Reality: An Essay in Cosmology*, ed. David R. Griffin and Donald W. Sherburne (New York: [Macmillan, 1929] Free Press, 1978), 29.

from other pieces, so knowing one particular situation can lead to greater understanding of other situations. Simply by being connected with one another, we share some common experiences and are able to learn about ourselves from the experiences of another.

The idea of internal relatedness carries with it some particularly provocative perspectives on case study methods. For example, even the dichotomy between the particular and universal is called into question. From a process perspective, the particular really is a unique particular, but not as a separate entity isolated from others; instead, it affects and is affected by the rest of the world.[20] A case study from this perspective would potentially uncover the uniqueness in a particular situation and some insight into the larger universe in which it participates.

Finally, *every unit of process has experience, enjoyment, and value.* This means that the world cannot be divided between those beings that experience and those that do not. Every actuality in the world experiences, and the experiences include both physical and mental responses;[21] every actuality has some degree of mentality, however small. This means that the actualities constituting a rock, tree, calf, and person will all experience reality, be capable of enjoyment, and be of value to the whole. They are of value not only for what they do for human beings, but also for what they contribute to one another. Even more basic, they are of value because they themselves are experiencing entities.

This idea has several implications. The most obvious implication is that though human experience is the highest exemplification of reality, there is no sharp distinction between human and nonhuman, or between living and nonliving actualities. Case studies should not focus soley on human beings and their experience of a situation. Such an idea is a sharp critique of case methods that have only rarely given attention to nonhuman, nonliving elements of cases. Jay McDaniel, a process theologian, has demonstrated the potential of reflecting on

---

[20]Ibid., 56–57, cf. 50. Whitehead reflects on this issue with some technical detail, relating this to his explanation of the solidarity of the universe. He concludes: "To be actual must mean that all actual things are alike objects, . . . and that all actual things are subjects, each prehending the universe from which it arises. The creative action is the universe always becoming one in a particular unity of self-experience, and thereby adding to the multiplicity which is the universe as many."

[21]Ibid., 108.

concrete situations in the animal world; he reflects theologically and ethically on the pelicans' practice of driving their secondborn from the nest, almost always to die.[22] Many issues are raised in this case such as a theology of reverence for life, natural selection processes, and animal rights.

Another implication is that cases should not be used simply to illustrate general principles or abstract truths, since every case and every particular feature of a case are of value. In theological education, for example, students might choose cases to prepare and study based simply on their inherent interests. This is different from choosing cases because they illustrate a psychological or theological principle. Both forms of case study have a place, but they function very differently. The uniqueness as well as the generalizability needs to be considered.

Still another implication is that cases can help us look at life during ordinary times; that is, we can use cases to study ordinary as well as extraordinary events. The tendency in education and the media is to look at extraordinary moments. Soap operas, for example, keep interest by injecting crises, and situation comedies usually include a major crisis and resolution in every thirty-minute segment. The curriculum reconceptualists have bemoaned this in education. William Pinar writes: "One critic's praise of the recent film 'Sunday, Bloody Sunday' had to do with its portrayal of the 'in-between' of life, not the periods of despair or of excitement, but of the middle range where most of us live most of the time."[23] By recognizing every moment as an event, process thought can open our eyes to these ordinary times. Case study is particularly conducive to helping us see the ordinary moments if the method is used for that purpose.

Assumptions of a Process-Case Study Method

A process-case method would not be exactly the same as the more common approaches to case study discussed above. Certain basic assumptions would be important for a process approach to cases.

---

[22] Jay B. McDaniel, *Of God and Pelicans: A Theology of Reverence for Life* (Louisville: Westminster/John Knox, 1989), 18, 41, 43, 45.

[23] William Pinar, ed., *Heightened Consciousness, Cultural Revolution, and Curriculum Theory* (Berkeley: McCutchan, 1974), 4.

Some of these assumptions are offered here as a prelude to the presentation of a re-formed method.

A first assumption is that *truth lies within the case, not just in the ideas and experiences that we bring to it.* Truth is known insofar as what we know from the case corresponds with the concrete realities of the case.[24] Case studies, then, should be an important approach to theology and to philosophical reflection as well as to teaching. In fact, any discipline concerned with truth could benefit from the use of case method. Seeking truth in the particular situation becomes important to theology, and case study is no longer a novel teaching technique, but a promising way to discover truth. Furthermore, the particularities of the case become as important as the theories we embrace, which means we need to bracket our preconceived ideas and theories as much as possible so the case can speak for itself.

A second assumption is that *the case is part of the flow of reality.* The past is present within it, and the future will be affected by it. It is a description of a frozen slice of reality, so it has been abstracted from the reality in two ways. The moments have been described through a process of gathering data and compiling the case, which inevitably abstracts the case from the actual concrete experience. The description is not the experience itself, and it can only partially reveal the experience. Furthermore, the actual events take place in the midst of a complex and ongoing process; they have been extracted and made static for purposes of study. We need to be aware that the past is present within the case and the future will be affected by it. The case needs to be approached with questions about how it is related to the process of reality; we cannot simply learn our lessons from it and throw it away as if the truths in this case would be true for all times and all places. This is quite different from the assumption of Lawrence Kohlberg that a case, or moral dilemma situation, has universal features that can easily be extracted from the flow of reality; the case situation cannot really be separated from the events that go before and after it and from the complexities that surround the situation in the present.

A third assumption from process theology is that *the case situation includes influences from God, from human and nonhuman reality, and from*

---

[24]Whitehead speaks of truth as coherence between propositions and nexus. See *Process and Reality,* 271.

the living and nonliving world. This is true whether or not these influences are made explicit. An awareness of this in compiling the case and reflecting on it would be important. Sometimes the geography, weather, soil quality, or animal life will have considerable influence in a case situation. In regions where forests or rich grazing land have become deserts, the effects of people on the land and the land on people are obvious. Sometimes, too, a case will focus on the soil itself or on a particular case in the natural world as Jay McDaniel does in the study of pelicans. Sometimes the gathering of case data will involve silence, a quiet listening and watching, in order to discern what is happening and to discern the movements of God.

Fourth, *the truths revealed in the case are disclosed by the case itself and by students of the case. The truths revealed are also limited by both.* In other words, no one truth can be found if the right techniques are used in writing or analyzing the case. The truths will always be relative and multiple. By relative, I mean that the truth drawn out of the case will be relative to the actual experience and also to the other experiences of the compilers and interpreters.

This does not mean that no standards of judging the validity of an interpretation exist. Some interpretations will be closer to the actual experience described than others. The easiest way to explain this is by illustration. Not long ago, I stood with a group of people on a street corner watching for a taxi. We saw a car approaching from a distance, and since it bore the familiar markings of a taxi, we hailed it. The car pulled up to the corner where we stood, and then we realized that we had hailed a police car. One member of our group apologized, and we all walked sheepishly to another corner to watch for a real taxi. Our interpretation had not been true in the sense that it did not correspond to the reality of the police car. The distance and angle had obscured our vision, not to mention our own hopefulness that this would indeed be a taxi. On the other hand, our interpretation was true in the sense that the markings on this police car were fairly close to taxi markings in our home cities (at least from a distance). Our interpretation was an approximate truth about the vehicle, but not a very useful one.

The same will be true of our case interpretations. The case description and the interpretation will always approximate the actual experience to a greater or lesser degree, and the usefulness will usually be greater when the degree of correspondence with reality is high.

Different descriptions and interpretations will always be possible, however, and each of these may correspond with some aspect of the reality and be useful to the case interpreters. Judgments can be made as to how closely any one description and interpretation corresponds to reality, but no one interpretation can ever be taken as the complete truth. This is an important assumption to consider because the danger of ruling out certain interpretations as false is probably greater than the danger of accepting too many interpretations as true. Certainly the work of liberation, feminist, and black theologians has raised awareness of the cultural biases in every perspective on reality. This makes urgent the recognition that the truth revealed in a case is influenced by the case itself and also by the students of the case. The truths drawn out will be multiple.

A fifth assumption emerging from process theology is that *all experience is not accessible in the case, however carefully the case is prepared. Only the experience that is selected by our consciousness is accessible*; therefore, the authors and interpreters need to respect what they will not know. Whitehead's idea is that consciousness follows experience and selects certain aspects of it to feature. This conscious highlighting intensifies the enjoyment of the experience.[25] With this in mind, we can see how case studies could be one means of highlighting or intensifying an experience. But we need, too, to be aware that aspects of the case will be beyond the reach of consciousness.

A related assumption is that case communication can be both verbal and nonverbal. Whitehead puts forth the idea that communication can be given and received without language. This idea implies a critique of the almost purely linguistic approach used in most case study, even in the comprehensive approach of Rom Harré and his associates. Whitehead's idea suggests that we need to look at what is expressed in ways other than language, and we need to know that some aspects we apprehend cannot be expressed at all. Whitehead says: "Yet Mothers can ponder many things in their hearts which their lives cannot express. These many things, which are thus known,

---

[25]Whitehead discusses the intensification of experience caused by intellectual feelings, which always include some degree of consciousness. Intellectual feelings concentrate attention and heighten emotional intensity. See Whitehead, *Process and Reality*, 272–73; cf. Cobb and Griffin, *Process Theology*, 17.

constitute the ultimate religious evidence, beyond which there is no appeal."[26]

With these assumptions in the background, we can now begin to re-form case study method from the standpoint of process theology and to re-form process theology from the standpoint of case method.

CASE STUDY METHOD RE-FORMED
BY PROCESS THEOLOGY

Much about the process approach to case method has been said above. Many aspects of present case methods would not be changed in a process reformulation, but some shifts would be suggested. In a process revision, case study would be more organic, especially in giving more recognition to the complexities in case situations—the multiple influences and perspectives on the case, and the processive nature of the case situation. To take account of these complexities in case methods, an approach is recommended below. The procedure is designed to include the basic elements of case method as traditionally understood, but re-formed by process theology.

Building a Case

Building a case begins with selection. In a process perspective, every case situation is significant and every one is related to the whole. But also from a process perspective, the actual case selected affects the learning situation. The selection is shaped by the perspectives and goals of the persons who make the selection, and the case is part of a web of relations before a group begins to work with it. In building the case, then, we need to be conscious of this complexity because the case will make a difference in the organic web.

Building a case requires a procedure for the data gatherers to bracket their own opinions as much as possible in the process of collecting the data. The first step, then, is to ask this question: *What assumptions*

---

[26]Alfred North Whitehead, *Religion in the Making* (New York: [Macmillan 1926] New American Library, 1954), 65.

or pre-formed ideas are brought to the case? In this way researchers acknowledge that they do not come to the case as blank slates, but as people with a history and relationships that color their choice of and approach to the case. Stating these assumptions at the outset helps the data gatherer set them aside to some extent and come back to them later in evaluating the case materials gathered.

The second step in data gathering is to ask the most obvious question: *What is going on here?* That includes what is going on in the human experience (both personal and communal), in the larger human social experience, and in the natural world. To do this requires more than describing what the major characters are doing, but also describing social patterns in the community, economic patterns, historical events, environmental context, and shifts in the natural environment. Educational case methods already involve broad descriptions, but the process perspective would push much further. Whether in medical, business, or ecclesiastical cases, the full range of influences needs to be considered.

A third step is to ask historical questions: *What historical elements are in evidence?* The case builder looks for evidence of the historical elements in such places as the community's buildings, the actions of the people, and the people's recollections of decisions and incidents. Here the formal history of the community is important, as well as the popularly remembered history and the historically formed customs and life of the community. A process perspective pushes below the surface to explore the less-than-obvious historical influences, recognizing that the historical influences will be extensive in any living community.

Finally, questions are needed about the future trajectory: *What future expectations or hopes are revealed?* Here the case builder is looking for expressed and unexpressed hopes, long-range plans, and demographic data on trends. In at least these ways, the future is already shaping the present situation, and in a process perspective, the future cannot be ignored.

In all of these case-building questions, we seek to describe the various elements in the situation and the way in which this case situation is related to the process of reality—past, present, and future. These questions cannot exhaust a case, but they can open it to a fuller view.

Interpreting the Case

Interpreting the case is also a multifaceted task. The facets are presented here as steps, and they do follow in a logical order. The order is not binding, however, and neither is the necessity of following all four steps. Various educational purposes may guide the choice of a case method, and the purposes should influence which steps are followed and in what order. At least four kinds of interpretive questions can be included, and each of these presents something to the full picture. Because a case already exists in a web of relationships and because every interpreter will bring different perspectives to it, these interpretive questions will yield fuller answers if addressed by a community working together. Diversity within the interpreting community will contribute even more to the fullness.

First are the *descriptive questions*. These are basically the same questions that researchers use in building the case. The attempt in these questions is to see and hear as much as possible. This again means setting aside prejudgments as much as possible, especially at the beginning of interpretation when preformed opinions are often blocks to learning something new from the case. The descriptive questions can follow the same steps outlined in the data-gathering process. Interpreters need to go through the process of identifying their assumptions and preformed ideas, setting them aside as much as possible, and asking questions of the case: What is going on here? What historical elements are in evidence? What future expectations or hopes are revealed? All of these queries, then, become data for further analysis as outlined in the steps below.

A second step in interpretation is asking the *analytical questions*. These help interpreters to discern how the particular case situation is part of the process of reality. Analytical questions might include: How has the past influenced the present situation? How are cultural, sociopolitical, economic, and environmental factors exerting influence? What is unique in this situation? What is its contribution to the future? These questions assume that the moments included in the case study are part of a larger whole, that they are themselves unique moments in the process, and that they will contribute to the future of the community and to the future of the world.

In view of process theology and its contribution to case study method, interpretation needs to include a third step of asking *theological questions*. Interpreters attempt to understand how God and the world are revealed through the case. Questions would include: What is revealed in the case about God? What is revealed about the world? What is revealed about the relation between God and the world? When a group of people reflects on such questions in relation to a concrete case, the divisive distinctions among conservatives, liberals, liberationists, and others can be placed in a larger perspective in which theological categories are less important than mutual exploration.

The questions most common to case study method are still important, and that is the fourth step of asking *prescriptive questions*. These questions help us judge how characters in the case should guide the future for themselves and how the students of the case can seek guidance from the case for their own actions. Prescriptive questions include: What needs to happen in this situation? And what needs to happen in my situation? As in all of the interpretive questions, prescriptions cannot be universalized because they are based on one case interpreted by one group of interpreters, but they are important nevertheless to guide the future. All knowing, including case study knowing, challenges people to respond.

Elaboration

In view of these basic procedures, process-case method can be elaborated in various directions. It can be included as part of a larger method of reflecting on the experience and action of the participants in an educational process. As such, it can be used as part of a long-range planning process. A case study of a church, synagogue, or educational institution can be a first step in decision making for the future.

In formal educational settings, cases drawn from the lives and work of the participants can raise situational and personal elements important to the future of the participants. Since these are cases that the students actually choose, they will actively contribute to the goals and subject matter of the educational process. Such cases can also contribute to sensitivity regarding concrete elements in their own lives and connections between their lives and others. Case study based on the participants' experience can be done effectively in situations featuring interpersonal relationships or ethical choices such as those found in business or medical settings. Carol Gilligan has discovered that people sometimes approach moral questions differently when the issues are drawn from dilemmas in their own lives. Thus she questions the universal patterns of moral development posited by Kohlberg.[27] Gilligan has discovered different patterns of moral development in women dealing with abortion decisions, for example. This finding further supports building cases from the life situations of the participants.

Another form of elaboration is the addition of steps to case analysis. For example, the students of the case might be asked to imagine the worst possible consequences that could arise from their decision. If these things do indeed happen and they believe they made the wrong decision, what would they do then? This calls attention to the case as part of an open-ended process that can have various outcomes and that will call for new decisions at every point. This is particularly relevant in light of Whitehead's idea that our past decisions and the consequences of those decisions continue to exist, but every moment is open for new decisions.[28] This also counters glib assumptions that decisions always have positive consequences or that case situations have easy or ideal answers.

Still another extension of process-case method is the introduction of content for reflection on the case. This extension is suggested by several approaches to practical theology in which various contents are brought into dialogue with concrete situations. The extension would also be supported from a process perspective as a way to bring historical and theoretical formulations into interaction with concrete situations. The content might be the heritage of the religious community or a theory of social interaction. This content becomes a perspective from which to analyze the case, and the introduction of the perspective can raise awareness that no case or case interpretation exists in isolation from the past events and interpretive frameworks that people carry.

---

[27]Carol Gilligan, *In a Different Voice: Psychological Theory and Women's Development* (Cambridge, Mass.: Harvard University Press, 1982).

[28]Whitehead's categories of freedom and determination explain the individual's freedom from external determination. Each actual entity is a self-determining subject that receives the external influences and decides how they are to be unified. (See Whitehead, *Process and Reality*, 27–28.) This suggests that every actual occasion is in some sense novel, never fully determined by the past. At the same time, the actual occasions of the past are always available as objective data for the becoming occasion. (See also pp. 210, 238.) The past does not go away, but it can be appropriated in new ways.

Robert and Alice Evans and Thomas Parker sponsor this kind of case interpretation very well, especially when they ask people to reflect on a case in relation to their particular theological beliefs. This is also the spirit of Thomas Groome's model of religious education as critical reflection on shared praxis. In Groome's approach, people reflect together on their own actions and stories; then they study the Christian story and vision; and, finally, they reflect on their particular actions and stories in light of that Christian story and vision. For Groome this is a dialogical process in which the Christian story and vision are also reflected on in light of the people's actions.[29] If this approach were extended to case studies, the content of Christian story and vision would be brought into active dialogue with the case itself, and each would be allowed to critique the other.

The kind of content introduced might also be a psychological or sociological theory. The theoretical framework from the social sciences can be brought into dialogue with a case to test the theory and to extend students' understanding of the concrete reality represented in the case.

PROCESS THEOLOGY RE-FORMED
BY CASE STUDY METHOD

This last consequence of the dialogue between process theology and case study method is perhaps the most challenging because it is the most strange to usual ways of thinking. Drawing on theological or philosophical systems to revise a method is sufficiently novel; thinking that the method could actually lead to revising the theological or philosophical system is especially brash. That is the hope here, however.

The most obvious challenge offered by case method to process theology is the possibility of actually using the method in theological reflection. To gather data and prepare a case and then to reflect theologically on it would contribute more empirical grounding for a theological system touted as empirical. This is especially important in light of the process view that the universe is revealed in particulars and

---

[29]Thomas H. Groome, *Christian Religious Education* (San Francisco: Harper & Row, 1980), 184–97, 207–23.

particulars contribute to forming the universe.[30] Some important benefits could come from using case studies in the reflective work of process theologians, especially the benefits of exploring the theory-practice relationship, human experience, and mystery.

Exploring the Intersection Between
Theory and Practice

Particularly promising in this approach would be the opportunity to explore the relation between theory and practice. Case method opens the way for this by offering a slice of concrete reality, a description of practice in which theories are already embedded and from which interpreters can reflect theoretically. In this way, interpreters can derive theoretical constructs or test them in relation to practice. Since so much of process theology has been directed toward applying process thought to aspects of the modern world, the possibility of furthering these discussions is invigorating. For example, the idea that process thought can offer answers to problems in ecology, economics, nuclear escalation, liberation, and education has been assumed by many process theologians,[31] but the idea that insights from these fields of study could inspire theological insight has been less common. The study of global practices in trade, loans, and business transactions reveals the interconnectedness of economics in wealthy and poor countries; a theory of interconnectedness follows that carries challenges for new actions. Likewise, the study of concrete social interactions could lead process theologians to deal with social patterns in a much more concrete and full way than Whitehead ever did. The

---

[30]See Whitehead, *Process and Reality*, 50, 56–57. This view is incompatible with views of reality that assume universal axioms that are independent and unaffected by particulars, or on the other hand, views such as deconstructionism that give no credibility to universals in any sense, even as cosmological generalizations. On this latter point, Grange argues a process view: "Abstraction does not aim at the replacement of the concrete. It seeks to protect the concrete by showing its connections, relations and interfusion with other parts of experience." See Joseph Grange, "Deconstruction and the Philosophy of Culture," *Process Studies* 17 (Fall 1988): 150, cf. 141–51.

[31]See, for example, Schubert M. Ogden, *Faith and Freedom: Toward a Theology of Liberation* (Nashville: Abingdon Press, 1979); Sheila Greeve Davaney, ed., *Feminism and Process Thought* (Lewiston, N.Y.: Edwin Mellen Press, 1981); Charles Birch and John B. Cobb, Jr., *The Liberation of Life: From the Cell to Community* (Cambridge: Cambridge University Press, 1981); Mary Elizabeth Moore, *Education for Continuity and Change: A New Model of Christian Religious Education* (Nashville: Abingdon Press, 1983).

plea for more social analysis in process thought has already been sounded by Lois Gehr Livezey and others,[32] but much of this work still lies ahead. Not only will process theory be re-shaped through such reflection on practice, but the re-formed theory will call for re-formed action.

Another matter of theory and practice highlighted by case method is the relationship between expressed beliefs and actions. This can often be seen in a case where both are described. The partial case I offered in the introduction of this chapter is but one example. The case presents my beliefs and actions, and this makes possible an analysis of the relationship between those beliefs and actions.

At the time of the case, for example, I was living in a new culture and my beliefs about the correctness of U.S. health-care practices had never been questioned. I believed that they were basically good, but I also believed that, above all, my way of relating to my English family should be flexible and agreeable. When these values conflicted, I was unable to deal with the conflict agreeably, so I left the room crying.

Reflecting on this case theologically, I observe my tendency to equate one particular government and culture (the United States) with correct practices in medical insurance, and my assumption that flexibility can be equated with smooth relationships and the absence of conflict. These two assumptions caused me problems, and tears flowed. But these two assumptions are not strange to theologians, who often perpetuate the idea that one government and culture is superior to others in every respect, and who often assume that harmony is the agreeable blending of different parts. We can easily argue against these ideas from a process perspective, but nevertheless the ideas are often associated with process theology as well, especially the emphasis on harmony.

Two of the most common criticisms of process theology are its apparent optimism about the goodness of concrete reality and human culture and its apparent emphasis on harmonious ends. Process theologians do argue convincingly that optimism is different from hope; they argue that they are not optimistic but hopeful that good can come from creation.[33] The emphasis on the depravity of human beings and

---

[32]Lois Gehr Livezey, "Women, Power, and Politics: Feminist Theology in Process Perspective," *Process Studies* 17 (Summer 1988): 70–71, cf. 67–77.

[33]Cobb is quite explicit about the evil and pain in the world in John B. Cobb, Jr., *God and the World* (Philadelphia: Westminster Press, 1969), 56, 94–95.

creation is not highlighted, however, and the explanation of sin is not usually developed in full.[34] The case considered here does raise that question; it asks theologians to consider where and how social critique can be done. Social critique needs to be more fully integrated into the process perspective.

The other criticism of process theology is its emphasis on harmony. My own attempt to maintain harmony in the case situation was tied to my own belief in the value of harmony. My actions were not compatible with the views of harmony that I held, and my actions actually led me to question the possibility of such an easy harmony. A process theologian might quickly say that harmony is best when accompanied by intensity, the consequence of differences held in contrast.[35] The process perspective is sometimes misinterpreted, however, as an optimistic view of harmony that does not take evil or conflict seriously— a view much like the one I held in the case situation. This suggests the importance for process theologians to reflect explicitly on conflict and tragedy in the world with the idea of asking what value process formulations have for those who suffer. This kind of reflection is taking place to some extent among process theologians; and, interestingly, those who participate most actively in these reflections are often engaging with concrete cases in some way.[36] The broader use of case

---

[34]The human condition is not the starting point of reflection for either Whitehead or Hartshorne. Whitehead introduces his pivotal *Process and Reality* as an essay in speculative philosophy (*Process and Reality*, 3), and he speaks of human issues in fairly general terms, reflecting, for example, on epochs of human history. Hartshorne goes to great pains to argue that the avenue to God's actuality is conceptual rather than perceptual. See Charles Hartshorne, *A Natural Theology for Our Time* (LaSalle, Ill.: Open Court Publishing Co., 1967), 77, cf. 66–89. Later process interpreters carry similar themes. Cobb, for example, does not feature human sinfulness in his own natural theology but focuses on human beings in relation to questions of freedom, value, and ethics. See John B. Cobb, Jr., *A Christian Natural Theology* (Philadelphia: Westminster Press, 1965), 92–134. While these broad themes do not deny human sinfulness, they do not take it as a starting point of theology. Cobb, like Whitehead, offers historical contexting of philosophy (ibid., 260–61) and acknowledges the relativity of philosophical thought (ibid., 270–72), but he, too, speaks of human issues in fairly general terms. Some more recent work, especially by feminist process theologians, moves toward more concreteness and particularity. See especially Catherine Keller, "Process Theology," *Process Studies* 17 (Summer 1988): 65; Livezey, "Women, Power, and Politics," 67–68; and Marjorie Hewitt Suchocki, *God-Christ-Church* (New York: Crossroad, 1982), esp. 7–10, 23–24, 28–32, 35–36, 117–18. On these pages, Suchocki uses cases as exemplars of process ideas. Interestingly, the movement to concreteness in the Livezey and Suchocki work is accompanied by a movement to greater attention to evil particulars in human life.

[35]Whitehead, *Process and Reality*, 111, 114, 249.

[36]Robert Brizee actually describes cases and reflects on the dynamics of suffering

study methods could well raise the issues of conflict, tragedy, and suffering to more intense levels.

These theological questions come out of the case offered in this chapter. Allowing concrete cases to raise theological questions can be very important to the future shape of process theology. By reflecting on this particular case, we can see how practices and beliefs influence and re-shape one another. We can also see how theological issues arise in the interplay of theory and practice.

Exploring the Meanings
of Human Experience

Case study method is also a reminder that human experience does have meaning, and this meaning is somehow accessible to the astute observer. This raises hope that the method might be used to take human experience much more seriously in theological reflection.

In particular, feminist theologians are urging theologians in general to take experience much more seriously in theological reflection. Marjorie Suchocki has discussed this in relation to process theology, which puts forth ideals of openness and mutuality but is not involved in practical efforts to enact those ideals and to reflect theologically on the action.[37] Suchocki's dialogical approach to the relationship between process metaphysics and feminist action begins to open the possibility that experience can be a source for theological reflection. Case study offers an approach for implementing this recommendation.

Specifically, the case discussed briefly in this chapter is revealing in regard to human experience. The values of flexibility and harmony were engendered in the training program of the Experiment in International Living, especially in the study of cases. But these values were tested in the evening discussion of medical insurance between

---

from a process perspective. His presentations of cases are moving and compassionate, but they are used primarily to pose questions for which process theology supplies answers. See Robert Brizee, *Where in the World Is God?* (Nashville: The Upper Room, 1987). This is an appropriate approach for a theological work (and one akin to Paul Tillich's method of correlation in practical theology). What I am suggesting here, however, is that cases might well challenge the very answers of process theology regarding harmony and suffering.

[37]Marjorie Suchocki, "Openness and Mutuality in Process Thought and Feminist Action," in *Feminism and Process Thought*, 62–82.

my English family and me. The explosion of my feelings was frightening, but my experiences of the family on the days following the
incident moved in a new direction. Those experiences did not re-
pudiate the values of flexibility and harmony, but they did transcend
those values. The family's gracious reaching out to me and the strength
I found in myself to face loneliness and doubts gave rise to a much
deeper understanding and appreciation among us. The experience of
grace was larger than the law of flexibility.

To realize that flexibility was not the most important value in the
situation was not easy to grasp or receive. On the other hand, the
experience itself spoke more loudly than my beliefs so that I had an
onrushing sense of grace. Furthermore, I began to raise questions
leading to a much more nuanced view of flexibility and harmony—
a view that could handle disagreement, conflict, and reconciliation.
The experience of transcendence was mediated through the family,
my friends, my inner sources, and humor. I named the transcendence God.

For process theologians, such a description of transcendence emerging from human experience is enlightening because the emphasis is
not on the emergence of concrete event after concrete event. The fact
of God's participation in reality is not simply an abstract theological
construct, but a revealed reality. Furthermore, it is a reality that seems
to come from beyond, but also through, normal social interchange.
This interchange may or may not be named God by those involved
in the interaction.

These ideas are highly compatible with the process view of God
as participating in the concrete emergence of events, luring the world
to a new reality. God participates in, but transcends, the world. However clear this is in process formulations of God and the world, the
participation of God in the details of the world and God's lure toward
a new kind of world are often addressed in terms more metaphysical
than concrete.[38] For this reason, the possibilities of process theology
as a source of meaning in the living of those details are often obscured.

---

[38]One exception to this generalization is Brizee's *Where in the World Is God?* where
he details experiences of suffering in relation to process philosophy. Another exception
is found in Delwin Brown, *To Set at Liberty: Christian Faith and Human Freedom* (Maryknoll,
N.Y.: Orbis Books, 1981).

Theologians write books about process theology in relation to liberation, politics, and ecology, but the particularities are often not accented. The fact of God's presence and lure in those particularities is
named but not detailed; liberation is endorsed but the particularities
of liberation movements are often not highlighted or guided.

These case reflections are not intended to be complete or conclusive,
but they do point to the way in which the meaning of human experience can be revealed through a case. What is revealed may well
be as important to understanding God and the world as other sources
of authority, such as those offered in traditional texts and theological
systems.

Exploring Mystery

Perhaps case method has as much to contribute by what it does not
do as by what it does. Case study inevitably reminds the reflectors
of what they do not know. Almost every time a case is discussed,
people ask questions that go beyond what is accessible in the case,
thus raising the question of how much can and cannot be known of
an experience in concrete reality.

This limitation on case material was discussed in relation to the
recognition in process theology that certain aspects of experience are
inaccessible to conscious perception. This insight in process thought
does offer a corrective in case method, a recognition that neither the
case material nor the interpretations can ever be complete and exhaustive.

The limitation also has a positive value, however, because con-
frontation with an actual case is a reminder to students of how much
they do not know. Thus, the case points to mystery. Ironically, the
attempt to describe adequately some aspect of reality leaves people
aware that reality can never be adequately described. The practice of
case method is often like the Buddhist reflection on a koan, such as
listening to the sound of one hand clapping. The very attempt to
reflect on the riddle of case or koan puts a person in contact with the
mystery beyond what is immediately evident.

This aspect of the practice of case study method does raise a question about the accessibility of truth. It also offers a critique of process
theologians' attempts to understand and explain as much of the world
as possible. The attempt to explain is not itself a problem. The problem

is when the effort to give comprehensive and adequate explanations of a broad, global sort draws attention away from particularities and mysteries experienced in the world.[39] The denial of mystery is also a denial of the relative and perspectival nature of our own theological system. The denial of mystery is a denial of the truth larger than what we grasp and understand.

Case study method, then, offers at least these three contributions to process theology: exploration of the theory-practice relationship, exploration of human experience as a source for theological reflection, and exploration of mystery. The fruits of the dialogue between process theology and case study method are the re-form of case method and the challenge to process theologians to engage more reflectively in practice, experience, and mystery.

---

[39]Most process literature is discursive and explanatory, with special attention to worldviews and patterns of thought. Neither indirect communication of poetry or narrative nor direct wrestling with particularities or mystery is common. Even Sallie McFague deals primarily with patterns of thought. She seeks more adequate metaphors for God and the world. Although she does this for the sake of invoking more ecological and global sensitivity, she deals very little with mystery or with particularities. Her models for God, then, are not as grounded in religious experience or particular life situations as they might be. See Sallie McFague, *Models of God: Theology for an Ecological, Nuclear Age* (Philadelphia: Fortress Press, 1987). We can find more concern for mystery in the works of Suchocki and McDaniel, however, both of whom have wrestled with large life problems in relation to particular experiences in the world. See Suchocki, *God-Christ-Church*, 191–223; Jay B. McDaniel, *Earth, Sky, Gods and Mortals: Developing an Ecological Spirituality* (Mystic, Conn.: Twenty-Third Publications, 1990); McDaniel, *Of God and Pelicans*, 85–110.

3
INTEGRATIVE
TEACHING

Gestalt Method

M y own interest in gestalt method is fueled by a double concern—that theology move in more active interaction with human science descriptions of human life, and that educators work with more openness in forming conclusions about the human dynamics in the educational process.

Too often, theology in general and process theology in particular are so focused on macro theories of God and the world that insights from psychology, sociology, and anthropology have little effect in shaping the theological response to ethical and other issues. The one very large exception is the whole cluster of liberation theologies which, fueled by their own concerns for human liberation in the world, have been deeply informed by the human sciences. Latin American liberation theologians have turned particularly to economics for insight, African-American theologians to sociology, and feminist theologians to psychology or social psychology. Since liberation theologians are concerned with different forms of oppression, they naturally turn to different human science tools, making choices in light of their own social location and liberation goals. What is most disturbing about the failure of many other theologians to relate significantly to the constructs of the human sciences is that this failure may well reflect a lack of self-consciousness about their own social location or a lack of goals for concrete life in the world.

On the educational side, the central issue is the tendency of educators to adopt a few favorite theories and to filter their own judgments in every situation through those theories. Of course, this human tendency is not fully escapable because people always come to any new situation with prejudgments and theoretical assumptions. Though prejudgments are inevitable, the concern here is with rigid and reductionistic prejudgments. For example, the psychoanalytic and developmental interpretive frameworks have been among the most fruitful in modern psychology. However, if teachers are limited to the insights of one or the other, and even that in a fairly superficial way, they are likely to apply the theory in a simplistic way to everyone, without much sensitivity to the complex human dynamics that exist in a given situation. This tendency is evidenced when a teacher assumes that all of a child's problems are family-based or parent-based. Such an assumption follows naturally from an introductory version of psychoanalytic theory, but it leads the teacher to ignore other factors in the social situation such as the child's own intentions or goals, peers, educational experiences, economic and historical influences, intellectual abilities, and biological tendencies. The teacher's interpretation may be so limited that the interventions offered are very narrow, and perhaps even harmful in the sense of adding more pressure to a family already overloaded with pressure.

Another educational dilemma is the tendency to rely on rote memorization and drill as principal approaches to learning. In religious education, memorization of verses and texts is sometimes taken to be the critical sign of whether good religious education is taking place. In general education, drill in basic reading and mathematics skills is often taken to be the critical sign of whether children are learning basics. In both cases, memorization and drill are rated out of proportion to other forms of learning and even out of proportion to their demonstrated value in the learning process. Rather than being used as one approach in a complex of approaches to learning, they become the pivotal focus of the learning process and the standard by which everything else is judged. This leads to an oversimplification of teaching and learning and a use of memorization and drill beyond the point when they are effective, sometimes even to the point of cruel force.

Gestalt, of course, is only one theory among others, and it is not offered here as the theory to displace all others. What gestalt theory offers in relation to the problems named above is a study of how human beings learn and organize their perceptions, on the one hand, and how they can open themselves to new insights and reorganization, on the other.

GESTALT METHOD

The gestalt method is much used in education, but not often identified as such. The impact of gestalt psychology is more often recognized in the counseling field than in education,[1] but many teachers use the method. I described it in chapter 1 as integrative teaching, or reaching out to the many facts and ideas and drawing them into unity. Basically, the gestalt approach presents many ideas in proximity to one another so that learners can put the ideas together in some sort of unity. The presentation does not follow a linear pattern toward a particular kind of unity, but sets forth a variety of images and concepts for the learners to draw together. In that sense it is an organic method in which the learners are active in the web of relationship.

Gestalt is a theory of perception and learning based on the ways people organize different phenomena into a unity greater than the sum of the parts. A work of music, for example, is more than an aggregate of notes; the composition as a whole has a quality that surpasses the cumulative effect of the parts. The word *gestalt* comes from the German word meaning "shape" or "form." Gestalt is the pattern that forms unity from the parts.

Max Wertheimer first began to talk about gestalt ideas in Germany in 1912. His only book, *Productive Thinking*, was edited and published after his death in 1945, so his ideas were enlarged and spread by others. Kurt Koffka developed the ideas in relation to learning, publishing *Growth of the Mind* in 1924 and *Principles of Gestalt Psychology* in 1935. Following in a similar line of gestalt thinking was Kurt Lewin, who moved in some new directions in his field theory, but stayed in the same family of ideas.

---

[1] The leading figure in developing gestalt psychotherapy has been Frederick (Fritz) Perls. See Frederick Solomon Perls, *Ego, Hunger and Aggression* (New York: Random House, [1947] 1969); Perls, Paul Goodman, and Ralph Hefferline, *Gestalt Therapy* (New York: Dell Books, 1951).

In the gestalt method of education, the teacher involves students in many experiences and ideas and encourages them to bring these together into a whole. It has a natural appeal to a process theologian; and Alfred North Whitehead's own educational aspirations were to bring the many together into one. He expressed his frustration with the "disconnection of subjects which kills the vitality of our modern curriculum."[2] His hope was for some kind of unity: "The problem of education is to make the pupil see the wood by means of the trees."[3] For some, this may mean unifying the elements of theory and practice; for others, unifying the insights from different disciplines or different art forms; and for still others, unifying the interpretations of different texts. In any case, seeking unity has been a common agenda for process theologians.

Another reason for the natural affinity between gestalt and process thinking is found in Whitehead's idea of concrescence. This is the process by which a new occasion or event emerges. All of the elements of past experience are brought into a unity in the becoming occasion, and the new occasion then becomes an element of experience for later occasions. Whitehead describes concrescence in this way: "The many become one and are increased by one."[4] In a real sense, each moment of experience is a gestalt (or unity) of experiences that have gone before.

Gestalt in Practice

Gestalt communication should seem quite natural to Jews and Christians whose Scriptures are often woven together in this organic way. The faith communities who shaped the scriptural texts often arranged stories and sayings in such a way as to communicate a dramatic whole. The arrangement of texts suggested a theme or question, but left enough openness that interpreters have worked for centuries to name and interpret those themes and questions. In Exodus 20, for example, we read that God reminded the people of their history before giving

[2]Alfred North Whitehead, *The Aims of Education* (New York: Free Press, [1929] 1957), 6–7.
[3]Ibid., 6.
[4]Alfred North Whitehead, *Process and Reality: An Essay in Cosmology*, ed. David R. Griffin and Donald W. Sherburne (New York: [Macmillan, 1929] Free Press, 1978), 21.

them the Ten Commandments: " 'I am the Lord your God, who brought you out of the land of Egypt, out of the house of bondage.' " (Exod. 20:2). Placing of this reminder immediately before the Decalogue suggests that God's deliverance of the people from bondage in Egypt is somehow intimately related with the Commandments. Together they form a gestalt, or whole, and they point to the wholeness of God.

One of the biblical writers whose arrangement of stories is particularly compelling is Mark. In the first half of his Gospel, Mark has grouped a long series of miracle stories, which build in intensity. In the middle of Mark is the dramatic moment when Jesus asks the disciples, " 'But who do you say that I am?' " (Mark 8:29). This question leads immediately into pronouncements regarding the cost of discipleship, namely, the requirement to take up the cross and follow. The rest of Mark's Gospel focuses on the passion and death of Jesus. Such an arrangement highlights the tension between the early miracles and the later passion, and it focuses attention simultaneously on the question of who Jesus is and what Jesus' disciples are called to do. Again, the arrangement is a gestalt; Mark has arranged the stories into a whole that communicates something more unified and powerful than the sum of the parts.

Gestalt method is particularly common in media communication, where a collage of pictures and ideas is presented in hopes that the viewer will bring the ideas together into some kind of unified understanding. A television special on Japanese-Americans during World War II is a good example. The special includes many interviews with Japanese-Americans who lived through the war era in internment camps or in the military. The interviews take place in their homes, in the empty internment camps, and on the farmland that was theirs before being confiscated. The camera's eye moves through the weathered camps and across the farmland; the narrator describes the actions that led to the camps and presents facts and figures about the period. One of the persons interviewed shares bitter memories, and another shares patriotic recollections of fighting in the war and losing a limb. Vignettes are told from the lives of some of the families. Together, all of these visual images, vignettes, statistical figures, and explanations make a story, but the story line is not simple. The beliefs of the producers are revealed in the presentation, but much is left to the viewers to bring the many parts into a unity. The parts are not presented in a logical, vertical way to produce one conclusion; they are presented as a collage to arouse the viewers' interest and stimulate them to draw their own conclusions.

Museums are often laid out in a gestalt way as well. The Museum of Westward Expansion under the Arch in St. Louis, Missouri, is a fine example. The museum is a collection of pictures, implements, a reconstructed frontier room, a tepee, a stuffed buffalo, excerpts from diaries, quotable quotes, facts and figures, and maps. Together, all of these things make a story, but the museum wanderer is left to draw out the story line. No set pattern is offered for going through the museum. The unity is not offered in completed form, but the very diverse and vivid presentation is an invitation to seek a unity.

Gestalt methods are often found in churches and synagogues, particularly those that are self-conscious about their architecture and art and music. Spending time in a cathedral can be an experience of many different art forms—architecture, painting, sculpture, mosaic, tapestry, spoken word, and music. These fit together into a unity, but the unity will not be the same for every person. When two people attend worship together in a cathedral, they usually have different stories to tell.

Basic Precepts of Learning

Gestalt psychologists put forth some basic precepts of how people learn, based on principles of perceptual organization. First, *people learn through central, cognitive processes*, not simply by the association of stimuli and responses. This means that learners acquire cognitive structures over time, rather than mindless habits. Furthermore, insight emerges in the process of problem solving rather than simply through trial and error.[5]

Gestalt psychology offers the idea of memory traces to explain learning by repetition. Associationism, on the other hand, focuses on

---

[5]Gordon Bower and Ernest Hilgard describe the context in which gestalt-learning theory arose. Psychology was dominated by Edward Thorndike's trial-and-error theories of connectionism and, increasingly, by John Watson's behaviorism. This was particularly true in the first half of the twentieth century in the United States, when gestalt theory was first introduced from Germany. See Gordon H. Bower and Ernest R. Hilgard, *Theories of Learning*, 5th ed. (Englewood Cliffs, N.J.: Prentice-Hall, 1981), 299–301.

the repetition itself—the repetition of a stimulus to produce a desired response. These stimulus-response theories have been influential both in the psychology of learning and in education. Learning by objectives is one result. Certain learning or behavioral objectives are set forth and learners are rewarded when they succeed in achieving the objectives. In many classrooms across this country, teachers set objectives for their students individually and collectively; the objectives can relate to any area of study or citizenship. A popular practice in recent years has been to practice discipline in the classroom by adding a marble to a jar every time the class or individuals in the class behave well. When the jar is filled, the students are rewarded for their good behavior. In this way, they are encouraged to become more consistent in that behavior.

Stimulus-response theories are critiqued by gestalt psychologists as offering a mode of teaching and learning that over-stresses repetitive drill to the point that perceptual organization skills may even be thwarted.[6] Gestalt psychologists do grant that habits are formed by repetition, but they explain the phenomenon in a different way. They claim that when an activity or idea is repeated, the individual memory traces are replaced by a memory trace system that is increasingly fixed and stable.[7] For example, we forget what we learned in our first swim lesson after many lessons, but we develop a memory system of how to swim. If we later fall into deep water, that memory system comes into action.

Another precept of gestalt psychology is that *learning takes place through problem solving.* Learning takes place as people interact with empirically perceived realities. This is different from formal logic, which emphasizes applying formulas to situations through reason. Formal logic gives little regard to what individuals actually perceive; the accent is on abstract principles.

Gestalt psychology does deal with insight but with the kind of insight that emerges from perception and problem solving rather than

---

[6]Ibid., 317–19.

[7]Kurt Koffka proposed what he thought was a more adequate view of learning through memory traces formed in the brain—a view in which the traces were seen to interact with the process of organization. This included a more adequate explanation of the role of repetition: repetition is effective because it creates, consolidates, and makes available trace systems. See particularly Kurt Koffka, *Principles of Gestalt Psychology* (New York: Harcourt, Brace & Co., 1935), 544–47; cf. 529–90, 429–31.

from the application of universal principles or from pure trial and error. The evidence of emerging insight is that persons faced with a problem to solve often pause to inspect or think, they are often able to repeat a solution after only one trial, and are able to generalize to other similar situations.

This last process is called transposition.[8] An example of transposition described by Max Wertheimer in 1945 is that when children are taught to compute the area of a rectangle, they will often be able to transpose that ability to compute the area of a parallelogram. They simply transpose the one shape into the other and use the same procedures to compute the area. They do not need principles of logic or blind repetition.[9]

The gestalt psychologists recognize that *insight learning is more likely under some conditions than others*, and this, too, has educational implications. Ernst Hilgard names some of these conditions.[10] First, insight is more likely when the subjects are more intelligent or more developed. Perhaps, then, the gestalt approach to education would be increasingly helpful with older youth and adults.

Insight is optimized also when learners are more experienced in an area of study. For example, students more experienced in geometry might be more successful in transposing their insights from rectangles to parallelograms. This idea fits well with Whitehead's idea that the stage of generalization in education follows the stage of precision. People need to know some details before they can form generalizations. For example, a person who knows some details about the context and literary structure of Mark's Gospel will be better able to draw out generalizations about Mark's messages.

Insight learning is also facilitated when the learning environment gives access to all of the elements and enables the patterning of the elements. This is exemplified in the Westward Expansion Museum. The Lewis and Clark expedition is presented all around the walls of

---

[8]The ability of persons to transpose ideas from one situation to the next has been important evidence of gestalt learning, or productive thinking. See Max Wertheimer, *Productive Thinking*, enlarged ed., edited by Michael Wertheimer (New York: Harper & Row, [1945] 1959), 66–68, 234–36, 253–55.

[9]Ibid., 13–78. Wertheimer also explains transposition in relation to transposing a tune from one key to another. (See 253–55.)

[10]Some of these conditions were identified in the earliest experiments of gestalt theorists. See Koffka's *Principles of Gestalt Psychology* and Wertheimer's *Productive Thinking* for some of the earliest findings regarding factors that influence insight learning.

the museum. If visitors enter the display at the beginning, they will find a map and a list of the explorers, followed by a chronological series of panels with scenic pictures and diary excerpts. Both the chronological order and the consistent style of presenting the pictures and excerpts form a pattern. The pattern facilitates the search for unity, even if visitors walk backwards through the display as I and many others have done. Likewise, the pattern creates a sense of visual unity even if museum goers jump around and visit only a few of the panels, as several parents with small children did when we were there.

Another form of patterning is offered in the same museum. In the middle area of the museum is a display of weapons of war, mixed together with large portraits of famous Americans and their impassioned statements for peace. Included in the display are Albert Einstein, Martin Luther King, Jr., Chief Joseph of the Nez Perces, General William Sherman, and Franklin D. Roosevelt. The numerous items in this section of the museum are displayed in various ways. However, the fact that they all relate to war and peace establishes a pattern that facilitates insight.

A fourth condition facilitating insight is that opportunities for trial and error increase the possibility for insight. This is particularly true if the trial and error is hypothesis testing, and if learners are encouraged to make thoughtful choices about what to try. For example, a mathematics teacher would usually discourage a child from haphazard guessing of answers to a problem. The teacher might instead encourage the child to think through the problem and then make a considered guess. In dealing with theological constructs, teachers might actually encourage persons to think through an idea of God by trial-and-error testing. In regard to the idea of the responsiveness and changeability of God, for example, learners might speculate that God is responsive to the world and changes in relation to the world. Then, they might test this concept by examining it in light of different biblical texts. They might also test the hypothesis by examining it in light of their experiences of God.

Insight learning is more likely under some conditions than others, and these have been sketched briefly. One last assertion must be made about gestalt learning: *Learning involves the whole person—cognitive and affective, mental and physical.* People have bodily responses to their environment as well as mental. This has been vividly revealed to me through our daughter's experience in liturgical dance. On one occasion, she was carrying the communion cup in a dance to "Let Us Break Bread Together." After the dance began, the dance director remembered that she had forgotten to tell Rebecca what to do during one of the verses. When the verse began, Rebecca slowly lifted the cup in a gesture of adoration—a gesture that fit the music beautifully. The dance director asked Rebecca afterwards how she had known what to do; Rebecca shrugged her shoulders and said, "It just seemed right." Rebecca's bodily response to the situation preceded her conscious awareness. She was responding to the whole of the situation, or to the gestalt.

Basic Precepts of Perceptual Organization

In addition to basic precepts of how people learn, gestalt psychologists also put forth basic precepts about how people organize their perceptions. Certain factors or laws affect how people organize their sense data, and these same factors can facilitate learning and retention.

The first and most basic law is the *Law of Pragnanz*. According to this law, individuals tend to organize their perceptions in the direction of a good gestalt, or good form. More specifically, they tend to organize in the direction of regularity, simplicity, and stability.

The *Law of Pragnanz* is the overarching law, and it is amplified by more specific laws that explain how people typically reach a gestalt. In learning situations, disequilibrium or tension often arises. Wertheimer put forth several particular laws to explain how the tensions get resolved.[11] Kurt Koffka expanded on the research and elaborated on the laws. Now four laws have become particularly familiar. The four laws describe how people organize their perceptions on the basis of similarity, proximity, closure, or continuation.[12]

According to the *Law of Similarity*, individuals tend to organize their perceptions into categories of similar items or similar movements. Children, for example, often organize their biblical knowledge by putting all of the "fleeing into Egypt" stories together. In the Lewis and Clark display, the similar forms of presentation contribute to the

---

[11]Wertheimer, *Productive Thinking*, esp. 234–37, cf. 234–59. Productive thinking happens in relation to wholes, rather than in a series of piecemeal events.
[12]Koffka, *Principles of Gestalt Psychology*, 106–176.

museum goers' ability to organize what they are seeing. In education, similarity of images, ideas, or presentation can be used to enhance integration.

The *Law of Proximity* asserts that people tend to organize their perceptions according to the nearness of the parts. In the Museum of Westward Expansion, the grouping of war and peace messages in the same vicinity fosters integration and intensifies the power of the messages. Likewise, persons often associate events that have taken place in the same time period or in the same part of the world.

According to the *Law of Closure*, people are motivated to complete incomplete figures, ideas, or series of events. They will seek closure and find satisfaction when it is achieved. This implies that open-ended questions, conflict situations, and pending decisions can create motivation for closure and can thereby contribute to learning. Rather than avoiding such situations, teachers should seek ways to maximize the learning opportunities inherent in them.

Finally, the *Law of Good Continuation* asserts that individuals tend to organize so that perceptual forms are continued in the same mode. For example, a straight line is assumed to continue as a straight line, and a curved line, as a curved line. Applied to theological thinking, the law of continuation would suggest that the idea of a faraway God would continue as a faraway God, and the idea of a responsive God would continue as a responsive God—unless new data presents a new idea.

If continuation is an operative principle, then persons may not grasp new ideas about lines or God easily because they will assume the continuation of the old ideas. When they do grasp a new idea, however, they will be able to continue it into other times and situations. A teacher can introduce a new idea without giving an example of every instance of the idea. If the learners grasp the idea in the first place, they will be able to extend it themselves. When a priest suggests to a family grieving over the death of a loved one that God is able to receive their anger, the view of God offered may be radically different from the ones they have known. The priest does not need to describe every aspect of that view of God and give a myriad of examples, however, because the family will be able to continue that idea of God into other situations if they grasp it in the first place.

One note should be added to this discussion of how people organize their perceptions. The gestalt psychologists give primary attention to the present field of experience, and past experience gets far less attention. Usually the past is a focal point primarily in relation to how it screens or influences new experiences. Koffka does speak of memories that enter into the present field, and he believes that these are organized according to similar perceptual laws. Also, the memory traces may be organized differently over time. For example, a father might exaggerate a memory of walking five miles to school over snow in order to fit better with other memories of being a more persecuted or heroic child than his own children.

Gestalt Method and Lateral Thinking

Gestalt learning theory challenges much of traditional educational method. This becomes even more important in the wake of the media revolution. Just as modern communication theory must take account of the revolutionizing influence of modern media, so modern psychological theories must take account of patterns in human perceptions and organization intensified by modern communications. Marshall McLuhan asserts that the birth of movies shifted the way people relate to the world. As a medium that addresses many senses at one time, the motion picture translates persons "beyond mechanism into a world of growth and organic interrelation."[13] This is a movement away from lineal connections to configurations; similarly, gestalt method is based on configurations. The dilemma is that much of today's education is based on the more lineal stimulus-response associations or formal logic, so gestalt theory poses a threat to many assumed patterns of teaching and learning.

Gestalt method promotes what Edward deBono calls lateral thinking. DeBono is concerned with how people achieve insight by creating new patterns out of available information. He distinguishes between vertical, or logical, thinking and lateral thinking. In lateral thinking, individuals approach a problem from different directions in order to see a new pattern and find an appropriate resolution. In vertical thinking, individuals use or build on a pattern that already exists. DeBono says, "Lateral thinking is useful for generating ideas and

---

[13]Marshall McLuhan, *Understanding Media: The Extensions of Man* (New York: McGraw-Hill, 1964), 12.

approaches and vertical thinking is useful for developing them."[14] The former is the kind of thinking facilitated by a gestalt approach to education.

This distinction between lateral thinking and vertical thinking becomes very important for education, which often assumes that communicating established ideas and collecting more information will be sufficient to create wisdom. DeBono argues that conflict can sometimes lead to new ideas, but that some kind of insight tool is needed. This is what lateral thinking offers, and it is closely akin to creativity. Lateral thinking is a critical complement to vertical thinking. He describes the relationship in this way:

> Lateral thinking enhances the effectiveness of vertical thinking. Vertical thinking develops the ideas generated by lateral thinking. You cannot dig a hole in a different place by digging the same hole deeper. Lateral thinking is used to dig a hole in a different place. The exclusive emphasis on vertical thinking in the past makes it all the more necessary to teach lateral thinking. It is not just that vertical thinking alone is insufficient for progress but that by itself it can be dangerous.[15]

Here is where gestalt theory has a distinctive contribution. In offering an analysis of insight learning and the methods by which people can be taught to pattern their perceptions into new insights, gestalt method can generate and enhance lateral thinking. Learners may be led to discover already established ideas about rectangles and parallelograms, but the exploration will often lead to new ideas as well. Learners will be encouraged to dig holes deeper and, also, to seek new places to dig.

PROCESS THEOLOGY AND
GESTALT METHOD

The kinship between process theology and gestalt method has been noted by several process thinkers in this century. Bernard Meland especially notes the kinship between Henry Nelson Wieman and the

---

[14]Edward deBono, *Lateral Thinking: Creativity Step by Step* (San Francisco: Harper & Row, 1970), 50; cf. 10–13.
[15]Ibid., 12–13.

gestalt psychologists; he sees the movement toward thinking holistically as undergirded by the psychologists of the gestalt school and the metaphysics of Alfred North Whitehead.[16] Some interesting discussions have taken place highlighting differences among Wieman, Whitehead, and Bergson.[17] However, the three of them were alike in that they were all writing in the early twentieth century during a period dominated by discussions of Charles Darwin's theory of evolution. In contrast to Darwin, they all were concerned with the inner dynamics of human beings in relation to external forces of nature.[18] Their work was highly compatible, then, with the more interactive views of human psychology deriving from George Herbert Mead and the gestalt psychologists.

Three ideas of process theology are particularly important to reflections on gestalt method. These are the ideas of concrescence, the dipolar nature of God, and novelty. Each of these ideas makes contact with gestalt theory and gives some basis for interchange between the psychological theory and the philosophical system.

Concrescence

The idea of concrescence was mentioned earlier in this chapter, particularly Whitehead's concept of the many becoming one and being increased by one. For Whitehead the most fundamental process of all of reality is this process of the many becoming one. It is the way that everything comes to be; all elements of experience are brought into

---

[16]Bernard Eugene Meland, *The Realities of Faith: The Revolution in Cultural Forms* (New York: Oxford University Press, 1962), 110–11, 119–20. This movement toward more holistic thinking in psychological field theories and process metaphysics has led to a new view of human beings, not as purely autonomous selves or as purely socially determined creatures, but as individuals in community. (See pp. 132–34.)

[17]One statement of the difference between Wieman and Whitehead is found in Gene Reeves and Delwin Brown, "The Development of Process Theology," in *Process Philosophy and Christian Thought*, Delwin Brown, Ralph E. James, Jr., and Gene Reeves, eds. (Indianapolis: Bobbs-Merrill, 1971), 24–25. Discussions of Whitehead and Bergson are found in Meland, *Realities of Faith*, 118–21, and in James W. Felt, "Intuition, Event-Atomism, and the Self," in *Process in Context: Essays in Post-Whiteheadian Perspectives*, Ernest Wolf-Gazo, ed. (New York: Peter Lang, 1988), 137–52. Felt finds Bergson's view more helpful in describing personal continuity through time (see pp. 138–48) and in presenting a more substance-like philosophy that corrects Whitehead's emphasis on event-atomism (see pp. 148–50).

[18]See particularly Meland, *Realities of Faith*, 124–27.

unity in the becoming occasion.[19] In a similar way, the gestalt psychologists understand the quest for unity to be a natural psychological process for organizing perceptions into a good form, or gestalt.

Concrescence is a fundamental concept for education from a process perspective because it explains how new experiences and past experiences come together in each moment. The image of the person at the intersection was a fundamental concept in my earlier book *Education for Continuity and Change*.[20] This image suggests that at every moment a person or a community enters a new intersection, or creative crossing. For both a person sitting in a classroom or a community facing a major decision, the intersection is a place where choices will be made (even if the choice is to continue in the same pattern). People bring their history, concerns, and previous knowledge into the intersection, and in that intersection they meet many new influences. At that point they have to decide which way to go. They may decide to stay on their original course, or they may change courses, but they will have to decide. Having made a decision, they will enter another intersection in the next moment, and the process continues.

Obviously, this process is not always conscious and we are not always aware of the decisions we make, but we always make them. Education is an opportunity to introduce new experiences and ideas to people at the intersection and to heighten their sense of being at a crossing in the road where they can make fresh decisions. At every intersection, human beings are confronted with God and the world of past, present, and future, and they are called to draw the many influences into a unity. This unity might be called a gestalt if the idea of gestalt can be extended to include not only conscious perceptions but also all of experience.

Whitehead's idea of concrescence is different from gestalt method in one important way. The emphasis in process thought is on the

---

[19]David Roy has also noted the relevance of Whitehead's view of concrescence to gestalt therapy. In Roy's view, the primary theme that emerges from a dialogue between process theology and gestalt psychology is integration, and the process of integration in process thought can be described as concrescence. See David Edward Roy, "Toward a Process Therapy: An Integration of Perception and Concrescence from Whitehead with the Self Modes and Gestalt Formation from Gestalt Therapy" (Ann Arbor, Mich.: University Microfilms, 1978), Dissertation, School of Theology at Claremont. See also Roy, "The Value of the Dialogue between Process Thought and Psychotherapy," *Process Studies* 14 (Fall 1985): 158–74.

[20]Mary Elizabeth Moore, *Education for Continuity and Change: A New Model of Christian Religious Education* (Nashville: Abingdon Press, 1983), 86–117.

influence of the past as well as the present. The dichotomy between past and present so common in psychology is rejected. According to process thinking, the past lives in the present, and also the past continues to have influence as past. A person, then, has memories that are organized and influential, but old memories can also come forth at any time to influence the person, even if the old memory has not been included as a major component in the more conscious memory.

As I described earlier, memory traces can explain how a person remembers how to swim, even though the specifics of different lessons may be forgotten. From a Whiteheadian point of view, any of the specifics from the past could come back to have an influence at any time, even though they may have long been lost from conscious memory. Most people experience this phenomenon from time to time. They think they have resolved a particular issue, but something in the present situation brings it into influence or consciousness and it arises again as a major issue. From a process theological perspective, this can happen with or without consciousness, and it can happen at any time because the past never dies and it is always to some extent accessible.

Dipolar Nature of God

Another foundational idea in Whitehead's metaphysics is background to the dialogue between process theology and gestalt method. This is the concept of the dipolar nature of God. God is understood as having two aspects, one that guides the world and one that is affected by the world. The first is called the primordial nature of God and the latter is called the consequent nature. God is one, but God acts in these different ways; hence, God's nature is dipolar. In God's dipolar nature, God is actually experienced in each moment, and God also experiences the world in every moment. God enters into the unity of every becoming occasion in concrescence, and every occasion affects the life of God. In sum, God is always creating, and God is always responding.

God is known in part by the creativity in the world because God is actively creating at every moment. This manifests God's primordial nature, subjectively entering into the world to influence it. The organic process perspective adds this element to gestalt assumptions, that

God is part of the process of reality. God envisions new possibilities for each becoming occasion, and God is working to enable the occasion to bring its past together into harmony. God is creating by being an active influence on every event and, also, by empowering each event to take shape.

In God's primordial nature, God provides an initial aim to every becoming occasion. This provides a pattern by which the many different elements of experience can be held together in harmony. The result is to increase the intensity of the whole. The initial aim makes concrescence possible and the converting of opposition into contrast.[21] This means that seemingly incompatible elements are brought into harmonious relationship. The harmony does not deny the differences among the elements, but it does make possible a unity. The initial aim is not the sole determinant on an occasion, however. In the process view, God acts through persuasion rather than coercion.[22] The emerging occasion will make its own decision about how it will take form. The decisive factor is the subjective aim of the occasion. God's aim for every occasion is real and influential, but it is not determinative in itself. The subjective aim will not always be the same as the initial aim from God.[23]

More specifically, God is working to maximize harmony and intensity. Intensity, for Whitehead, does not refer to the volume or loudness of experience, but to the variety that is held in contrast. Intensity has to do with bringing together many parts into a new pattern of relationship that allows different ideas and experiences to be held together. As explained earlier, gestalt methods actually encourage people to explore variety and seek to bring the many parts into harmony. From a process perspective, such a method would offer the possibility of maximizing intensity. Since intensity is valued in a process perspective for connecting disparate elements, the gestalt method seems very promising.

In God's consequent nature, God is responding as well as creating; thus, God not only influences people, but also people affect God. The

---

[21]Whitehead, *Process and Reality*, esp. 244–45, 249–50, 109, 111–15.

[22]This idea is developed with particular fullness in Lewis S. Ford, *The Lure of God: A Biblical Background for Process Theism* (Philadelphia: Fortress Press, 1978).

[23]These ideas are particularly developed in Whitehead, *Process and Reality*, 108, 244–45, 27–28.

way a person or community brings unity out of many elements will influence God. For example, if a young man brings unity out of a series of broken relationships by bitterly abandoning all relationships, God may react with sadness and may work in and around the young man to bring about more enjoyment, or more harmony. Likewise, if an oppressed people bring unity out of the many acts of violence against them by giving up their struggle for a better life, God surely will feel their pain and work in every possible way for their liberation.

This dipolar activity of God, as creating and responding, is at the heart of the God-world relationship. As Whitehead states: "What is done in the world is transformed into a reality in heaven, and the reality in heaven passes back into the world. By reason of this reciprocal relation, the love in the world passes into the love in heaven, and floods back again into the world. In this sense, God is the great companion—the fellow-sufferer who understands."[24] No unity in the world, then, is isolated from God. God will influence and be influenced by it.

Novelty

The third process idea in the background as we converse between process theology and gestalt educational method is novelty. Whitehead describes a becoming occasion as influenced both by the collective past and by novelty.[25] The occasion is not limited to old and new combinations of past influences, but is affected by new influences as well. The idea of novelty explains how new forms of unity can emerge, both from new patterns of organizing the past and from new influences.

Within Christianity we certainly have evidence of many forms of unity that claim to give witness to the Christian faith. Unity in worship is found in one way in the Episcopal Church, in another way in the United Church of Canada, and in another way in the Russian Orthodox Church. None of these unities exhaust all of the possibilities, however. All of these have emerged through influences of the past and of newness.

---

[24]Ibid., 351.
[25]Ibid., 21, 187, 88, 65–67.

New forms will continue to appear, always influenced heavily by the past, but also subject to the influence of novelty entering in the world anew. This is what Marjorie Suchocki refers to as the openness in process thought. She says, "The future is the creation of new values through the creative response to relationships of the past."[26] Suchocki believes that process theology is helpful in articulating how novelty enters into reality, but she finds feminist action even more helpful in embodying the openness to new realities.

Novelty originates in God who is "the organ of novelty aiming at intensification."[27] Novelty enters into a becoming occasion in response to God's initial aim, and it is embodied through the subject's unique response to God's aim and the inheritance of the past. Furthermore, the embodied novelty enters back into the life of God, thus contributing to "the creative advance into novelty."[28] God and the world thus contribute novelty to one another.

The subject's response to God and to the inheritance of the past is called the subjective form.[29] The subjective form of every becoming occasion is a unique response, but some are more novel than others. Worship changes are introduced when a worshiper or worshiping community experiences the old forms with new feelings, and this leads to critique and reform. One vivid example is Alexander Campbell's experience of alienation in the Presbyterian church when worshipers were required to present tickets in order to take communion. Campbell's experience, and that of others like him, led eventually to the formation of the Disciples of Christ denomination and a new form of communion ritual. Most of us have had numerous experiences of seeing a familiar situation in a new light; this results from a subjective form different from those that have gone before.

The idea of novelty is quite compatible with gestalt assumptions, for people may have new insights for organizing the elements available to their perceptions. This aspect of gestalt method is akin to deBono's lateral thinking. People are not bound to perceive reality in the same logical sequence every time; they may dramatically reorganize their

---

[26]Marjorie Suchocki, "Openness and Mutuality in Process Thought and Feminist Action," in *Feminism and Process Thought*, ed. Sheila Greeve Davaney (Lewiston, N.Y.: Edward Mellen Press, 1981), 63.

[27]Whitehead, *Process and Reality*, 67.

[28]Ibid., 349.

[29]Ibid., 23.

perceptions and have new insights into problems as a result. Gestalt method fosters this kind of thinking.

The idea that novelty is introduced into experience from God may seem strange to gestalt method, however. God fosters novel integrations of the past and introduces novel elements from the divine experience. This idea suggests that novel patterns of unity might go beyond those that can be explained by the gestalt laws of perception.

The emergence of novelty can be an ordinary life event. One good example comes from deBono's story of his efforts to repair a broken lamp in his apartment after a friend had spent the weekend there in his absence. After deBono worked unsuccessfully on the bulb, the fuse, and the plug, he decided to try the wall switch and the light came on. His friend had simply turned off the lamp at the wall.[30] Many a dramatic engineering feat, such as the St. Louis Arch or the Cathedral of Notre Dame, also represents novelty, a new pattern of putting together building materials and engineering details. The resulting pattern itself may be very simple, but the details that enter into it are highly complex.

The fact that novelty can contribute to the creative process does not mean that novelty is an end in itself. From the perspective of process theology, the value of novelty is the degree to which it contributes to the enjoyment of intense experience. In fact, both order and novelty are of value insofar as they add to that enjoyment.[31] The implication for teaching is that order and novelty are both important, and novelty for the sake of novelty is not always fruitful. The existence of novelty is promising for the educational task, but the introduction of novelty does not guarantee that the task will be done effectively.

GESTALT METHOD RE-FORMED
BY PROCESS THEOLOGY

The dialogue between gestalt method and process theology calls attention to the complementarity between them. From both perspectives, the process of organizing the many into one is seen as basic to

[30]Edward deBono, *The Use of Lateral Thinking* (Harmondsworth, Eng.: Penguin Books, [1967] 1979), 122.

[31]Whitehead, *Process and Reality,* 161; John B. Cobb, Jr., and David R. Griffin, *Process Theology: An Introductory Exposition* (Philadelphia: Westminster Press, 1976), 161.

reality. For gestalt method, certain laws of learning and perception have been identified to explain how people organize their perceptions and ideas. For process theology, certain assertions about God have been made that call attention to the experience of God's presence and to God's initial aim that fosters the process of the many becoming one. Now we turn attention to the shape of a gestalt method informed and reshaped by process theology.

Major Elements in Teaching

Teaching in a process-gestalt method would have three major action elements—to experience the many, to seek unity, and to preserve the complexity of detail. The first two derive from both gestalt and process perspectives, but the third introduces an accent from process theology usually dismissed or given less attention in gestalt method. All three seem obvious from what has been said above, but they are not obvious in the context of traditional teaching methods. Introducing many different facts and ideas can be dangerous if teachers want to teach students to believe only in a certain way. Seeking after unity is dangerous if teachers do not want to risk new visions of the world that threaten conventional ways of thinking and acting. Preserving the complexity of detail is also dangerous if teachers want to perpetuate a dominant way of thinking and to discourage ideas and actions that emerge on the fringes of the community. The word *heresy* derives from a root meaning "to choose" or "to choose for oneself." If a community wants to discourage choice, it will advocate dominant beliefs, values, and practices and dismiss the complexity of detail that does not fit dominant patterns.

The first element in teaching is *to give opportunity for students to experience the many*. The teacher offers some variety of facts and ideas or invites these from students. The group, then, can look at a concept from many different perspectives, such as studying the work of Christ from different historical perspectives. The teacher may also offer presentations and explorations in many different media or may approach a subject using different methods of research, such as library research, interviews, and field trips. Part of the power of Mary Tully's teaching, as described by Maria Harris, was her creative use of many forms of expression and her thoroughness in creating an environment for teaching. She created an environment for students to explore—an environment that engaged many senses.[32] The structure was guided, but students had much freedom to explore the materials and their own responses.

At this point, process theology might raise one potential limitation of such an environmental approach to teaching. Environmental exploration can be so focused on what is sensed in the immediate environment that the elements of knowledge outside of ordinary sense data get very little attention. From a process perspective, the building blocks of knowledge include more than sense data. The building blocks come from total experience, and our education is faulty if we attend only to sense data; this leads inevitably to selective attention.[33] In this way, we can easily miss internal dynamics or large social and economic movements not immediately accessible to the senses.

What we need is multiple forms of reflection, including imaginative, critical, and depth reflection so that our inquiry will open many dimensions of experience, rather than be limited to ordinary sense data. From both gestalt and process perspectives, knowledge emerges from the interaction of external and internal dynamics. Thinking, then, needs to include both critical reflection on the events of the world and depth reflection into inner experience.[34] Human thinking and action need to take account of sense data that is perceived and, also, the internal purposiveness of the perceiving subject.[35]

In addition, the process perspective reminds teachers that the range of events includes events across the world and throughout history; since the range is wider than we can receive as sense data in the immediate environment, our education needs to be broad. Also from a process view, the dichotomy between ultimacy and immediacy is overridden. Ultimacy is the dimension of depth in every immediate event;[36] thus, every event has significance in relation to the whole and in relation to ultimacy. Teaching gives opportunity for students

---

[32]Harris presents a case study of Mary Tully's teaching at Union Theological Seminary in Maria Harris, *Teaching and Religious Imagination* (San Francisco: Harper & Row, 1987), 119–41.

[33]Robert S. Brumbaugh, "Whiteheadian American Educational Philosophy," in *Process in Context*, 57–61.

[34]Moore, *Education for Continuity and Change*, 127–32; Felt, "Intuition, Event-Atomism, and the Self," 142–44.

[35]Lois Gehr Livezey, "Women, Power, and Politics: Feminist Theology in Process Perspective," *Process Studies* 17 (Summer 1988): 70–75.

[36]Meland, *Realities of Faith*, 116, cf. 114–16, 121–22.

to experience the many, and every one of the many will point to ultimacy. If the ultimate is accessible in the immediate event, our education needs to be deep. And so we are led back to the importance of multiple strategies for teaching—strategies that foster education with both breadth and depth. Introducing multiple views and means of expression can free learners from the limited options they have seen heretofore and can free them to seek a more adequate view of the world, a wider and deeper understanding, and a fuller means of expression.

The second element of teaching in a process-gestalt method is *to seek unity*. The act of teaching involves leading students toward unity, however difficult that might be. The search for unity has to do with searching for the whole that is greater than the sum of the parts. The search for unity in a given period of history may be a search for unifying themes or for the spirit of the whole. The search for unity in a work of art may be a search for the total experience of the work.

The search for unity is often done by setting the many experiences or facts alongside one another to see what insights and patterns emerge. For example, a community might experience many forms of sharing together to gain some whole sense of what it means to be a sharing community, or *koinonia*. A group might look at the views of various commentators on a political event and see what central insights they glean. Many teachers and pastors search for unity when they spread out their research notes and seek to make them into a whole lecture, class plan, or sermon. The act of trying to decide what is most important to do or say is an act of seeking unity.

Of course, teachers and pastors can easily prepare a lecture or sermon without seeking unity in a string of apparently disconnected pieces. From a process theological perspective, to avoid the search for unity is to avoid the search for harmony among disparate elements or to settle for the triviality of chaos. Likewise, to settle for the most obvious form of unity—and avoid probing the depths of experience for more significant forms—is to settle for trivial harmony.[37] The consequence is a loss of intensity in experience.

---

[37]Whitehead expresses concern that trivial order involves trivialized actual entities. He says, "Unless some systematic scheme of relatedness characterizes the environment, there will be nothing left, whereby to constitute vivid prehension of the world." (*Process and Reality*, 254.) Also, for Whitehead, order is necessary for depth of satisfaction; chaos yields triviality but some forms of order provide trivial satisfaction themselves. He concludes, "Thus, if there is to be progress beyond limited ideals, the course of history by way of escape must venture along the borders of chaos in its substitution of higher for lower forms of order." (Ibid., 111; cf. 110.)

The search for unity can also take place when a teacher or teaching community presents material with the gestalt laws of perception in mind. The movement in Christian education to organize communal life around the liturgical year or the lectionary is a move in that direction, though no one has claimed that this is a gestalt form of organizing. One of the writers who most clearly articulates this approach to Christian education is John Westerhoff. Westerhoff has proposed organizing all of the church's community life and administrative committees around the seasons of the Christian year.[38] Such organization would coordinate the many aspects of community under a similar theme, thereby aiding its members in forming a gestalt, or unity, around the different events in the life of Jesus and the early Christian community.

The danger, of course, is that organizing around the life of Jesus eliminates other important aspects of the Christian tradition such as Hebrew Bible traditions, later traditions of the church, or events taking place in the world today. These are all viewed through the organizing principle of the life of Jesus, which tends to highlight certain aspects and ignore others. An example is that most lectionaries select Old Testament texts as they relate to New Testament selections. Many parts of the Old Testament are ignored in this way.

On the other hand, organizing church life around the seasons of the Christian year does offer significant guidance to Christians seeking unity. From a process theological perspective, patterning around the life of Jesus is important in a Christian community because its identity is based in Jesus Christ.[39] The community needs to remember, however, that patterning in this way does not exhaust all of the elements in its tradition. Neither does the approach exhaust all of the possible patterns that would have integrity in the tradition.

Still another way for a teacher or community to help people seek unity is to ask questions, especially basic questions of meaning. The questions, of course, will vary according to the purpose of the educational enterprise, but they may include such questions as: What is

---

[38]John H. Westerhoff III, *A Pilgrim People: Learning Through the Church Year* (New York: Seabury Press, 1984).

[39]See, for example, Cobb and Griffin, *Process Theology*, 105–6. Here they recognize that the incarnation in Jesus Christ is actually enhanced as we "deliberately place ourselves in his field of force, and as we renew our contact with his teaching." This basic idea will be explored more fully in chapter 4 of this book.

the most important aspect of your community life? What is your main purpose in this study? What is the thesis of your paper? What is your most important idea? What is the center of the Jewish faith? The purpose of such questions is to encourage learners to seek significant wholes and not settle for trivial harmony.

In Jewish and Christian contexts, another kind of question would also be important in light of a process perspective on God's participation in the dynamics of creation. Leaders would ask questions such as: What is God doing here? How is God creating and leading? To what kinds of unity are we being pulled? Such questions invite people to be open to transcendence in their midst.

Some cautions have been raised in discussing teaching that seeks after unity; these lead to a third element in process-gestalt teaching— *to preserve the complexity of detail.* The very unwillingness to settle for one or two organizing principles is a corrective offered by process theology because in that perspective the elimination of complexity and detail would be considered a major loss.[40] The very thrust of the creative process is to bring the many into one and to convert opposition into contrast. Contradictions within the tradition are cause for wrestling, not cause for simple interpretations that eliminate the details that do not fit. This concern for detail and complexity is an important contribution of process theology to gestalt method. In process theology the balance between identity and diversity is seen as very important for contrast.[41] Pure identity yields no contrast, only repetition. Pure diversity yields no contrast, only incompatibility. This suggests a perceptual law that is compatible with gestalt method, but enlarges on it. The law is that the intensity of experience and fullness of perception are maximized when complexity holds identity and diversity in balance.[42]

---

[40]Complexity is very important for contrasts, for intensity of experience, and for the aesthetic ideal. See Whitehead, *Process and Reality,* 255, 278–80.

[41]Whitehead describes this as "balanced complexity," and he understands balance as "the adjustment of identities and diversities for the introduction of contrast with the avoidance of inhibitions by incompatibilities." (Ibid., 278.)

[42]This law moves in a different direction from the four gestalt laws of perception presented earlier in this chapter. This law has less to do with perceiving a good form, or gestalt, and more to do with sensing that which is beyond the bounds of the good form. Some acknowledgment of this complexity is given in gestalt therapeutic theory. One specific example is Roy's addition of de-structuring to the therapeutic process. See Roy, "Toward a Process Therapy," 81–87. Roy, however, has seen this more as an early stage of formation than as part of the final stage or the whole process.

If teachers took this law of perception seriously in teaching, they would ask questions of unity, such as: What are the central insights? What is most important here? What is the main purpose? What is the thesis? What is God doing here? But they would also ask questions about the marginal and subterranean themes, such as: What insights do not fit with the central ones? What is important to the minority voices? What are the secondary and tertiary purposes? What are the undercurrents and subtheses? What is not revealed about God's actions?

The three elements in process-gestalt teaching suggest a rhythmic approach in which teachers and learners would begin with exposure to many details, seek to unify the details into a whole, and acknowledge the details that do not fit into the unity.[43] The rhythm naturally leads to unifying wholes and, then, back into details and a renewed search for unity. Teaching is a continual process of searching for wholes and preserving awareness of the inadequacy of any unified conclusion.

The Teacher's Role

Having named the major elements of teaching, I need to be more specific about the teacher herself or himself because much responsibility in the gestalt method lies in the hands of this person or group of persons. A few of the specific roles, or responsibilities, will be outlined here.

DO RESEARCH   One obvious responsibility of the teacher or teaching

---

[43]This rhythm is somewhat different from Whitehead's rhythm of education described in *The Aims of Education* (15–28), and developed further by Robert S. Brumbaugh in *Whitehead, Process Philosophy, and Education* (Albany: State University of New York Press, 1982). The rhythm described by Whitehead begins with romance, moves to precision, and finally yields to generalization or satisfaction. The rhythm described here is quite compatible; in both, the movement is toward wholes. Whitehead's stage of romance would emphasize the importance of capturing the interest of students in the initial presentation of details or existing forms of unity. The stages of precision and generalization would be much like the rhythm being described in this chapter in which students wrestle with many details and finally bring them into a whole, or into a generalization. The stage being added in this chapter is the stage of acknowledging that some details will still not fit and will reopen the questions to be pursued again. This is not incompatible with Whitehead's rhythms of education, but it is not so explicit in the educational philosophy as in Whitehead's metaphysics discussed throughout this chapter.

community is to do research or to collect the data and ideas relevant to the life and work of the learning community. When a learning community is struggling with conflict, research might be done into the various psychological explanations of conflict and conflict management. Or, research in a religious community might focus on how conflict has been interpreted and handled in the traditions of that community.

PLAN THE PRESENTATION   A second role of the teacher is to open access to the various parts of the data by presenting them in a patterned way. This would not necessarily be a logical, or vertical, presentation (to use deBono's term), but a presentation that follows a gestalt pattern. The presentation might group the data according to similarity or proximity, for example. The teacher might base the pattern of presentation around the contexts, senses, and forms of expression relevant to the learners and the subject matter. A study of creation can be approached through music, dance, poetry, biblical story, historic Hebrew liturgies, creation myths in other cultures, or church creeds. Any of these forms of expression can be used to offer a pattern for learners to use in seeking a unified vision of creation.

ENCOURAGE PEOPLE TO FIND PATTERNS   Another teaching responsibility is to help people seek the patterns in the data. Offering many different expressions of creation may not be sufficient in itself if some holistic view of creation is being sought. At the end of a study of creation, the teacher might ask group members to write their own belief statements, write a creation myth, or prepare a community celebration. Any of these might inspire the group to seek patterns of unity.

REMAIN OPEN AND ENCOURAGE OPENNESS IN OTHERS   What is needed is openness to questions unanswered, to data that do not fit neatly into the available interpretative frameworks, to conflicting interpretative frameworks, and to data never before acknowledged as data. These sore points are important subject matter for study if a community wants to explore new modes of integration and interpretation.

One of the more difficult roles of the teacher is to remain open to new ideas and forms of unity. A teacher needs to realize that there is not one single pattern of unity to be taught. A teacher needs to be able to offer genuine encouragement to learners in trying out various patterns. This might involve inspiring and giving permission to a religious community or a local school board to brainstorm possible decisions on an issue at hand. A teacher also needs to realize that novel patterns might emerge that no one in the learning community has envisioned before. Furthermore, these novel patterns might just be the wisdom of God. The teacher, then, is one who awaits novelty and encourages others to live with the same expectancy. In a Jewish or Christian community, this waiting might be described as listening for the voice of God or listening for wisdom from those who live on the margins of society.

PRESENT ONE'S OWN VIEWS One more role of the teacher can be helpful as persons seek to bring the many into one. The teacher may present her or his own view so that it can be considered among the many different views. This can be a way of guiding learners toward unity by offering a form of unity that has meaning for the teacher or teaching community.

These various teaching roles are important if the teacher is to enable students to have rich experiences and to seek the unity in those experiences. These roles are important so that the many can become one.

PROCESS THEOLOGY RE-FORMED
BY GESTALT METHOD

The dialogue between educational method and theology always moves two ways when we are standing on the bridge between the two disciplines. Some proposals have been made regarding the reform of gestalt-teaching method in light of process theology. Proposals are also in order for the reform of process theology in light of gestalt theory.

The primary challenge of gestalt theory is the idea that certain laws or principles can be generalized to explain learning and perception. The process theological view of the unique and free subjective aim of every becoming occasion tends to emphasize the atomic event and give less attention to common patterns in human experience.[44] Certainly a process metaphysics has much to offer in describing the basic dynamics of experience, such as the initial aim and objective data that come together in the subjective form of every becoming occasion. Unfortunately, middle psychological principles that explore patterns of human growth, perceptions, and relationships are not usually included in a process metaphysics. This leads to an uneasy relationship between process theology and psychological theory in general. It also leads to a tendency in process thinking to ignore common patterns in human life.

Process theologians do speak of the inheritance of the past as a way to explain the continuity of becoming occasions with those that have gone before, but the idea of common patterns is not emphasized. One exception to this is the work of Catherine Keller who has drawn connections between Jungian archetypes and process theology, thus proposing some psychological dynamics and structure compatible with a process view of the world.[45] The richness of human understanding that emerges from her work signals the importance of exploring psychological descriptions of human experience in relation to process theology.

Gestalt theory moves in a somewhat different direction in introducing the idea of perceptual laws or principles that function in human life. This offers a distinctive contribution to process theology, particularly in describing how human beings interact with their environment and how their environment becomes a matrix (or field) for human self-development. The dynamics of interaction between human beings and their environment receive considerable attention from gestalt psychologists, and their findings could be fruitful for process theology. Kurt Koffka defines the task of gestalt psychology as "the study of behavior in its causal connection with the psychophysical field."[46] The psychophysical field is very broadly understood, taking account of the human being and the entire environment: "We must

---

[44]Felt discusses similar difficulties in Whitehead's descriptions of human experience. ("Intuition, Event-Atomism, and the Self," 137–52.) He sees the problems as related largely to the event-atomism in Whitehead's thought. The aspect of the problem that particularly concerns him is the difficulty of describing personal continuity across time.

[45]Catherine Keller, *From a Broken Web: Separation, Sexism, and Self* (Boston: Beacon Press, 1986).

[46]Koffka, *Principles of Gestalt Psychology*, 67.

not forget that our psychophysical field exists within a real organism which in its turn exists in a geographical environment."[47] Certainly, process theologians would agree that human beings are formed in relation to their own organism and the entire geographical environment, but attending so little to structures of relationship, they are not able to deal with some of the practical issues that emerge in human life, such as how to organize an educational curriculum or how to foster healing in psychotherapy.

James Felt thinks we may need a more "substance-like" philosophy to correct Whitehead's event-atomism.[48] I suggest that theorizing on middle principles of psychology and sociology would be even more promising; we could avoid any tendencies to slip from a "substance-like" philosophy into a substantive one.[49] Process theology could make unique contributions to the consideration of form and structure. From a process perspective generalizations about form and structure would include not only structures of human experience, but also structures of all experience in the natural world. Because all actuality experiences, from a process view, the experience of the whole cosmos is subject for investigation, and generalizable laws could be important from any part of the whole.[50] Furthermore, the process perspective would leave open the possibility that even the generalizable laws of nature could change. They may not be universally true for all times and places because even these laws would be in process and would be subject to transformation. This could be a significant contribution from process theology if process-oriented theologians entered more actively into discussions with structure-oriented psychologists.

Gestalt theory confronts process theology with the idea that structure, form, and pattern may be a very important aspect of human life. In other words, certain patterns of human perception and ways of organizing knowledge do exist. Acknowledging these patterns may even accentuate the process emphasis on relatedness and cancel any

---

[47]Ibid.

[48]Felt, "Intuition, Event-Atomism, and the Self," 148–50.

[49]Ibid. Actually, Bergson's work does help us move in that direction, and Felt has offered one important clue to new directions.

[50]Jay B. McDaniel identifies generalizable laws of child-rearing practices among pelicans, and he demonstrates how these raise questions for human decisions about animal rights and care. See Jay B. McDaniel, *Of God and Pelicans: A Theology of Reverence for Life* (Louisville: Westminster/John Knox, 1989).

tendencies of process theoreticians to deal with occasions of experience in microcosmic and macrocosmic ways, with little attention to middle principles. The attention to structure, form, and pattern may further encourage process theoreticians to give attention to social and environmental structures that affect the lives of people and the earth. Analysis of psychological patterns has been the province of gestaltists and other psychologists, and analysis of social patterns has been the province of sociologists and political theorists. Perhaps the gestalt challenge to process theology is to take these structural analyses more seriously in explaining the life of human beings and the earth.

4

INCARNATIONAL TEACHING

Phenomenological Method

The Word, for our sake, became poverty clothed as the poor who live
   off the refuse heap.
The Word, for our sake, became agony in the shrunken breast of the
   woman grown old by the absence of her murdered husband.
The Word, for our sake, became a sob a thousand times stifled in the
   immovable mouth of the child who died from hunger.
The Word, for our sake, became rebellion before the lifeless body of
   Gaspar Sanchez Toma, "scientifically" murdered.
The Word, for our sake, became danger in the anguish of the mother
   who worries about her son growing into manhood.
The Word became an ever-present absence among the 70,000 families
   torn apart by death.
The Word became Light,
The Word became History,
The Word became Conflict,
The Word became Indomitable Spirit,
and sowed its seeds upon the mountains, near the river and in the
   valley
and those-of-good-will, heard the angels sing.
Tired knees were strengthened,
trembling hands were stilled,
and the people who wandered in darkness,
saw the LIGHT!

—Julia Esquivel[1]

---

[1]Selections from Julia Esquivel, *Threatened with Resurrection: Prayers and Poems from an Exiled Guatemalan* (Elgin, Ill.: Brethren Press, 1982), 31–35.

T he passion that stirs behind this chapter is the passion for openness—openness to what is revealed of God and the world in this
moment. Incarnational teaching is teaching that expects God's revelation in the world, teaching that respects the preciousness of life
wherever it is found. Incarnation is God's enfleshment or presence
in the world. It can be expected in the teacher-student relationship,
in the qualities of life of every person in the educational process, in
the lives of those excluded or marginalized by the educational process,
in the joys or tragedies of the moment, and in acts of compassion and
acts of anger toward injustice.

Teaching that is not open is dry and lifeless, often a rote recitation
of facts collected in some bygone time. A teacher who is not open
often deals with students as problems to be fixed, as types and stereotypes who have no uniqueness, or as empty receptacles of the
teacher's knowledge. A teacher who *is* open may actually discover
new insight in the midst of problems, may revise typologies and
dismiss stereotypes in light of the uniqueness of the people in the
educational process, and may share knowledge with the expectation
that new discoveries will be made in the teaching interchange.

Another passion that stirs behind this chapter is the passion for
intersubjectivity, for encountering and engaging others subject to subject. Intersubjectivity in education is an engagement of persons with
one another, with other persons in remote times and places, with
ideas, with the earth, and with themselves. Serious engagement itself
requires openness. It requires exposure to others, encouragement to
take others seriously, and opportunities for genuine interchange. Intersubjectivity is seriously impaired, for example, when curriculum
materials present stories and pictures of only one ethnic group, or
when literature classes draw literature from only one cultural tradition.
In the United States, the attempts to limit communication to English
only, to draw literature largely from European and Euro-American
traditions, and to encourage independent and competitive styles of
learning are all practices that discourage intersubjectivity. Likewise,
religious curriculum resources that minimize exposure to a breadth
of ethnic, cultural, and theological traditions limit intersubjectivity. In
such a learning context, people are likely to engage only those people,
ideas, and events most like themselves.

One other passion underlies this chapter—the passion for caring.
Caring for others is part of teaching; it is not an extracurricular activity

that some do because they are "nice." Caring for others is an important quality in the teaching-learning process and an important goal. Such caring will be displayed in various ways, and it will not always look like niceness. It may be revealed in many different ways—in listening or professing, in encouraging individual decisions or communal projects, in forgiving or holding accountable, in removing expectations or adding them. Caring has to do with responding to an entire situation and to the individuals within the situation—responding with a hope for justice and wholeness.

PHENOMENOLOGICAL METHOD

Phenomenological methods are those in which persons reach into themselves and others and draw forth meaning. The process is like reaching into a well and drawing water. It is based on assumptions that relate in interesting ways to the organismic philosophy of Alfred North Whitehead.

The most relevant assumption in process theology for this discussion is that God is incarnate in the world, incarnate in everything that is. Two other pertinent assumptions are grounded in this one. One is that reality reveals God: everything is holy and can reveal meaning. The other is that everything is interconnected in a web of meaning. The first is an important assumption for phenomenology because every perceived reality—and every single human being—is approached as a source of meaning. The second is important because the connections among human beings, and between humans and other beings, imply a connection of meanings among particular entities. We can talk, therefore, about a web of meaning, and we can expect that what is revealed in the life of one person or community will be related and significant to the life of others. The similarities and distinctions between the phenomenological and process assumptions will be discussed later.

When phenomenological methods are used in education, teachers and students seek meaning in human life. The approach is intersubjective, and it has two basic dimensions. The first dimension is reaching into oneself and others to observe life experience. Teachers and students listen to people's stories and observe their actions. The second dimension is drawing forth the meaning in the life experiences.

This is the interpretive task, and it is usually done in collaboration or dialogue. Teachers and students share and try to understand what they perceive.

By Definition

Phenomenology itself is a method of reflecting on experience and letting conclusions emerge from those reflections. Aspects of this method were introduced into the religious community by Anton Boisen, the founder of clinical pastoral education. He did in-depth study and theological reflection on the lives of people (including himself), which he called the study of "living human documents."[2] Boisen was working in the context of early-twentieth-century United States, when theological reflection was usually limited to the study of written texts. The serious interpretation of human experience was an innovation that led to new methods in theology and, also, in education and counseling.

The more formal definition of phenomenology is "a branch of science dealing with the description and classification of phenomena."[3] The word derives from the Greek word *phainomenon*, meaning "to come to light" or "to appear." Phenomenology, then, deals with what appears (what is accessible through perception) and with the inner experience of the perceiving subject. It has developed into a method and a philosophical perspective. The starting point for both is the "facticity" of existence.

Maurice Merleau-Ponty defines phenomenology as "a philosophy for which the world is always 'already there' before reflection begins."[4] To this he adds the idea that "all its efforts are concentrated upon re-achieving a direct and primitive contact with the world, and endowing that contact with philosophical status."[5] We can conclude that phenomenology is first and foremost descriptive, beginning with a person's sense experience of the world.

---

[2]Anton Boisen, *The Exploration of the Inner World* (New York: Harper & Brothers, 1936).

[3]*Webster's Third New International Dictionary*, 1968, s.v. "phenomenology."

[4]Maurice Merleau-Ponty, *Phenomenology and Perception*, trans. Colin Smith (New York: Humanities Press, 1962), vii.

[5]Ibid.

Phenomenologists have been very much opposed to philosophical ideas that divide human consciousness from the world and give credibility only to one or the other. They have been quite critical of René Descartes and other philosophers who have focused on the ego or cogito at the expense of the world, as if the world only exists as a concept of mind. On the other hand, they have been critical of the scientists who have rejected ordinary sense data and attempted objective study of phenomena by standards derived from physics.[6] The one fallacy is idealistic speculation, and the other is scientific reductionism, both of which were dominant in philosophical approaches of the nineteenth century when Edmund Husserl began to develop phenomenology. Neither approach deals adequately with what it means to be a being-in-the-world, a subject in relation to the world.

Being a subject in relation to the world implies the need to study the fullness of the world and our own experience of that fullness. For example, a hiker may encounter a mountain stream as a medley of rushing sounds, a source of thirst-quenching water, a potential threat during years of heavy snow, and a beautiful spectacle of dancing waters on rock. To eliminate all of these experiences of water and speak of the stream only as a creation of human consciousness or only as a body of water moving at a certain velocity is very limiting. Much of the facticity or surplus of meaning is eliminated by such approaches. Phenomenologists want to preserve both the facticity and the surplus of meaning.

The phenomenological method is characterized by a bracketing process in which people suspend their own judgments as much as possible in order to name, describe, and understand experience. In Husserl's later work and in existential phenomenology, the attempt is to go beyond external and obvious perceptions and to understand the intentionality of both the experiencing subject and the experienced other. In other words, the phenomenologist will seek to understand the intentions of those involved in a given situation. The very act of bracketing, or suspending judgments, is an effort to avoid reductionism in the study of experience and to discern intentions, or meanings.

---

[6]This discussion is summarized in William A. Luijpen, *Phenomenology and Humanism* (Pittsburgh: Duquesne University Press, 1966), 3–11, 25–29. See also Merleau-Ponty, *Phenomenology and Perception*, ix.

For that reason, conclusions about experience are reserved until description is done; for example, we do not judge that a father and his child are in perpetual conflict until we first observe and describe the situation. We then attempt to go beyond the obvious observations and to explore what the father and child intend as they interact with one another.

For Edmund Husserl, the originator of the phenomenological method, the bracketing is part of a reduction process; it is an attempt to return to the things themselves. Merleau-Ponty describes the aim of this effort: "To return to things themselves is to return to that world which precedes knowledge."[7] All knowledge, theories, and scientific measures actually refer back to the "things themselves"; the hope in the reduction process is to bracket the knowledge, theories, and scientific measures in order to let facticity appear. Even the search for the essence (*eidos*, or defining characteristics) of a phenomenon is intended "to bring the world to light."[8] The essence is intuited out of various concrete cases. In sum, the bracketing process is a methodological commitment to perceiving the phenomena as they reveal themselves. Husserl, Merleau-Ponty, and other phenomenologists are not saying that the experiencing subject is disengaged from the world with no relation to the things themselves. What is bracketed is the status of the person's engagement with the world; thus, the person can be open to new discoveries.

This approach to the description of human action is not usually based on naive assumptions that prejudgments can be set aside completely. It is simply an attempt to allow phenomena to speak for

---

[7]Merleau-Ponty, *Phenomenology and Perception*, ix.

[8]Ibid., xvi, cf. xiv–xvii. This search for essence is called eidetic reduction by Husserl. He distinguishes this from psychological reduction and transcendental reduction, but the distinctions have not always been made by later phenomenologists, and they are not important for this work on education methodology. A relationship is drawn between reduction and psychotherapeutic theory and practice in Henri F. Ellenberger, "A Clinical Introduction to Psychiatric Phenomenology and Existential Analysis," in *Existence*, eds. Rollo May, Ernest Angel, and Henri F. Ellenberger (New York: Basic Books, 1958), 95–97. Ellenberger also elaborates three main phenomenological methods used in psychiatry (see pp. 95–117). The most controversial form of reduction is transcendental, in which the phenomenologist brackets whether phenomena and the world exist. This form of reduction is thought by some to be unnecessary and by others to be contradictory to other aspects of the phenomenological philosophy. Luijpen pointed out that bracketing questions of whether things that appear are ultimately real is not necessary. He argued that Husserl already assumes the reality of things in his concept of intentionality because intentionality is based on the belief that subjects consciously intend toward the phenomena of the world. See Luijpen, *Phenomenology and Humanism*, 18–21.

themselves as much as possible. This is quite different from the more common approach to the human sciences in which researchers study human experience in order to prove or disprove a preformed theory. The attempt instead is to accept the world as it appears without prejudgments and scientific concepts that replace the lived world, and without a priori theories that eliminate some possibilities of meaning. Husserl's idea of getting back to the things themselves is an attempt to seek the world of original experience with its multiplicity of meaning.

One further aspect of the phenomenological method should be noted in the definition; that is the attempt by many later phenomenologists, especially existential phenomenologists, to perceive and interpret the inner meanings in people's experience. The attempt is to understand the inner world of the individuals studied by understanding how they experience the elements in their life worlds. This is particularly significant for education.

The phenomenological method is so very different from other methods in philosophical and scientific inquiry that even explaining it is difficult. It is more an art to be practiced than a theory to be learned. Hence, Martin Heidegger explains that he did not really understand Husserl's phenomenology until he spent some time with Husserl, who led him into phenomenological "seeing."[9]

Phenomenology in Educational Practice

Phenomenology is an important method in education and ministry because it involves listening to the voice of the people and of God at work in the midst of people. Just as Jews and Christians seek meaning in the biblical witness by reading biblical texts to discover God's revelation, teachers and learners can also seek meaning by reading human lives to discover God's revelation through those texts. Through phenomenological method, teachers and learners can come to know a community or life situation better than they would simply by studying

---

[9]Don Ihde cites this experience of Heidegger and further adds that phenomenology is almost impossible to understand without the experience of doing phenomenology. See Don Ihde, *Experimental Phenomenology* (New York: G. P. Putnam's Sons, 1977), esp. 13–16. See also Martin Heidegger, *On Time and Being*, trans. Joan Stambaugh (New York: Harper & Row, 1972), 76–78.

statistics, dates, and selected leaders and events. History, for example, is more than a series of events involving monarchs and political leaders, and religious history is more than a series of events around rabbis, popes, bishops, and leaders.

The phenomenological method takes every detail of historical and contemporary phenomena seriously; it allows people to speak for themselves and to give birth to meaning. The teacher has a midwife role, according to Ross Snyder, and assists in the birthing process.[10] In this sense, it is closely akin to case study in which the teacher functions largely as a midwife. Finally, the phenomenological method moves toward a more honest listening to students; the teacher is not so much involved in controlling or directing the students as in joining with them as a colleague in search of meaning.

We can imagine many contexts in which the phenomenological method would be valuable, such as a visit to another faith community for the purpose of better understanding. Phenomenological methods can also be valuable for encountering another person's life story or a film or work of art. Some common approaches to education fit with the phenomenological method, particularly those derived from humanistic and existential theories. Some will be considered here as instances of phenomenological method in practice.

CARL ROGERS The chief architect of humanistic psychology was Carl Rogers, who wrote a book on educational practice in his later years. *Freedom to Learn* is an application of Rogers's psychological and counseling theories in educational settings.[11] His basic thesis is that students should be given freedom and support to learn in their own ways. He, therefore, proposes student-centered education in which learning is individualized and organized by contract between teacher and student. This kind of teaching stresses respect for the students and their individual needs, goals, and learning styles. The kinship with phenomenological method lies in the attempt to organize education in relation to the particular students and situation and to nurture the inner resources and goals of the students.

---

[10]Ross Snyder, "Ministry to Youth Is a Ministry of Meanings" (Nashville: General Board of Education of the Methodist Church, 1961), 2.

[11]Carl Rogers, *Freedom to Learn* (Columbus, Ohio: Charles E. Merrill, 1969).

ROSS AND MARTHA SNYDER   Ross and Martha Snyder have done more than any other educators to introduce phenomenology formally into religious education. Influenced by Rogers and by progressive religious education, they have developed several specific methods to enhance intersubjectivity. One example is the way in which Ross Snyder recorded Dietrich Bonhoeffer's writings on tape so that students could listen and experience being in relation with Bonhoeffer himself.

Another more elaborate example is the Institute for Meaning Formation designed by Ross and Martha Snyder. The purpose of the institute is to help participants look into their own experiences and find meanings there to foster interiority. One method the Snyders use is to lead six three-hour sessions in small transgenerational groups. Participants write short essays about their lives and then share and interpret these with the other members of their group. In writing, they report each of the following: (1) *lived moment*—an experience significant to the person; (2) *psychohistory*—a record of several lived moments during a period of time, along with the feelings that were part of these moments; (3) *manifesto*—a record of a time when the person risked self; and (4) *saga*—an account of the person's own life or journey with the holy or "wild energies of God."[12] As each of these essays is written, participants reflect with their group on the writing. The emphasis in the transgenerational groups is on listening, helping one another give birth to meaning (as a midwife) and reflecting on the decisions and strengths that sustained each person through difficult times.

The relationship of this work in meaning formation to phenomenology is apparent. Group members are encouraged to reflect on the particulars of their experiences and to draw meaning from their experiences and those of others. One man told in his manifesto about a time he risked himself while serving as scoutmaster with a Boy Scout troop. The boys were annoyed with a Scout who was a slow learner and did everything differently from the rest. One day the scoutmaster realized that the situation was destructive for everyone, especially for the boy. When this boy was away, he told the other boys that he was concerned about the situation, but he was going to let them discuss

---

[12]Ross and Martha Snyder, "Formed Meanings-to-Live in the Second Half of Life" (Institute of Meaning Formation, San Rafael, Calif., unpublished monograph, 1980).

it and decide how to handle it. They were free to decide whether the boy should leave their troop, or stay. The scoutmaster left the room. He was risking the decision to the boys. The boys, in fact, decided that the outcast boy should stay, and they made further decisions about how they would deal with him in the future. The young boy soon found the Scout troop to be his most important community. He later grew to be a beloved and valued member of his small town, probably in large part because of that decision of a group of boys. As the scoutmaster retold his manifesto many years later, he became aware how important that moment of experience had been for him as well.

RECONCEPTUALISTS   Closely related to the humanistic educational theories are the recent existentialist movements in education. Many of the reconceptualists, in fact, are reconceptualizing on curriculum in light of existentialism. The reconceptualists begin with problems in modern United States society that also plague education. William Pinar believes that we are estranged from ourselves (from our essence) and that estrangement leads to a "search for dignity and satisfaction outside ourselves."[13] He further notes that being absorbed with externals, we do not attend to our inner lives.[14] Heightened consciousness has to do with getting some distance from our public selves in order to explore the inner life.[15] The reconceptualists accent the exploration of meaning and inner life for the sake of a richer and more humane existence.

BERNARD LONERGAN   Parallel to existential movements in education is the transcendental method in theology. Bernard Lonergan has developed this method. Again, the attention is on meaning and consciousness. Lonergan speaks of the way meaning is communicated intersubjectively, as when we sense another person and respond with spontaneous, natural gestures. When a person smiles at us, we naturally smile in return. This is intersubjective communication, and it

---

[13]William Pinar, ed., *Heightened Consciousness, Cultural Revolution, and Curriculum Theory* (Berkeley: McCutchan, 1974), 3.
[14]Ibid., 4–5.
[15]Ibid., 13–15.

can take place through art, symbols, or language. It often takes place incarnately through human lives.[16]

Lonergan recommends the transcendental method as a way of "heightening one's consciousness by objectifying it."[17] The process involves becoming aware of our own experience, understanding the unity of that experience, affirming the reality of it, and deciding to act in accord with the norms found in that experience.[18] In short, the method is to sense, interpret, and affirm our own experiencing and, then, to make judgments and decisions based on those experiences. The norms are drawn from the experiences themselves and then used to guide future actions.

Phenomenology in the Study of Human Behavior

Phenomenology is also an important method for the social sciences because it involves a careful observation of social phenomena. It is closely akin to ethnography, or participant observation, in social anthropology and to qualitative research, such as grounded theory, in modern psychology.[19] The contribution of phenomenology to human science research also adds to the practice of education by offering an approach to the study of human experience that can serve the research interests of educators and be useful as an investigative approach to classroom teaching.

STRENGTHS Three strengths of phenomenology commend it particularly for the study of human behavior. The first strength is that *the method offers more direct observation in a natural setting than some other*

---

[16]Bernard J. F. Lonergan, *Method in Theology* (London: Darton, Longman & Todd, 1971), 57–73.

[17]Ibid., 14.

[18]Ibid., 14–15.

[19]Victor Turner describes his own ethnographic method as an attempt to observe what is going on in the ritual life of a people and to learn what those rituals mean to the people themselves. He has learned that the observer's perspectives on rituals are seriously limited if the people are not asked to give their interpretations of the rituals. See Victor Turner, *The Ritual Process: Structure and Anti-Structure* (Harmondsworth, Eng.: Penguin Books, 1969), 9–11. A description of grounded theory is offered in Barney G. Glaser and Anselm L. Strauss, *The Discovery of Grounded Theory: Strategies for Qualitative Research* (Chicago: Aldine Publishing, 1967); Barney Glaser and Anselm Strauss, *Theoretical Sensitivity: Advances in the Methodology of Grounded Theory* (Mill Valley, Calif.: Sociology Press, 1978).

varieties of experimental and empirical research. The researcher actually enters into the natural setting, or interacts with the subjects, as much as possible.

Phenomenological methods are different from experimental methods in which researchers place subjects in a controlled situation where certain variables are manipulated in order to observe the effects on other variables. Experimental research is quite useful in identifying the causes of certain behavior, such as acts of aggression, but it cannot adequately predict behavior in more natural settings. In a laboratory, researchers can discover that most subjects exhibit violent behavior after watching a violent television program or interacting with an aggressive adult. However, this does not predict how the same persons will react within a natural context of multiple, uncontrolled stimuli, nor does it describe the persons' inner experiences of the aggression.

Also standing in contrast to phenomenology are the interview and questionnaire methods, which depend on subjects' verbal or written responses to questions. These methods uncover much about what people believe or do, but the researcher is left to wonder how close is the fit between the subjects' words and their actual experiences and actions. The interview and questionnaire approaches are not completely unlike phenomenology, especially since phenomenologists often include verbal questions in their studies. The approach of the phenomenologists, however, would be less likely to follow preformed questions, and it would give more attention to hearing persons' stories as they choose to tell them and hearing the meanings expressed by these persons.

Compared to interviews, questionnaires, and experimental research, phenomenological methods offer a more direct look at what is going on in a natural situation. Not only will this contribute to understanding human behavior, but also it has educational value. This method can be a way for teachers and learners to come to better understanding of themselves and their situation, or to explore more deeply the lives and situations of others. For example, field trips and *encuentros* are often valuable learning events because people enter into the life situations of others in order to see and hear and understand.[20]

---

[20]William Kennedy has elaborated on the possibilities of learning through encuentros. See: William B. Kennedy, "Encuentros: A New Ecumenical Learning Experience," *Study Encounter* 24 8, no. 2 (1972): 1–8.

In such interactions, people usually learn more and have more subject-to-subject experience of others than they do when they read a book or listen to a lecture.

A second strength of the phenomenological method is that *it allows the living texts (the situation and the people) to speak for themselves.* Experimental, interview, and questionnaire methods are usually based on hypothesis testing. The researcher forms an hypothesis, designs research to test it, collects the data, evaluates the hypothesis in light of the data, and reformulates the hypothesis. Phenomenologists attempt to bracket their own hypotheses in order to observe closely and allow hypotheses to emerge from the observations.

A third strength in the phenomenological method is that *it moves toward a kind of searching that is more honest than that of positivistic science.* Positivistic science attempts objectivity by the researcher's using experimental methods to control the situation being observed. This is done by creating an artificial situation or by formulating a list of questions. Phenomenologists attempt to open themselves to the situation as much as possible so that the conclusions will conform as closely as possible to the situation itself.

STEPS Ross and Martha Snyder have given considerable attention to the study of human behavior and its role in the educational enterprise. They have defined their method of studying human behavior as "phenomenologizing," and they outline a series of steps: observing, describing, looking for patterns, theorizing, and practicing or testing.

The first three steps involve gathering and organizing the data of perception. The first step is *observing*, allowing the people or situations to speak for themselves as much as possible. In this step, the method of bracketing is important because the purpose is for learners to perceive what is happening and not to analyze their own prejudgments. The second step is *describing* what has been observed, including specific details about what the subjects said or did. The third step is *looking for patterns*, or searching for relationships among the details observed. After observing and describing a community, for example, learners might look for patterns in the relationships between men and women, or patterns in the ways adults speak to children or react to personal questions.

The next step is *theorizing*, or postulating what these patterns mean. When we ask questions of personal or theological meaning, we have begun to theorize. This is a move toward abstraction, which seems to run counter to the phenomenological stress on describing phenomena as they appear. The move is appropriate, however, as long as we remember that the abstraction does not take the place of the phenomena. Gabriel Marcel speaks to this point by describing the step of abstraction as a methodological move necessary to the attainment of a goal.[21] It is a move that necessarily eliminates some descriptive detail, and it is problematic only if the full detail is eliminated and treated as if replaced by the abstraction.

The last step of phenomenologizing according to Ross and Martha Snyder is *practicing or testing the theories*. To practice a theory is to make decisions and act differently in light of the theory. New actions, then, become subjects for further observation, description, and theory building. To test a theory is to repeat the whole process in different situations and to compare the theories that emerge in the various contexts. The practice of theories is important if the purpose of phenomenologizing is to do education; the testing of theories is important if the purpose is to study education. In either case, the process is circular, sending the teacher or researcher back through the steps repeatedly.

Ross and Martha Snyder have used these steps for many years in diverse contexts. Much of their work has been done with groups of youth and adults, and much has been developed in the nursery school associated with Chicago Theological Seminary. They have used the methods particularly to help students probe the meanings of their own experiences and to help teachers reflect on meanings in their students' life worlds.

PROCESS THEOLOGY AND PHENOMENOLOGICAL METHOD

The relationship between process theology and phenomenology may not seem immediately obvious. Process theology is grounded in an

---

[21]Gabriel Marcel, *Man Against Mass Society*, trans. G. S. Fraser (Lanham, Md.: University Press of America, 1985), 155. Luijpen continued this line of argument by pointing out that abstraction is useful unless it becomes artificial and loses its relation with lived experience. See Luijpen, *Phenomenology and Humanism*, 62–63.

historical biblical tradition and a metaphysical system. Phenomenologists focus largely on present experience, and they attempt to bracket
metaphysical questions. In Alfred North Whitehead's early work,
however, his own concerns with experience corresponded in some
striking ways with the phenomenologists' concerns.

Among Whitehead's early books were *An Enquiry Concerning the
Principles of Natural Knowledge* and *Concept of Nature,* published in 1919
and 1920 respectively. In both he attempts a philosophy of science in
which scientific abstractions are tested in relation to experience, or
nature. In the first book he reflects particularly on geometry, asking
the question, "How is space rooted in experience?"[22]

In both books Whitehead is studying the object of perception rather
than the inner experience of the perceiving subject. He says: "We are
concerned only with Nature, that is, with the object of perceptual
knowledge, and not with the synthesis of the knower with the known.
This distinction is exactly that which separates natural philosophy
from metaphysics."[23] Herein lies a commonality and a divergence from
phenomenology. On the one hand, Whitehead is concerned with the
objects of perception as are the phenomenologists. On the other hand,
Whitehead is distinguishing between the knower and the known and
focusing on the latter. His interest in setting aside metaphysics to do
natural philosophy is akin to the interest of phenomenologists, but
they deal actively with the interaction of the knower and the known,
and they are very concerned with the inner experience of the knower,
or experiencing subject.

In Whitehead's second book, he even strengthens his critique of
metaphysics in the philosophy of science: "The immediate thesis for
discussion is that any metaphysical interpretation is an illegitimate
importation into the philosophy of natural science. By a metaphysical
interpretation I mean any discussion of the how (beyond nature) and
of the why (beyond nature) of thought and sense-awareness."[24] Whitehead does, in fact, bracket such how and why questions. Herein we
discover an anomaly, however. Whitehead's accent in his two early

---

[22]Alfred North Whitehead, *An Enquiry Concerning the Principles of Natural Knowledge*
(New York: Dover Publications [1919, 1925] 1982), v, cf. vi.

[23]Ibid., vii; see also Alfred North Whitehead, *Concept of Nature* (Cambridge: Cambridge University Press, [1920] 1971), vii–viii, 28.

[24]Whitehead, *Concept of Nature,* 28.

books is on definitions and basic concepts, such as duration, extension, and congruence; his explicit starting point is not experience so
much as systems of thought. He begins by critiquing dominant phi-
losophies and defining the philosophy of science. He proceeds with
logic to develop some key concepts in relation to one another and
existing theories. Whitehead appeals to experience only as a test of
those systems of thought.[25]

The concern for congruence between ideas and experience has been
prominent in the work of process theologians; however, their attention
is usually directed toward applying process ideas to experience rather
than reflecting on experience itself. Process theologians have generally
followed Whitehead's pattern of analyzing systems of thought rather
than analyzing experience. In time, Whitehead's own efforts were
even more focused on cosmological explanations in relation to philosophical systems and broad sweeps of history.[26] His concern with
describing particularities of experience faded farther into the background.

Basic Concepts in Process Theology

The conceptuality of process theologians does have more congruence
with phenomenology than does their method. The process conceptuality on experience begins with the process view that God is incarnate in everything. This and the concept of internal relations form
the basic ideas around which dialogue can take place on the bridge
between process theology and phenomenological method.

INCARNATION Whitehead speaks of God as present in everything,
and Christian process theologians have elaborated the concept of

---

[25]For example, Whitehead evaluates geometries in relation to their fit with nature.
Ibid., 121–24.

[26]Alfred North Whitehead, *Process and Reality: An Essay in Cosmology*, ed. David R.
Griffin and Donald W. Sherburne (New York: [Macmillan, 1929] Free Press, 1978), xi–
xv. In this preface Whitehead describes his purpose: "The true method of philosophical
construction is to frame a scheme of ideas, the best that one can, and unflinchingly to
explore the interpretation of experience in terms of that scheme" (p. xiv). Whitehead
proceeds with this method of inquiry because he assumes that all constructive thought
is guided by such a scheme, even if unexplicit; he opens the conceptual schemes for
critique and reform by making them explicit (p. xiv). He acknowledges that prejudgments influence human imagination, but the role of experience is to test schemes of
thought rather than to give them birth. Whitehead's metaphysical interests were stronger by this time, but a similar concept-based method was also dominant in his earlier
work.

incarnation. John Cobb speaks of Logos incarnate in the world as Christ.[27] For Cobb, the views of divine incarnation through creation and through the Christ are quite compatible, although the two views have not always been seen as compatible within Christian tradition. Furthermore, people in other traditions have often experienced Christians as denying the revelation of God in any form other than Jesus Christ. The claim that divine revelation is only in Jesus Christ has, in fact, been used often by Christians to justify rejecting the revelatory claims in other traditions.

Whitehead accents the idea of God's participation in every becoming occasion. Because God contributes an initial aim to every emerging event of experience, God touches everything. Insofar as that initial aim is appropriated by the experiencing subject, God influences and dwells in that subject. The idea of divine revelation or incarnation in creation has been important in much of Christian tradition and also in other religious traditions. However, it stands in tension with some Western habits of thought, including those that infuse Christianity with the idea that God is revealed or incarnate *only* in Jesus Christ. Though some parts of Christian tradition affirm God's revelation in all of creation, they reserve the term *incarnation* for Jesus Christ. Some interpretations accentuate the incarnation in Jesus Christ as a unique, solitary event such that other revelations of God are underplayed or taken to be beyond human discernment.

Many common expressions in the English language betray the common belief that God is *not* incarnate in all of the world. Such expressions as "God-forsaken country" or "out in the middle of nowhere" suggest that some places are beyond the touch of God. Further, the most common approaches to biblical interpretation are to search for what the Bible says about God and God's relationship to humanity, with little or no mention of the rest of creation. If we take the process view of incarnation seriously, however, we are faced with the idea that the smallest element of reality can reveal God. Everything is holy, so we listen for the word of God in all that is.

Having heard the word of God all around us, we then must test the spirits in order to make judgments about what speaks of God most fully or most truly. If God is incarnate in everything, the revelation of God in the full human and earth community should be taken

---

[27]John B. Cobb, Jr., *Christ in a Pluralistic Age* (Philadelphia: Westminster Press, 1975).

seriously. If God is incarnate in everything, the riches of history should also be taken seriously. Thus, attention is given not simply to the immediate person in the immediate situation, but the experience of this person is considered in relationship to all that is and all that has been.

The incarnation of God in everything does not detract from the specific idea expressed by many Christian process theologians that God is most fully incarnate in Jesus Christ. John Cobb and David Griffin express their view in this way: "Whereas Christ is incarnate in everyone, Jesus *is* Christ because the incarnation is constitutive of his very selfhood."[28] The revelation in Jesus Christ offers a vision that helps to interpret and judge other revelations. Jesus' life calls attention to what Whitehead describes as "the tender elements in the world, which slowly and in quietness operate by love."[29] The overarching view in process theology is that Jesus reveals God to the world as creative-responsive love. As such, Jesus' life has offered an ideal possibility to the world. This ideal judges our reality and pulls us toward something better. Whitehead describes the Galilean ethics as "a gauge by which to test the defects of human society. So long as the Galilean images are but the dreams of an unrealized world, so long they must spread the infection of an uneasy spirit."[30] The vision incarnate in Jesus Christ is both ideal and judge.

Furthermore, our encounter with the life and teachings of Jesus can actually enhance the incarnation of God in us. The incarnation is enhanced as we perceive the incarnation in Jesus, as we "deliberately place ourselves in his field of force, and as we renew our contact with his teaching."[31] For the church, the relation with Jesus is most consciously enhanced by listening to the Word and by participating in the sacraments.[32] In the language of Christian tradition, these are means of God's grace; they bring us into relation with Jesus so that the work of Christ can be more active in our lives.

---

[28]John B. Cobb, Jr., and David R. Griffin, *Process Theology: An Introductory Exposition* (Philadelphia: Westminster Press, 1976), 105.

[29]Whitehead, *Process and Reality*, 343.

[30]Alfred North Whitehead, *Adventures of Ideas* (New York: [Macmillan, 1933] Free Press, 1961), 17.

[31]Cobb and Griffin, *Process Theology*, 105–6.

[32]Ibid., 106.

INTERNAL RELATIONS   Closely related to the concept of incarnation is the concept of internal relations. Whitehead's idea is that God and the world are data for every becoming occasion, and they enter into every occasion insofar as they are prehended and incorporated. The initial aim from God and the objective data of the past are available to every experiencing subject, and these come together in the process of concrescence, which is finally guided by the subjective aim of the becoming occasion.

The relationship that a becoming occasion has with God and the world is internal. Both God and the world dwell in the emerging event. We can say, then, that two people who are friends are not just side by side, but each has entered the experience of the other. This means that a broken relationship between the two friends will not really end the relationship because the internal connectedness will continue; the relationship, however painful, will persist and have continuing influence.

In spite of the fact that the data of the past and the aim of God enter into all of our experiences, they do not become engulfed and erased by new occasions. Our experiences of them do not replace their presence in reality. They exist as past data and as influences on future occasions. We can say, then, that the Christian Bible (New Testament) incarnates the Hebrew Bible (Old Testament), but the New Testament does not include fully or take the place of the Old Testament. Neither does the Hebrew Bible take the place of ancient Middle Eastern religious myths. Likewise, we can say that a person's experience of Christ incarnates Christ because the reality of Christ has entered into and shaped that person's life. This does not mean, however, that Christ now exists only in the life of that person. In fact, Jesus the Christ continues as past datum and as one who dwells in the life of the present world. As such, the influence of Jesus as historical person continues, as well as the influence of Christ in others through the centuries.

Furthermore, each individual also dwells in God and the world. Every part of creation contributes to the life of God and to cosmic value.[33] Internal relations are mutual, and they turn us back to incarnation. God and the world are incarnate in each individual, and

---

[33]Griffin makes a case for the influence a person's soul has on God's work and on

each individual is incarnate in God and the world. Such a view attributes high value and responsibility to every subject.

Dialogue with Phenomenology

The challenges of these process theological reflections for phenomenological method are rooted in the concepts of incarnation and internal relations. Some striking similarities in assumptions appear; but, likewise, we find some striking differences.

POINTS OF SIMILARITY   Both process theology and phenomenological method are based on the primary assumption that experience is accessible. For neither process thought nor phenomenology does consciousness equal reality; consciousness gives access to reality. The consciousness of a tree and cloud is not the same as the tree and cloud, but the awareness of them opens access to their reality. Building on that idea is the practical assumption that we can learn about ourselves and the world by probing the meaning of experience. In other words, the human perception of the world and interpretation of experience give access to knowledge.

In addition to these epistemological assumptions are some shared assumptions about experience itself. First is the assumption that experiencing is the act of a subject who is in relationship with the world. The act of experiencing is a meeting or encounter between subject and world; we cannot really think of one without the other. This is quite different from the Cartesian cogito in which each person is perceived as "an isolated interiority" separate from the world.[34] A second assumption naturally follows: that external phenomena influence human experience because people are encountered and affected by elements in their situation. A third assumption is that an experiencing subject makes choices as to what and how it experiences; these

---

others. See David Ray Griffin, *God and Religion in the Postmodern World: Essays in Postmodern Theology* (Albany, N.Y.: State University of New York Press, 1989), 125. The importance of individuality to education is stressed by Robert S. Brumbaugh, "Whiteheadian American Educational Philosophy," in *Process in Context: Essays in Post-Whiteheadian Perspectives*, ed. Ernest Wolf-Gazo (New York: Peter Lang, 1988), 66–67.

[34]Luijpen, *Phenomenology and Humanism*, 122. Luijpen points out that if people are viewed as isolated interiority separate from their world "we can imagine someone could have a clear conscience in a decaying world."

choices are not always conscious. These three assumptions, taken together, picture human beings as subjects who are always experiencing and judging the reality around them.

POINTS OF DIFFERENCE   Process theology does present a somewhat different view of reality, however. Whereas the phenomenological method centers on human perception and conceptualization on experience, process theology yields four ideas that run counter to phenomenological method. One is that *some experience is beyond people's conceptualization.* The fact that some aspects of reality are not prehended by human beings does not mean that the reality does not exist. Furthermore, much experience is beyond consciousness and is, thus, beyond the realm of conscious human perceiving or interpreting.

A second process concept that runs counter to phenomenology is that *all of creation experiences, whether human or nonhuman, living or nonliving.* All aspects of creation have some degree of mentality and subjectivity, however slight this might be in some entities (such as a cell or a molecule).[35]

Thirdly, *the assumption in process theology that all of reality is internally related would suggest that the web of relationships is much more extensive than the obvious physical encounters among persons.* Human beings are connected to other human beings and the earth far beyond their realm of immediate conscious, or even subconscious, knowledge. They are shaped in part by social structures, historical events, and ideological forces. People are internally related to the world because these other people, events, structures, and ideas actually dwell in them. For these reasons, we should cast our net broadly when we seek to understand relationships and influences, and we should consider not only intersubjective relationships, but also broad social relationships and intrasubjective relationships in which influences internal to the subject can be considered.[36]

---

[35]Whether we speak of occasions of experience at the submicroscopic level or of animals and humans, subjectivity is present. The degree varies, of course. Jay McDaniel concludes "that the entire cosmos is alive with subjectivity, with aims and interests, and hence with intrinsic value. All of nature's existents—from plants and bacteria to rivers and stars—either are intrinsically valuable or are aggregate expressions of energy events with intrinsic value." See Jay B. McDaniel, *Of God and Pelicans: A Theology of Reverence for Life* (Louisville: Westminster/John Knox, 1989), 77.

[36]This point of difference is really grounded in the epistemological differences noted earlier. From the phenomenological standpoint, process theology goes beyond what

Finally, *the process view of internal relations means that we can generalize from one experience or situation to another.* From a process perspective, we can speak of generalizable truths without making universal claims. Our community's experience may resemble the experience of other communities because all communities are interrelated. This is quite different from William Luijpen's claim that many worlds exist and, therefore, many separate systems of meaning exist that cannot be added together like a mosaic. His point of view virtually eliminates cross-disciplinary dialogue as well as other forms of communication among different persons with different attitudes.[37] The process view would acknowledge many worlds or attitudes but would see them as related and, therefore, accessible to communication and integration.

The last two points of difference require some elaboration to understand more fully the extensive implications. Process theologians generally hold a much more social view of human life than do philosophers and educators in the phenomenological tradition. The highly individualistic tendencies of someone like Jean-Paul Sartre and the difficulties of the early Edmund Husserl in dealing with intersubjectivity are modified by later phenomenologists such as Maurice Merleau-Ponty, William Luijpen, and Stephan Strasser. These philosophers put much more accent on social relations, but for them, the emphasis is still on the conscious intentions toward others more than

---

can be known through the experience of the experiencing subject, entering into speculative thinking not grounded in experience. From a process theological standpoint, phenomenologists allow themselves to be narrowly trapped by the limits they place on epistemology. This issue is not simply an epistemological debate among process and phenomenological thinkers, however. Critical theorists in education are also raising the issue of social relationships that are underplayed by phenomenological educators, especially forces of social and economic power. See Kathleen Weiler, *Women Teaching for Change: Gender, Class and Power* (South Hadley, Mass.: Bergin & Garvey, 1988), 12–13.

[37]Luijpen, *Phenomenology and Humanism*, 63–75. Luijpen puts forth the idea that we can find as many worlds as subjects' attitudes. The attitudes are affected by such factors as a person's occupation or place in history (pp. 63–65). Because systems of meaning are influenced by different attitudes, they remain separate. Each discipline needs to have its own attitude in order to progress; the findings of one cannot be added to the other. Luijpen concludes "that those who pursue different disciplines should not be expected to communicate with each other as long as they remain within the attitude peculiar to their disciplines. If, in fact, they do make sense to each other it is because one of them has temporarily taken over the attitude inherent in the other's discipline and lives in his [sic] world" (pp. 74–75). These conclusions differ from those of Merleau-Ponty, who asserts that the existence of multiple perspectives is all the more reason to approach a subject from different perspectives and to seek the existential meaning in each one. See Merleau-Ponty, *Phenomenology and Perception*, xviii–xix.

on the way in which others enter into the very internal being of the experiencing subject.[38]

Strasser bemoans the fact that Husserl was unable to deal adequately with the social dimension of human existence.[39] Strasser's solution is a dialogical phenomenology in which meaning is constituted in social interaction, or in dialogue among people in relation to their culture, their bodies, and their world.[40] Strasser argues that relationships are at the base of human existence. Unlike Sartre, who believed human beings are born with absolute freedom and later choose to enter relationships, Strasser says that human freedom actually grows from relationships in the first place; then, people can choose to enter further relationships.[41] Strasser's point is significant for this discussion because his idea has moved the phenomenological tradition closer to the organic tradition of internal relations in process theology. Rather than view persons as individuals to be nurtured so that they can enter relationships (as would be characteristic of Carl Rogers's student-centered, individualized learning), Strasser proposes that humans are fundamentally social.

This is also the view of most process theologians, for whom all of reality is seen as interconnected in a complex web. Process theologians would tend to emphasize that web even more than someone like Strasser, giving attention to how all entities (not just humans) are affected by their social web. Each entity is both determined and free in that the influences of the social past enter into every becoming occasion. The becoming occasion may prehend more or less of that past, but the influence is always there, as well as the subjective decision about how to respond.

PHENOMENOLOGICAL METHOD
RE-FORMED
BY PROCESS THEOLOGY

The groundwork for re-formulating phenomenological method has been laid already in what has been said about similarities and differ-

---

[38]We find this quite clearly in Merleau-Ponty when he speaks of taking up experiences, or "taking our own history upon ourselves." See Merleau-Ponty, *Phenomenology and Perception,* xx.

[39]Stephan Strasser, *The Idea of Dialogical Phenomenology* (Pittsburgh: Duquesne University Press, 1969), xii.

[40]Ibid., 65–68.

[41]Ibid., 112.

ences. Basically, the method is strongly affirmed from the standpoint of process theology, particularly the value of beginning with experience as a source of knowledge and proceeding to interpret the experience.

The strengths in the method lie particularly in the following attributes: the respectful approach to each moment of experience and each experiencing subject, the recognition that every experience is unique and will not necessarily follow known laws, the corresponding attempt to let each experience speak for itself rather than interpret it through a preformed theory, the attempt to discern the meaning in experience, the recognition that multiple perspectives will exist for any experience, and the insistence on thinking of the subject and world in relationship. These strengths will be important to maintain in a process reformulation.

Challenges from a Process View of Incarnation

Five challenges derive from the process view of incarnation; they are offered here to those who would use the phenomenological method. One challenge is already accepted by some who use the method, but it is often an absent or minor feature in the practice of the educational method. This is the challenge *to open access for learners to meet traditional sources of authority subject to subject*. Within this challenge is the idea that the Bible and the historical tradition are sources of knowledge through which persons can encounter important aspects of experience. Teaching these sources is a means of grace, alongside preaching the Word and celebrating the sacraments. They are incarnations of God in the world, and they are neither replaced nor made obsolete by present experience. They are still objective data of the past that continue to have influence.

Furthermore, what is incarnate in the beliefs and values of an historical religious tradition calls attention to aspects of reality (both positive and negative) and mediates the holy. Through intersubjective experience of the historical traditions, the range of experience consciously available to persons is expanded. The beliefs and values can also become incarnate in the individuals who experience them subject to subject and incorporate them into the way they perceive reality. The historical traditions are more than a norm to judge present experience, although judgments from the past *and* present will emerge. The historical traditions are subjects to be experienced, subjects that mediate God and the world to us. Through those traditions we will meet tragedy and evil, and we will meet grace and good, but we *will* meet the world.

Teachers who take this challenge seriously will introduce students to historical texts and invite them to engage those texts seriously. They will encourage students to understand the work of historical figures, viewing them within their own contexts and values, and not simply through the lenses of contemporary opinion. When students are discussing an historical figure's thought, they can be encouraged to limit their discussion initially to that person's thought and try to understand what the person believed and why. Students' opinions about the person are thus bracketed until some depth understanding emerges; then, students may proceed with evaluating the person's thought. Using the same approach, students could explore the fuller experience of historical persons without limiting the inquiry to the persons' thoughts. Diaries, biographies, and autobiographies are some of the resources that could greatly enrich the phenomenological study of historical figures.[42]

The challenge also calls teachers to introduce students to ordinary persons and events of history and to encourage students to listen for silent voices. To do this, teachers and students alike need to work at the art of research, seeking to go beyond the bounds of most textbooks that feature dominant figures, cultural groups, and events of history. The research that Phyllis Trible and Elisabeth Schüssler Fiorenza are doing with biblical texts, and Ann Taves with historical texts, includes listening for silent women's voices and exercising logic and imagination to find missing pieces of the puzzle.[43] This approach to research

---

[42]James McClendon has initiated considerable discussion of the use of biography in theological reflection. I am proposing that his work could guide phenomenological investigation, especially as he encourages the depth study of persons who embody the convictions of a community. McClendon takes seriously the individual and the community in relationship. See James W. McClendon, *Biography as Theology* (Nashville: Abingdon Press, 1974).

[43]Phyllis Trible, *Texts of Terror: Literary-Feminist Readings of Biblical Narratives* (Philadelphia: Fortress Press, 1984); Elisabeth Schüssler Fiorenza, *Bread Not Stone: The Challenge of Feminist Biblical Interpretation* (Boston: Beacon Press, 1984); Fiorenza, *In Memory of Her: A Feminist Theological Reconstruction of Christian Origins* (New York: Crossroad, 1983); Ann Taves, *Religion and Domestic Violence in Early New England: The Memoirs of Abigail Abbot Bailey* (Bloomington: Indiana University Press, 1989).

suggests how a phenomenological teacher could proceed, seeking to discover and understand the experience of historical individuals not normally featured in historical studies but important to understanding the experience of the community and world during a particular era.

A second challenge is *to seek the past and future dwelling in the present*. This follows from the process idea that emerging occasions receive the past and future possibilities into themselves. The process of concrescence is discussed in chapter 3, so here we will look particularly at human experience of past and present. In *Education for Continuity and Change*, I use the metaphor of an intersection to describe a moment of human life.[44] At each moment a person enters an intersection where a decision is made regarding the future. The person enters the intersection with a heritage of past events and decisions and a range of future possibilities; these enter into the new decision, but they do not determine it. The past is received, and the person decides in each moment how to respond—to repeat the past, ignore it, or transform it.

With this view, teachers are challenged to encourage students to reflect on their own experience and the past dwelling therein. How have their experiences been shaped by their own religious and cultural traditions? How have historical events and socioeconomic contexts influenced them? Teachers will also lead students in probing current issues, seeking to understand how contemporary social experience is affected by the heritage of the past.

The third challenge is *to listen to the poor and to political and social experiences for revelation of meaning*. If God is incarnate in all actuality, then we need to give special attention to listening and watching for God through people whom we usually ignore. The human experiences most often explored as sources of knowledge and meaning are those of the elite, the persons whose social position and education make it possible for them to take the time and use their reflective skills in

---

[44]Mary Elizabeth Moore, *Education for Continuity and Change: A New Model of Christian Religious Education* (Nashville: Abingdon Press, 1983), 86–117, esp. 92. One implication of such a processive view of persons is that educational method needs to include transmission, reflection, and transformation. All are dynamically interwoven (pp. 127–32). Gordon Jackson has drawn implications for pastoral care. See Gordon E. Jackson, *Pastoral Care and Process Theology* (Lanham, Md.: University Press of America, 1981), 1–9.

interpreting their experience. If God is incarnate in everyone, however, we are limiting our view of God by limiting the experiences that we are willing to explore. We need to seek out the poor and marginalized as sources of authority and means of grace. We also need to seek out those who cannot engage in conscious witness to their experience, such as young children or individuals who are handicapped in communication. One priest said that the church baptized infants so that God can come to us through them. With this statement he introduced an infant baptismal service and reminded the persons present that God is revealed in those who cannot yet speak. Likewise, God is revealed in those who can speak but who are silenced or ignored because of social structures. These are the people we need to meet as one subject to another.

The fourth challenge is *to open access for intersubjective communication with animals, plants, earth, and sky.* This statement sounds bizarre outside of certain mystical traditions, but in a process perspective, it would be an essential component of the phenomenological method.[45] Since God is incarnate in all actuality, including those parts of the world normally considered to be nonliving, the experience of the whole world is important for theological reflection. Access to that experience is difficult in a highly verbal society, but the discipline of silence practiced by the religious mystics would be one means of access.

The final challenge deriving from the process view of incarnation is that *part of educational practice should include prayer and meditation to allow mysteries incarnate in the world to touch the learners and to encourage a sense of the mysteries they will never be able to touch.*[46] This challenge is a natural conclusion of the other four; each encourages engagement with an enlarged circle of experience. When we become aware of how large the circle of experience really is, we are face to face with awe and mystery.

---

[45]Jay McDaniel is a process theologian whose focus on animals, plants, and earth leads him to formulate a "biocentric spirituality." See Jay B. McDaniel, *Earth, Sky, Gods and Mortals* (Mystic, Conn.: Twenty-Third Publications, 1990); McDaniel, *Of God and Pelicans,* 85–92.

[46]Some suggestions in this regard are made in Mary Elizabeth Moore, "Meeting in the Silence: Meditation at the Center of Congregational Life," in *Congregations: Their Power to Form and Transform,* C. Ellis Nelson, ed. (Louisville: Westminster/John Knox, 1988), 141–65.

Challenges from an Internal Relations View

Just as some challenges derive from the process theological view of incarnation, other challenges derive from the view of internal relations. Naming these will provide a prelude to the next section in which I propose steps for theological reflection. Particularly important is that *the phenomenologist, in observing and listening, needs to take heed of the complex network of social relations.* If, in fact, human beings are internally related to people they have known and the world all around them, the phenomenological approach needs to open access to those internal relationships. From a process point of view, the whole dwells in each part, so any particular experience will be connected to the experience of the universe.[47]

Concretely, *learners using the phenomenological approach to study experience need to consider the social web in which the experience is grounded.* The social web includes the immediate environment (such as the individuals a person knows) and, also, the complex of social structures and environmental and cultural dynamics that influence the experience. Both interpersonal relationships and broad social systems are important to take into account.

Further, *learners should also consider the potential influence of this experience on the future.* What is the unique contribution of this event or person or community to the world?

Phenomenologists also need to build in some precautions to minimize the influence of their own prejudgments and to make these accessible for interpretation. The attempt to bracket personal judgments while doing the

---

[47]The false distinctions between the particular and universal have concerned process theologians, and this was a persisting theme in Whitehead's writing. In his first book, he writes: "Perception is an awareness of events, or happenings, forming a partially discerned complex within the background of a simultaneous whole of nature. . . . This background is that complete event which is the whole of nature simultaneous with the percipient event, which is itself part of that whole" (Whitehead, *Principles of Natural Knowledge*, 68). Building on this, Whitehead identifies the relationships among events as both temporal and spatial; thus, events are grounded in a matrix of time and space through which the relations among component events are discerned and expressed (Whitehead, *Concept of Nature*, 166–68; cf. *Principles of Natural Knowledge*, 8). Continuing in *Process and Reality*, Whitehead describes the importance of viewing events relationally. He critiques the common understanding that one particular is not necessarily related to any other particular. He concludes: "The principle of universal relativity directly traverses Aristotle's dictum, 'A substance is not present in a subject.' On the contrary, according to this principle an actual entity is present in other actual entities. In fact if we allow for degrees of relevance, and for negligible relevance, we must say that every actual entity is present in every other actual entity" (Whitehead, *Process and Reality*, 5).

descriptive work is not so simple as it may sound; in fact, it is impossible. The interconnectedness of the observer and observed will make mutual influence inevitable. The observer may bracket prejudgments, but these will continue to play a part in what is perceived and described. The observer may try to be unobtrusive and uninfluential on the other person's experience, but the observer's influence will play a part. Several precautions can be helpful in bracketing and, then, in exploring what is in the brackets.

One last note is needed as we reflect on internal relations. The quality of interaction with the world of experience is as important as the recognition of inherent relationships in the social web. The process affirmation of God's love is an affirmation that God loves the whole and every particular part.[48] *The quality of love incarnate in teaching encourages in the student a deep respect and appreciation for the persons or events being studied.* It encourages a respect for their subjectivity and an appreciation for the sacred realities incarnate in their experience.

Having led students in many studies of human experience, I do not think that this point can be overemphasized. We are culturally conditioned to think of the human sciences and theological analysis in terms of objective analysis, and to think of the students' role as bringing some impressive insight to bear on the situation, usually from their own storehouse of human science and theological ideas. These traditional approaches have merit in many situations, but the reformed phenomenological approach would focus more on uncovering the insight present within the situation itself. This is very much like uncovering the insight present within a biblical text rather than reading it only through our own prejudgments; it is like respecting the integrity of that text and expecting sacred reality to be revealed in it. Both the human experience and the biblical texts will reveal evil as well as good, but they *will* reveal, and to approach them as subject to subject will open access to their revelation.[49]

---

[48]McDaniel summarizes this view: "Limitless love is both universal and particularized. It is unsurpassably broad and, with respect to each creature, unsurpassably deep." See McDaniel, *Of God and Pelicans*, 21, cf. 41.

[49]Mary Boys has been helpful in identifying the role of religious education in opening access to the Bible. She speaks of religious education as making accessible tradition and transformation. See Mary C. Boys, "Access to Traditions and Transformation," in *Tradition and Transformation in Religious Education*, ed. Padraic O'Hare (Birmingham, Ala.: Religious Education Press, 1979), 9–34.

Steps in Theological Reflection on Experience

Several teaching suggestions have been made for a process-phenom-enological method. This section now concludes with a practical pro-posal for steps in theological reflection on experience. The experience studied may be any part of the universe—including human experi-ence, which has been so well attended by phenomenology. The steps could also be applied to reflecting on the subjects of the natural sci-ences; indeed, process theology would urge us to do that. These steps are not the only conceivable way to proceed, but they do offer a significant pathway into understanding the depths of experience. They can also offer clear guidance to teachers who wish to implement phenomenological reflection.

The first step is *to identify the experience that is the focal point of study*. This step sounds self-evident, but the choice will affect what students learn. As discussed above, the choices need to be broad, reaching deeply into history and broadly across the range of human experience in the present. Furthermore, the choices need to include the experi-ences of the whole natural world, and not just the human world. If the choice of subjects is limited, especially to individuals who are much like the students and teachers in social location, then learning may be more narrow. If the choice of subjects is broad, learning can be broadened at the same time that deep insight from experience is drawn forth.

The second step is *to identify and bracket one's own prejudgments and assumptions about the experience*. The observer needs to discuss and record personal responses to such questions as: What do I expect to learn? What assumptions do I carry about this subject, the social context, the situation? This step, especially when done in a group, can be very helpful in identifying the group's stereotypes, theoretical perspectives, and human science knowledge, any of which could unconsciously dominate the group's observations, or even close the door to fresh observation. The bracketing process sets aside prejudg-ments for the sake of openness and records them in such a way that the group can return to them for analysis. The group may later discover that the prejudgments are confirmed, rejected, or transformed or that they are not particularly relevant to what was discovered in studying the experience.

The third step is *to observe and describe the experience*. Here the pur-pose is to be attentive to every detail of the experience, whether observers are exploring their own inner experience or observing another's experience. The recording needs to be as complete and as descriptive as possible, bracketing analysis and theoretical conclusions as much as possible.

One helpful device for bracketing comes from anthropology. The student or researcher describes an event without analyzing. When an analytic insight emerges, the student records the insight in brackets or on another sheet of paper. For example, the student can write "(O.C.: . . .)" into the description to denote "observer's comment." This preserves the insight for later reflection, but sets it aside from the more descriptive observations. I have discovered in my own research and teaching that this skill is worth developing. Despite the fact that bracketing can never be complete, the discipline of setting analytic judgments aside does, in fact, open the observer to fresh insight and to a much fuller analysis of the experience at a later stage.

The fourth step is *to analyze the experience*. At this point the observer asks such questions as: What themes emerge in the experience (e.g., common words, symbols, actions)? What patterns do I see in the details observed? What is the relationship of this particular experience to historical-political events, interpersonal dynamics, cultural values, socioeconomic location, and geography? How have my prejudgments been confirmed, disconfirmed, transformed, or replaced by judgments more significant to the actual experience? These analytic questions begin with the observed experience, move toward broader social experience, and then consider the analytic judgments made along the way.

The fifth step is *to reflect theologically on the experience and the analytic insights that have come from it*. This is a time for seeking the meanings that arise in the experience. Questions again are helpful: What does this experience mean to me? What does it mean to those most intimately involved in it? What theological issues are raised? What sacred reality is incarnate in the experience?

Another important part of the theological reflection is to interpret this experience from the point of view of other experiences and from the point of view of theological traditions. Why is this human experience different from that of another cultural group, or an earlier historical era, for example? Or, how is this experience of the land related to Christian theologies of nature? These questions invite dialogue back and forth across culture, history, and systems of thought.

One last step is *to make a decision for action*. What does this moment of experience demand of me in response? What does it demand of others? These questions are important in light of the effect of any experience on the future. Making a conscious decision for action is an appropriate goal of the educational process. The decision is made in light of the experience itself and the observer's reflections on it. Observers may, for example, decide to learn more, to act differently toward the land, to value their own inner experience more, to confess their sins, or to take some political action. In any case, people make a decision, and this is an important part of the method from a process-phenomenological perspective.

These steps offer one very fruitful approach to incarnational teaching. Students are capable of extraordinary insight using this approach, and teachers can foster sensitivity to the sacred incarnate in the world. The approach is quite flexible in contexts, style of questions, and specific goals. In a public school setting, the questions would not be explicitly theological, but questions of meaning could be asked. With children, the questions might be reduced and simplified. In an informal setting, the questions might be discussed as they emerge rather than in a structured way. Many other adaptations are possible.

PROCESS THEOLOGY RE-FORMED BY PHENOMENOLOGICAL METHOD

The encounter with phenomenological method highlights some strengths in process theology, and it also calls attention to some areas in need of reform. Both strengths and challenges will be examined here, and some new directions for process theology will be projected.

Strengths in Process Theology

The basic strengths in process theology have been hinted at earlier. Process theology takes experience seriously (every bit of it); it poses the idea that God is part of that reality to be experienced; it offers a view of reality in which the description of reality emerges from experience rather than from some ideal realm of categories that are only actualized in experience; it explains the interconnectedness of experience; it explains subjectivity and how attitudes can affect perception; it describes an active relationship between beings and the world, such that the world is always open to change. In these various strengths, process theology is quite compatible with phenomenology, with the possible exception of the process affirmation of God. God is acknowledged by some phenomenologists and not by others. More will be said of this below.

Challenges to Process Theology

The first challenge is *to give more attention to theoretical reflection on experience*. Process theologians have given their primary attention to theoretical analysis; analysis of experience has been limited largely to analyzing applications of theory. The phenomenological challenge would be to draw theory from experience itself and to return to experience for testing and developing the theory. Marjorie Suchocki has actually proposed such a revised approach to experience in the process encounter with feminist theology. In her point of view, process theology gives account of experience while feminist theology draws more actively from it.[50] Process theology has heretofore had no systematic method for analyzing bits of experience and drawing theory from the analyses. This would be possible as process theology draws insight from phenomenological method.

This particular challenge is not foreign to process theology. Although in his later work Charles Hartshorne never gave priority to the analysis of experience, Alfred North Whitehead and many recent process theologians have. As discussed earlier in this chapter, Whitehead's own approach to experience was to take it seriously as the ground of all reflection. He especially emphasized this in his earlier work, although the accent persisted. Neither Whitehead nor later process theologians have pursued a careful analysis of experience, however, especially as a starting point for theoretical reflection.

Whitehead puts forth a method of inquiry clearly grounded in experience. He likens the method of discovery to the flight of an

---

[50]Marjorie Suchocki, "Openness and Mutuality in Process Thought and Feminist Action," in *Feminism and Process Thought*, Sheila Greeve Davaney, ed. (Lewiston. N.Y.: Edwin Mellen Press, 1981), 62–82.

airplane: "It starts from the ground of particular observation; it makes a flight in the thin air of imaginative generalization; and it again lands for renewed observation rendered acute by rational interpretation."[51] The method begins and ends with experience, but is amplified by imaginative generalization in between. Gregory Reichberg describes this approach as induction (*epogoge*) in the classic Greek sense, since Whitehead was seeking general principles in particular cases.[52] Certainly Whitehead and others have proceeded in this way, giving strong attention to induction peppered with imagination.[53]

What is missing, however, is a method that actually begins and ends on the landing field. Process thinkers often spend most of their time in the flight of imaginative generalization, often even taking off from the imaginative generalizations of others. Whitehead describes final generalities as the goal of discussion rather than the origin. He elaborates: "Metaphysical categories are not dogmatic statements of the obvious; they are tentative formulations of the ultimate generalities."[54] In practice, however, process theologians have given primary attention to metaphysical categories, moving from those to application.[55]

---

[51]Whitehead, *Process and Reality*, 5.

[52]Gregory Reichberg, "Imaginative Generalization as Epogoge," *Process Studies* 17 (Fall 1988): 152, cf. 152–62. Reichberg calls the method abstractive induction because "it involves the drawing out of the universal from the particular instance."

[53]Reichberg argues that this is the distinctive aspect of Whitehead's induction, distinctive from Baconian reliance solely on direct observation without the aid of imagination. See particularly Reichberg, "Imaginative Generalization," 154–55. See also Alfred North Whitehead, *Science and the Modern World* (New York: [MacMillan, 1925] Free Press, 1953), 43–44.

[54]Whitehead, *Process and Reality*, 8.

[55]One example of the tendency to begin with ideas and to focus primarily on the influence of those ideas on the quality of life is found in the work of David Griffin. Though Griffin clearly expresses his concern with the concrete realities of the world, he approaches them primarily by analyzing the ideas that live in the world and then by considering how those ideas influence such concrete practices as spirituality and nuclearism. See, for example, Griffin, *God and Religion in the Postmodern World*. Griffin himself moves into more actual dialogue with concrete realities of the modern world in the second volume of the same series in which he and other authors engage questions that emerge in the modern world. He introduces the volume as contrasting with the first and third volumes, "which deal with the nature of postmodern worldview." He describes the second volume as "concerned with what it would mean, for persons and societies, to live in terms of some such worldview." See David Ray Griffin, "Introduction: Postmodern Spirituality and Society," in *Spirituality and Society*, David Ray Griffin, ed. (Albany: State University of New York Press, 1988), 1. This introductory comment by Griffin is stated in the form of applying postmodern worldview to practice, but the very exercise of that application does lead the various essayists to interchange more

A second challenge to process theology is *to take human subjectivity more seriously*, recognizing how dramatically perceptions and life on this planet can be shaped by human intentions. Human perceptions are not passive. Human beings are active in attending to an object, so their grasp of meaning is active in relation to the object. This idea was touched earlier in relation to Whitehead's own belief that people come to a study with prejudgments. Quite early he wrote, "Your audience will construe whatever you say into conformity with their pre-existing outlook."[56] Whitehead continued to recognize the prejudgments and worldviews that people bring into any situation.

What aspect of human subjectivity is less emphasized in process theology? The most notable gap in process reflections is attention to the inner experience of the subject. The phenomenological emphasis on subjectivity makes us aware of the meaning and influence of each human existence, the personal character of a person, and the interpersonal character of relationships. This can be too easily overlooked in process language about the movement and interconnectedness of reality. Such language focuses so strongly on the relations among the tiniest bits of reality that the personal qualities of human beings and of God are often pushed to the background. The language can also be so focused on the history of ideas and worldviews that other aspects of subjectivity are underplayed. How, for example, do people's life goals and fears and hurts affect their view of the world and their decisions for action? Such questions as these are not often featured by process theologians.

The challenge of subjectivity is not to abandon the processive and relational quality of reality, but to become more conscious of the subjective and intersubjective character. One benefit of such consciousness would be to develop more concern for love as guiding values for ethics. One process theologian has made this a major feature of his work. Daniel Day Williams features subjectivity and the issues of human life that come to the fore when subjectivity is pursued. Interestingly, he even acknowledges the contribution of phenomenology to theological analysis. He affirms Søren Kierkegaard for offering a

---

actively between theory and practice and between imaginative generalizations and concrete realities on the landing field. This is a step in the direction recommended here.

[56]Whitehead, *Concept of Nature*, v.

phenomenological description of anxiety as the occasion of sin, and of despair and loss of selfhood as the consequence. He recognizes this internal history of human sin as important for theological reflection on the human condition.[57] What Williams is offering a subjective approach to theological reflection, and this approach needs further probing in the next era of process theologizing.

One other benefit in attending to subjectivity is the attention that can be given to the qualities of human beings and God. One process theologian who has attended to the qualities of God is Lewis Ford. He has been guided largely by philosophical analysis, concluding that God works through divine persuasion rather than through coercion.[58] Ford establishes a lively dialogue between philosophical and biblical knowledge, distinguishing what can be known of God from philosophical reflection and from the Bible. What he has not done, however, is to interact with the subjectivity of the biblical texts in drawing conclusions about God's attributes. This is another work for the next era of process theologians.

A third challenge to process theology emerges naturally from the second. Process theologians need *to attend more thoroughly to God incarnate in history.* It was acknowledged earlier in this chapter that one of the process contributions to phenomenology is attention to the past; now, the challenge is to pursue that strength to greater depth. One of the ironies of a philosophical tradition that attends so thoroughly to the interconnectedness of the past, present, and future is that the revelations of the past are often not attended as thoroughly as the disciplines of philosophical analysis.

Lewis Ford's work is one example, for he has taken the biblical account of God's activity very seriously. He concludes that God has both necessary and contingent qualities; the necessary qualities are best discerned by philosophical analysis, and the contingent qualities, by historical testimony.[59] Both are important in Ford's view, the former for the sake of systematic statements on the nature of God, and the

---

[57]Daniel Day Williams, *The Spirit and the Forms of Love* (New York: Harper & Row, 1968), 143–45.

[58]Lewis S. Ford, *The Lure of God: A Biblical Background for Process Theism* (Philadelphia: Fortress Press, 1978), 15–28.

[59]Ibid., 25–28.

latter for the sake of experiencing our salvation.[60] The challenge offered by phenomenology, however, is to suspend metaphysical judgments about God to a much greater degree and to engage intersubjectively with the revelations of the biblical and historical traditions.

The incarnation of God in the lives of the people of Israel and in the life of Jesus Christ need to be engaged as significant sources of revelation and starting points for theological reflection; hence, Jewish and Christian communities need to ground theology thoroughly in biblical and historical traditions. These historical witnesses are not the only sources revealing God incarnate, but they are vital. Ignoring them can be a way of masking revelation. For Daniel Day Williams, God's relation with Israel and gift of Jesus Christ reveal the meaning of love; for Isabel Carter Heyward, Jesus reveals humanness and the power of justice and right-relation; for Rita Nakashima Brock, Christology reveals erotic power.[61] What is left masked if such explorations are not made? Organic theology requires encounter with God incarnate in the past in relation to the present and with God incarnate in the present in relation to the past. The particularities of human experience with God are not replaced by metaphysical concepts or systematic doctrines.

Although process theologians have given primary attention to the doctrine of God, less attention has been given to Jesus Christ as the incarnation of God. Lewis Ford notes the lack of attention to Christ by Whitehead, Hartshorne, and most process theologians in the earlier period of this century, and he proceeds to offer a christological position based in the resurrection and in the Christian community that emerged from it.[62] For Ford, the emphasis is on the incarnation of God in the community, which is made possible by the life of Jesus. The subjectivity of the risen Christ is incarnate in the ongoing community.[63]

---

[60]Ford actually deals more extensively with the philosophical task in reflecting on God, but his conviction about the authority of the biblical testimony is stated clearly: "Since it is in the particular, historical way that God was able to intensify his purposes through the agency of Israel that we experience our salvation, the Bible as the historical record of that way possesses authority for our lives" (ibid., 28).

[61]Williams, *The Spirit and the Forms of Love*, 155–72; Isabel Carter Heyward, *The Redemption of God: A Theology of Mutual Relation* (Lanham, Md.: University Press of America, 1982), 31–59; Rita Nakashima Brock, "Beyond Jesus the Christ; A Christology of Erotic Power" (Unpublished paper presented to the American Academy of Religion, Boston, Mass., December 1987).

[62]Ford, *Lure of God*, 45–50, 71–79.

[63]Ibid., 78–79. Marjorie Hewitt Suchocki puts forth a similar view in *God-Christ-Church* (New York: Crossroad, 1982), 125–26, 129–30, cf. 93–121.

Other Christian process theologians have given considerable attention to Jesus Christ in recent years, carrying concerns similar to those of phenomenology. The very exploration of the doctrine of God has led some, like Norman Pittenger and John Cobb, to explore the "reality known to us in Jesus Christ."[64] For others, like Schubert Ogden, the dilemma is to articulate a constructive, post-liberal statement on Christ. Ogden's conclusion is that Jesus' ministry spoke more *of* the God-human relationship than *about* it, thus enabling us to encounter the full existential reality of that relationship.[65] For both Cobb and Ogden the heart of Christology is to meet God in the Christ—a subjective meeting. This subjective meeting would be encouraged and amplified in a phenomenological perspective.

A fourth challenge to process cosmology is the need *to recognize a plurality of lived worlds.* Whenever we take seriously the effects of people's differing attitudes on their life worlds, we have to recognize that every life world is somewhat different from every other one. We cannot, then, propose universal theories about human life (or any other life for that matter) and expect the theories to hold true for all times and places. In fact, we can expect uniqueness; we can beware of overly grand theories that make overly large claims.[66] We can generalize about human experience because of the interconnectedness of life, but the uniqueness of each person's experience will be fully as important as the generalizations.

The study of uniqueness has not been prominent in process thought, despite the fact that most process thinkers speak of metaphysical generalizations as tentative and affirm the plurality of lived worlds. The uniqueness of a particular life world or a particular cultural context gets less attention from process theologians than do generalizations that apply broadly. The process philosophers who have given most attention to particularities have often been educators or

---

[64]John B. Cobb, Jr., *God and the World* (Philadelphia: Westminster Press, 1969), 42. Cobb has since expanded on the multiple ways to meet Christ—as Logos, as Jesus, and as Hope. See: Cobb, *Christ in a Pluralistic Age;* W. Norman Pittenger, *The Word Incarnate* (New York: Harper & Brothers, 1959).

[65]Schubert M. Ogden, *Christ Without Myth* (New York: Harper & Brothers, 1961), 162.

[66]Robert Brumbaugh sounds this warning: "We should learn that the clearer things are—whether sensations or ideas—the more selective and hence the more incomplete they are." See Robert S. Brumbaugh, "Some Applications of Process and Reality I and II to Educational Practice," *Educational Theory* 39 (Fall 1989): 386, cf. 385–90.

counselors themselves.[67] The phenomenological challenge is again to bracket those metaphysical generalizations more fully and to attend to the uniqueness of the particular.

Related to this is another challenge, that is, *to hold a healthy skepticism about our own most fundamental convictions*. Process theologians need greater consciousness about how their own life worlds are affected by their social locations and attitudes. The internal processes of selective perception and interpretation play a much larger role than the microcosmic theories of becoming occasions sometimes indicate. Though process theology is not without tools to explain the complexity of human attitudes, affections, and will, these have not been explored fully in process theories of human behavior. For some process theologians, such as Charles Hartshorne, such inquiries are not even in the purview of philosophical inquiry.[68]

All judgments about the processive and relational nature of reality and the participation of God in all actuality are influenced by prejudgments. Such judgments should be open always to review, just as the opposite judgments of a nonprocessive, nonrelational, nonliving, or mechanistic existence should be open to review. We can never escape the influence of our prejudgments, and they should therefore be subjects for further questing. Certainly, process theologians have tended toward revision of their basic theological insights, but questioning those insights in relation to their social locations and attitudes has been less explicit.[69] One valuable addition to theological reflection would be to include more exploration of the inner experience of the

---

[67]Brumbaugh especially emphasizes the importance of concrete seeing. Robert S. Brumbaugh, *Whitehead, Process Philosophy, and Education* (Albany: State University of New York Press, 1982), 85–88, 95–96, 124; Brumbaugh, "Whiteheadian American Educational Philosophy," 63–64, cf. 57–68; Brian Hendley, "Robert Brumbaugh: Towards a Process Philosophy of Education," *Process Studies* 17 (Winter 1988): 227–31. Gordon Jackson also encourages attention to the uniqueness and complex, processive nature of people so as to avoid the "diagnostic trap." See Jackson, *Pastoral Care and Process Theology*, 8–11. Of the process theologians who attend to particularity of human experience, Bernard Lee stands out, although his presentation of particularity is fairly general and Whitehead's metaphysics is placed in the foreground. See Bernard Lee, "The Appetite of God," in *Religious Experience and Process Theology*, Harry James Cargas and Bernard Lee, eds. (New York: Paulist Press, 1976), 369–84.

[68]Charles Hartshorne, *A Natural Theology for Our Time* (LaSalle, Ill.: Open Court Publishing Co., 1967).

[69]One who has moved in the direction suggested here is John Cobb, who introduces his Christology in the context of his personal journey and the pluralistic cultural context in which his views of Christ were formed. He also recognizes the lack of completion in his effort. See particularly Cobb, *Christ in a Pluralistic Age*, 13–28.

theologians and reflecting communities as part of theological inquiry. This seems especially appropriate in light of Whitehead's conviction that philosophy's "ultimate appeal is to the general consciousness of what in practice we experience."[70]

In concluding this chapter, the last challenge really is addressed to process theologians, phenomenologists, and general readers. It summarizes all of the other challenges named in this chapter: *to develop more thoroughly incarnational understandings of relationships—with more reverence toward the presence of the holy in all actuality and more alertness to the internal relationships people have with one another and with the whole natural world.*

The most obvious contrasts between process thought and phenomenology are differences in primary convictions about relationships with God and the world. The process emphasis on internal relations with God and the world stands in tension with the phenomenological emphasis on subjective relationships based in the consciousness of self-conscious subjects. Further, process theologians and phenomenologists often make different primary assumptions about God. For example, Sartre and Merleau-Ponty assume that God does not exist, and Whitehead assumes that God is an active part of reality. William Luijpen points out that Sartre and Merleau-Ponty have actually built the nonexistence of God into their meaning systems by defining existence solely in terms of the subject in relation to the mundane world.[71] On the contrary, Whitehead has included God in his meaning system by describing existence in terms of subjects in relation to all of actuality, including the actuality of God.

From the standpoint of a practical theology done on the bridge between phenomenological method and process theology, we can see that the phenomenological assumptions about reality do not necessarily have to exclude God or the world from human existence. We can emerge from the bridge, then, with a phenomenological method much more open to the experience of God and the natural world, and we can emerge with a process philosophy much more concerned with perceiving the facticity of experience and exploring the subjectivity of human existence.

---

[70]Whitehead, *Process and Reality,* 17.
[71]Luijpen, *Phenomenology and Humanism,* 94–96.

5

RELATIONAL TEACHING

Narrative Method

I come to narrative method with another set of passions—passions for people to connect with other persons and events across time, to root deeply in the cultural and religious stories of their own people, and to cross boundaries into the stories of other peoples and the earth. I am appalled by teaching that divides everything into small bits and pieces to be learned one at a time. We expect students then to be able to integrate knowledge that was artificially split in the first place. Focusing on small pieces is often important, and integration is certainly a skill to learn, but we cannot focus adequately on a part without some awareness of the whole. We cannot teach integration in the context of schools and churches and synagogues in which learning is compartmentalized and the whole is torn asunder.

I have been teaching and writing about narrative theology and education for several years now, and every year I make new discoveries. I discover how one story generates another; how sharing stories binds people together, even across ideological divides; how stories ground people in their heritage and give expression to their present situation; how stories enflesh social critique; and how stories give hope for the future. I also discover how narrative teaching gives meaning to abstract concepts and specific skills, presenting them within contexts in which interest is stirred and people can view the parts in relation to the whole.

Concepts and skills have actually been extracted from narrative contexts in the first place, so placing them back into these contexts is a way of sending them home. Justice is an abstract concept, but a story of people living justly (or unjustly) with one another and the earth is *embodied* justice; the relationships show. Reading and biblical exegesis are important skills to learn, but they can easily be disconnected from any meaning in persons' lives. They are often approached through drill and dry practice of the technical apparatus, whether in kindergarten or theological education. The skills can be reembodied, however, when approached in relation to stories in students' lives. In this way, the skills are taught in relation to life as a whole; they are approached through stories to be read and biblical texts to be exegeted.

So what are the possibilities? Reading skills can be learned while engaging significant literature; writing skills, while recording significant stories of our own lives. Exegetical skills can be learned while engaging meaningful texts, the relations among texts, and the relations of a particular text to the multiple communities in which it was born and has lived. Even basic principles of science will have more meaning if viewed in the context of stories of discovery.[1]

The central assumption of this chapter is summarized by my husband's comment one day when he emerged from a bookstore, "If you take time to read, the whole world is spread before you in books." That sense of wonder of the world revealed in narratives and that sense of being related to the world give inspiration and spirit to this chapter. I hope our stories will be read and told and danced and painted and sung until we know ourselves in relation to all that has been and all that is to come.

NARRATIVE METHOD

Teaching narratively calls forth images of storytelling, simulation gaming, dramatization, and ritual reenactments. But teaching narratively is more than a set of techniques that can be thrown into an eclectic bag of tricks. Narrative is a significant mode of human communication,

---

[1] I am indebted to Robert Brumbaugh for this proposal, letter, 1989.

a bearer and critic of culture, and a potentially profound and far-reaching educational method.

In *Zorba the Greek*, Nikos Kazantzakis portrays the simple character of Zorba—a man who is simply complex, a man of rich experience whose life is so full of stories that his crude philosophy is full of wisdom. In his wisdom, Zorba constantly shames his well-read, intellectual companion who works as his boss and narrates his story.

Zorba's life is a bundle of narratives, and he himself communicates primarily through narrative. His storytelling is so organic and involving that he does not even need words to tell a story. In one scene Zorba tells his boss of his days in Russia. He tells of meeting a Russian man in the tavern where he spent every evening after working the copper mines by day. Together Zorba and the Russian drank vodka and began to talk. Even though Zorba's Russian vocabulary was limited to five or six words, he and his newfound friend wanted to share their stories. Zorba explains how they managed:

> We had come to an arrangement as well as we could by gestures. He was to speak first. As soon as I couldn't follow him, I was to shout: 'Stop!' Then he'd get up and dance. D'you get me, boss? He danced what he wanted to tell me. And I did the same. Anything we couldn't say with our mouths we said with our feet, our hands, our belly or with wild cries: Hi! Hi! Hopla! Ho-heigh![2]

Zorba narrates his friend's story of the Russian revolution, and then he proceeds with his own:

> And then, after that, it was my turn. I only managed to get out a few words—perhaps he was a bit dense and his brain didn't work properly—the Russian shouted; 'Stop!' That's all I was waiting for. I leapt up, pushed the chairs and tables away and began dancing. Ah, my poor friend, men have sunk very low, the devil take them! They've let their bodies become mute and they only speak with their mouths. But what d'you expect a mouth to say? What can it tell you? If only you could have seen how the Russian listened to me from head to foot, and how he followed everything! I danced my misfortunes; my travels; how many times I'd been married; the trades I'd learned—quarrier, miner, pedlar, potter, *compitadji*, *santuri*-player, *passa-tempo* hawker, blacksmith, smuggler—how I'd been shoved into prison; how I escaped; how I arrived

---

[2] Nikos Kazantzakis, *Zorba the Greek*, trans. Carl Wildman (New York: Simon & Schuster, Touchstone Books, 1952), 73.

in Russia. . . . Even he, dense as he was, could understand everything, everything. My feet and my hands spoke, so did my hair and my clothes. . . . When I had finished, the great blockhead hugged me in his arms. . . .[3]

Such is narrative! It can cross cultures, speak through the whole body, and bind people together in a depth of understanding. The response of the Russian to Zorba's story was a hug; the response of Zorba's boss later that night was a feeling of shame that his own life was not so rich:

> I was a long time getting to sleep. My life is wasted, I thought. If only I could take a cloth and wipe out all I have learnt, all I have seen and heard, and go to Zorba's school and start the great, the real alphabet! What a different road I would choose. I should keep my five senses perfectly trained, and my whole body, too, so that it would enjoy and understand. I should learn to run, to wrestle, to swim, to ride horses, to row, to drive a car, to fire a rifle. I should fill my soul with flesh. I should fill my flesh with soul. In fact, I should reconcile at last within me the two eternal antagonists.[4]

In fact, the two eternal antagonists of soul and flesh are reconciled in story. Story, whether told in words or in dance, is embodied communication. A good story is richly textured: the characters are full and embodied; their lives are interwoven, and their ideas and actions are interwoven. Of course, stories are told for various reasons; for example, some are designed primarily to convey certain ideas or morals. What is recognized here, however, is that stories are more aesthetically rewarding if they are more richly textured.

These qualities of story naturally attract an organic theologian, who naturally cares about the relation between soul and flesh, between one person and another, between one culture and another, and between ideas and actions. When we begin theorizing about education from an organic, weblike view of the world, we begin by assuming that the world is thoroughly interconnected and by seeking modes of communication that are themselves organic and weblike. When we begin theorizing about education from an organic view of time, we begin by assuming that the present is intimately related to the past

---

[3]Ibid., 73–74.
[4]Ibid., 74.

and future and by seeking modes of communication in which the dynamic process of life can be viewed through time. Narrative communication is a natural, and it invites a closer look.

Narrative Method in Modern Education

In surveying the literature for contemporary educational reflections on narrative method, I was struck by the relative absence of such reflections. In reviews of teaching and learning theories, the absence is striking.

Narrative method is mentioned with somewhat more frequency in reviews of teaching techniques or strategies. One example would be Aimee Dorr Leifer's essay entitled "Teaching with Television and Film," published in N. L. Gage's *The Psychology of Teaching Methods*, a widely read yearbook of the National Society for the Study of Education.[5] In this essay, Leifer summarizes what has been learned from various psychological studies of television and film narratives, but the limited range of the studies limits the vision of narrative teaching she puts forth. Particular attention is given to the kinds of content communicated through such narratives (cognitive, social and emotional, information-processing skills, implicit messages, and modes of learning) and to the processes and potential of learning from television and film. Though Leifer casts her net broadly, she focuses mainly on television and film, and she functions within the constraints of the psychological research, which itself deals largely with cause-and-effect questions and with carefully selected variables, one or two at a time. Her review suggests broader possibilities for narrative, but those broader possibilities are not the intent of her essay, nor of the volume and others like it. In fact, another widely used volume on teaching methods, written by Bruce Joyce and Marsha Weil and now in its third edition, does not even mention narrative as a method.[6]

One notable exception to the absence of narrative method in education is Mildred McClosky's *Teaching Strategies and Classroom Realities*.[7]

---

[5]Aimee Dorr Leifer, "Teaching with Television and Film," in *The Psychology of Teaching Methods*, N. L. Gage, ed. (Chicago: University of Chicago Press, 1976), 302–34. This book was the Seventy-fifth Yearbook of the National Society for the Study of Education, and it has been one of the most broadly used of the yearbooks.

[6]Bruce Joyce and Marsha Weil, *Models of Teaching*, 3d ed. (Englewood Cliffs, N.J.: Prentice-Hall, [1972] 1986).

[7]Mildred G. McClosky, ed., *Teaching Strategies and Classroom Realities* (Englewood Cliffs, N.J.: Prentice-Hall, 1971).

In this edited volume, McClosky includes a large number of case studies written by teachers and telling of their experiences using drama, simulation techniques, filmmaking, and literature related to social values and ethnic issues. Although this volume points to extensive possibilities in narrative teaching, its purpose is to deal with particular techniques rather than a full and systematic method.

Two possible conclusions might be drawn from the scarcity of attention to narrative as an educational method. One is that most teaching and learning theories are based on the research and theory of modern psychology, which has not focused primarily on complex forms of communication and reception. In fact, narrative knowing is only now being rediscovered as a critical research strategy in the human sciences.[8] Another conclusion is that technique is often separated from method and methodology, which are the more comprehensive terms. Method is a systematic approach for reaching a goal or doing inquiry; methodology is theoretical reflection on method. The ease of separating technique from method and methodology has made it easy in turn to deal with narrative as a helpful technique without considering the large possibilities in narrative method. Narrative techniques have been clearly demonstrated as effective, but reflection on narrative method has been done very little.

Narrative Method in Religious and Moral Education

The picture of narrative method in religious and moral education is somewhat different. In recent years an awakening to the power and multivalence of story has stirred considerable interest in storytelling, story sermons, narrative theology, and literary approaches to ethics and values. A review of this literature will not be attempted here, but some interplay with the literature will illuminate the movement.

The importance of storytelling in the religious community is well vivified by storytellers in the Jewish community today.[9] The Jewish

---

[8]Donald E. Polkinghorne, *Narrative Knowing and the Human Sciences* (Albany: State University of New York Press, 1988).

[9]Notable among these are Elie Wiesel and Isaac Bashevis Singer, as well as communities of women seeking to compose modern midrash. See, for example, Elie Wiesel, *Messengers of God: Biblical Portraits and Legends* (New York: Random House, 1976); Wiesel, *The Fifth Son*, trans. Marion Wiesel (New York: Warner Books, 1985); Isaac Bashevis Singer, *The Penitent* (New York: Fawcett Crest, 1983); Jane Sprague Zones, ed., *Taking the Fruit: Modern Women's Tales of the Bible* (San Diego: Woman's Institute for Continuing Jewish Education, 1981).

people are part of an ancient tradition of telling, interpreting, retelling, and forming anew the stories of God and God's people.[10] Further, communication through story has long been central in some cultural traditions of Christianity. Narratives have been central to theological reflection in many Asian communities, often providing the starting point for theological and political discourse.[11] Storytelling and music have always been prominent in African-American communities, and narratives are given a significant place in theological reflection within those communities today. Delores Williams approaches theology and culture through the analysis of African-American women's narratives.[12] Cornel West, an African-American philosopher of religion, insists on the significance of narratives for theological reflection; he argues for the historical and political significance of narratives because they deal more adequately with social embeddedness and diversity than do metaphysical formulations.[13]

At the same time, literature on the subject of storytelling and story sermons is burgeoning in many Christian communities today.[14] Though this can easily become a faddish technique, much of the work available is provocative and substantive. Also growing in importance and attention is the art of narrative theology.[15] Some of this work has

---

[10]Some discussion of this tradition is found in William Scott Green, ed., *Approaches to Ancient Judaism: Theory and Practice* (Missoula, Mont.: Scholars Press, 1978); Jacob Neusner, *Midrash in Context: Exegesis in Formative Judaism* (Philadelphia: Fortress Press, 1983).

[11]See, for example, C. S. Song, *The Tears of Lady Meng* (Maryknoll, N.Y.: Orbis Books, 1981); C. S. Song, *Tell Us Our Names: Story Theology from an Asian Perspective* (Maryknoll, N.Y.: Orbis Books, 1984).

[12]Delores Williams, "Women's Oppression and Lifeline Politics in Black Women's Religious Narratives," *Journal of Feminist Studies in Religion* 1-2 (1985–1986): 59–71.

[13]See particularly Cornel West, "The Politics of American Neo-Pragmatism," in *Post-Analytic Philosophy*, ed. John Rajchman and Cornel West, (New York: Columbia University Press, 1985); West, "The Historicist Turn in Philosophy of Religion," in *Knowing Religiously*, Leroy S. Rouner, ed. (Notre Dame, Ind.: University of Notre Dame Press, 1985); West, "Dispensing with Metaphysics in Religious Thought," *Religion and Intellectual Life* 3 (Spring 1986): 53–56.

[14]William J. Bausch, *Storytelling: Imagination and Faith* (Mystic, Conn.: Twenty-Third Publications, 1984); William R. White, *Speaking in Stories* (Minneapolis: Augsburg Publishing House, 1982); Fred B. Craddock, *Overhearing the Gospel* (Nashville: Abingdon Press, 1978); Craddock, *Preaching* (Nashville: Abingdon Press, 1985); Ralph Milton, *The Gift of Story* (Toronto: Wood Lake Press, 1982); Richard A. Jensen, *Telling the Story: Variety and Imagination in Preaching* (Minneapolis: Augsburg Publishing House, 1980); James A. Sanders, *God Has a Story Too: Sermons in Context* (Philadelphia: Fortress Press, 1979); Amanda Joann Burr, *New Life for the Old, Old Story: A Guide for Developing Story Sermons* (Arlington, Va.: Thornsbury Bailey & Brown, 1989).

[15]See, for example, George W. Stroup, *The Promise of Narrative Theology* (Atlanta:

been studied in direct relation to Christian religious education,[16] but most of it has yet to be mined for its possibilities.

Finally, some observers view narratives as a significant pathway for reflecting on values. One notable example is Robert Coles who has, for years, been a listener to stories and who now reflects on the importance of stories in teaching and moral imagination.[17] Coles finds novels and poetry to be a significant mode of communication, not to *save* students in a simple cause-and-effect way, but to *engage* them and to make a difference in their lives.[18]

Theoretical Reflections on Narrative Method

Having made a case for the absence and presence of narrative method in modern education, I can identify a few persistent themes that appear in the broad literature of educational theory, philosophy, and theology. Some general attention will be given to these various areas of inquiry in order to identify some important themes.

First, *imagination is being revalued as an important ingredient in education.* Beginning with the idea of imagination itself, Elliot Eisner, writing in general education, and Maria Harris, writing in religious education, are calling attention to the role of imagination in the educative process. Eisner has offered a persistent critique of the overdependence of education on science, modern technology, and narrowly defined learning processes and content. He has spoken to the importance of artistry in teaching, and the importance of educational imagination throughout the entire system of schooling.[19] Of artistry

---

John Knox Press, 1981); Amos N. Wilder, *Jesus' Parables and the War of Myths: Essays on Imagination in the Scriptures* (Philadelphia: Fortress Press, 1982); Robert W. Funk, *Parables and Presence* (Philadelphia: Fortress Press, 1982); Robert Paul Roth, *The Theater of God: Story in Christian Doctrines* (Philadelphia: Fortress Press, 1985); Sallie McFague, *Speaking in Parables* (Philadelphia: Fortress Press, 1975).

[16]See particularly Mary C. Boys, "Access to Traditions and Transformation," in *Tradition and Transformation in Religious Education*, Padraic O'Hare, ed. (Birmingham, Ala.: Religious Education Press, 1979), 9–34; C.A.M. Hermans, "Understanding Parables and Similes qua Metaphors: A Cognitive-Linguistic Approach to the Learning of Parables and Similes in Religious Education," *Journal of Empirical Theology* 1 (1988): 21–50.

[17]Robert Coles, *The Call of Stories: Teaching and the Moral Imagination* (Boston: Houghton Mifflin, 1989).

[18]Ibid., 110–11, 120–21.

[19]See especially Elliot W. Eisner, *The Educational Imagination: On the Design and Evaluation of School Programs* (New York: Macmillan, [1979] 1985), 183–86, 354–80.

in teaching, he says: "Artistry is important because teachers who function artistically in the classroom not only provide children with important sources of artistic experience, they also provide a climate that welcomes exploration and risktaking and cultivates the disposition to play. To be able to play with ideas is to feel free to throw them into new combinations, to experiment, and even to 'fail.' It is to be able to deliteralize perception so that fantasy, metaphor, and constructive foolishness may emerge."[20] Similar themes are struck by Maria Harris, who sees imagination at the very heart of religious education.[21]

A second theme is that *narratives are an important source of imagination*. This theme has been developed by persons like Bruno Bettelheim, who has demonstrated the healing value of fantasies for young people with emotional and other disorders.[22] The theme has also been emphasized by Northrup Frye, who explicitly describes the value of fairy tales in inspiring imagination. Such tales restore the primitive perspective of myth that relates the human and natural worlds.[23] William Bausch is one of many religious educators who specifically identifies the role of story in linking theology and imagination.[24] In the area of story and imagination, religious educators have perhaps been more attentive than general educators because of the consciousness that religious traditions are carried largely by story.

Yet another theme in the educational literature is that *narrative is a source of human consciousness and social critique*. On the subject of human consciousness, Jerome Bruner calls attention to the distinctive role of narrative. The two natural modes of human thought, according to Bruner, are paradigmatic thought (logico-scientific thinking that rests on description, explanation, and verification) and narrative thought that weaves together action and consciousness.[25] Consciousness is the thinking, feeling, and willing of the human person. To

---

[20]Ibid., 183.

[21]Maria Harris, *Teaching and Religious Imagination* (San Francisco: Harper & Row, 1987).

[22]Bruno Bettelheim, *The Uses of Enchantment: The Meaning and Importance of Fairy Tales* (New York: Alfred A. Knopf, 1976); Bettelheim, *Truants from Life: The Rehabilitation of Emotionally Disturbed Children* (New York: Free Press of Glencoe, [1955] 1960).

[23]Northrup Frye, *The Educated Imagination* (Bloomington: Indiana University Press, 1964).

[24]Bausch, *Storytelling: Imagination and Faith;* see also White, *Speaking in Stories;* Milton, *Gift of Story.*

[25]Jerome Bruner, "Narrative and Paradigmatic Modes of Thought," in *Learning and*

focus entirely on paradigmatic modes of thought is to pull away from attending to consciousness and, therefore, to the human act of sense making. Unfortunately, according to Bruner, the tendency in psychology has been to ignore the narrative mode of thought. He says: "For some reason, the nature and the growth of thought that are necessary for the elaboration of great stories, great histories, great myths—or even ordinary ones—have not seemed very attractive or challenging to most of us. So we have left the job to the literary scholars and linguists, to the folklorists and anthropologists. And they have studied not the process, but the product, the tales rather than the tellers."[26] We are left, then, with little understanding of consciousness in the learning process and little attention to it in the educational process.

The accent on narrative and consciousness is being most clearly sounded in educational theory today by Maxine Greene, who is herself both a literary scholar and an educator. She draws extensively on literature, both in teaching and in writing, and she has been active in advocating the importance of education that fosters human consciousness. Meaningful learning, for Greene, involves " 'going beyond' what has been."[27] This can involve imagination and subjectivity, but is not limited to these modes of thought. Consciousness involves an awareness of the world and our own experiences of the world, and also an effort to make sense of the world.[28] In her teaching Greene draws a relation between the dawn of consciousness and social critique. In the process of arousing consciousness and stirring imagination, narratives raise people's awareness of the social situation and of new social possibilities. This theme recurs in Greene's writing, as she points to the inherent link between the individual's consciousness and the social reality, a link fostered by narrative teaching.

Still another aspect is the consciousness of being part of an intellectual, social, and historical context. Jonathan Z. Smith sees narrative

Teaching the Ways of Knowing, Elliot Eisner, ed. (Chicago: University of Chicago Press, 1985), 97–115. This volume is the Eighty-fourth Yearbook of the National Society for the Study of Education. The inclusion of Bruner's article in the yearbook could signal a growing interest in narrative methods of education.

[26]Ibid., 103.

[27]Maxine Greene, "Curriculum and Consciousness," in *Curriculum Theorizing: The Reconceptualists*, William Pinar, ed. (Berkeley: McCutchan, 1975), 302.

[28]Ibid., 299–317.

as a way of raising that consciousness.[29] He recommends turning "narratives into problems," highlighting judgments made by an author in writing a text, and by the author and others in editing it and interpreting it through different periods of history. He also recommends that teachers explain their own judgments in selecting the text for a class reading. Smith sees this kind of consciousness as especially important for college introductory courses, where the capacity to be critical and make judgments needs to be nurtured. Narratives here are not just texts, but also the narrative contexts of these texts. Smith's rationale is relevant to youth and adults studying together in a church or synagogue, as well as in a college classroom; in fact, his position is important in any religious community where texts are taken to be revelatory subjects for study. The story of a text is important to understanding it.

The fourth theme in the literature comes from philosophy and theology rather than from education. This is the idea that *story is a form of indirect communication that conveys truths that cannot be communicated directly*. The idea of indirect communication was especially developed by Søren Kierkegaard, who was a philosopher, theologian, and literary figure. He, in fact, communicated through story in his own work, interpreting at length the story of Abraham and Isaac, and creating parabolic stories to convey his insights into the human condition. He also sought to develop a theory of humor, always searching for the comic dimension in the human "contradiction."

Kierkegaard speaks of irony as the means by which human beings make the transition from aesthetic to ethical awareness, and humor as the means for making the transition from ethical to religious awareness.[30] Through irony people realize they cannot settle the tension between possibility and necessity, but must live with the tension. Humor offers a means for responding to contradiction and suffering with it. An example of Kierkegaard's humor of contradiction is the story of the shipmates who frenetically try to make their ship orderly, all the while their ship is sinking.[31] For Kierkegaard, humor is an

---

[29]Jonathan Z. Smith, "Narratives into Problems: The College Introductory Course and the Study of Religion," *Journal of the American Academy of Religion* 56 (Winter 1988): 727–39.

[30]Søren Kierkegaard, *Kierkegaard's Concluding Unscientific Postscript*, trans. David F. Swenson and Walter Lowrie (Princeton: Princeton University Press, [1941] 1960), 446–68, esp. 448.

[31]Ibid., 493.

important avenue for human growth, precisely because it is able to communicate something of the human condition that cannot be communicated adequately in other ways.

For similar reasons, storytelling is an essential method in philosophical discourse. Kierkegaard often employs story to carry some of his major philosophical themes, such as the contrast between experiential and theoretical knowledge. He tells the story of a conversation between a troubled man and a parson. The parson was trying to give the man some consolation about everything working together for the good. To prove his point, the parson quoted from a book, citing that, after all, God is love. To the parson's surprise, the troubled man revealed that he was the author of that book.[32]

Another prominent theme in Kierkegaard's work is the human failure to be self-aware. In *Sickness unto Death*, he tells the story of a peasant who sought to put on a new self and new clothes. He became inebriated and lay down in the road to sleep. When he saw an approaching wagon, he told the driver to drive over his legs because they were not his anyway; he did not recognize them with his new shoes.[33] With such stories Kierkegaard is able to convey truth that is elusive in direct communication.

Kierkegaard's approach to truth through story has directly influenced Fred Craddock, who has developed a theory of indirect communication within the context of the Christian church. He sees indirect communication as the way to preach and teach the Gospel to those who have already heard.[34]

Within Christian theology the attention to story as truth-communicator is also emerging with great power among Asian theologians. Minjung theologians in Korea communicate largely through stories of the *minjung*, or the people. They tell biblical stories of Jesus responding to the common people, and contemporary stories of the people in Korea, especially those who are oppressed or suffering. Another Asian theologian from Taiwan, C. S. Song, usually begins his writings with story, followed by interpretation.[35] He does not use

---

[32]Søren Kierkegaard, *Christian Discourses*, trans. Walter Lowrie (Princeton: Princeton University Press, [1940] 1974), 206–7.

[33]Søren Kierkegaard, *Fear and Trembling* and *Sickness unto Death*, trans. Walter Lowrie (Princeton: Princeton University Press, [1941] 1968), 187.

[34]Craddock, *Overhearing the Gospel.*

[35]Song, *The Tears of Lady Meng*; Song, *Tell Us Our Names.*

the stories to illustrate the commentary, but the commentary elaborates and interprets the stories.

One last theme in narrative method emerges from the theological literature. This is the idea that *stories have the power to form and transform the world*. Different kinds of stories function in different ways, but stories do function to form or transform individuals in their worldviews and life-styles. Dominic Crossan has developed this point of view; he describes myth as the form of story that functions primarily to establish world, and parable as the form of story that subverts world.[36] Recognizing the different social functions of different kinds of stories offers a route into a more nuanced educational theory of the narrative method.

This discussion of dominant themes in modern educational theory is not intended to be comprehensive and complete, but to point to some important work evidenced in the educational, philosophical, and theological literature. The work is being done without much collaboration and cross-fertilization, and no comprehensive educational method of narrative has been developed. Some very fruitful insights are available that could be formative elements in such a method.

Assumptions About Learning

Inside these glimpses of narrative method are some assumptions about learning that need attention for the sake of theory development. These assumptions are implicit and explicit in the works reviewed above.

One foundational assumption is that *human beings are imaginative creatures—capable of imagination and in need of it*. Imagination is important to mental health, human growth, cross-cultural understanding, and social critique. Imagination opens the way for people to gain perspective on their own lives, to perceive the world of another person or culture, and to envision alternate possibilities for life on the earth.

A second assumption about learning is that *persons learn through stories*. Story is a stimulus to imagination, as well as to greater self- and social-awareness. Story stirs imagination, and it also points to realities not easily communicated in conceptual forms.

---

[36]John Dominic Crossan, *The Dark Interval: Towards a Theology of Story* (Niles, Ill.: Argus Communications, 1975), 47–62.

A third assumption about learning is that *social learning takes place through stories* so that cultural beliefs and values and patterns of action are actually formed and transformed through storytelling. Story is, therefore, an important factor in social stability and change.

PROCESS THEOLOGY AND
NARRATIVE METHOD

The organic philosophy of Alfred North Whitehead offers potential for valuing and re-forming narrative method. Unlike Søren Kierkegaard or C. S. Song, Whitehead did not employ a narrative method. He did, however, emphasize the educative value of reflecting on ideas within an historical matrix, and his philosophy has fostered accents on interconnectedness and historical process highly compatible with narrative method. Here I will probe some major accents in Whitehead's cosmology that may reinforce and illuminate narrative teaching.

Even the use of the word *cosmology* is illuminating. Whitehead describes his work in *Process and Reality* as an essay in cosmology,[37] and cosmology is itself a theory, or story, of the universe. Whitehead's use of the term *cosmology* undoubtedly leans more toward the connotation of theory than of story, but his attempt to put forth a holistic picture is undeniable. He wanted to move beyond a philosophy that was simply a "criticism of detached questions" and work toward constructive thought.[38] He believed that "the true method of philosophical construction is to frame a scheme of ideas, the best that one can, and unflinchingly to explore the interpretation of experience in terms of that scheme."[39] Further, he believed that all constructive thought is guided by such a scheme, whether or not that scheme is acknowledged; the role of philosophy is "to make such schemes explicit, and thereby capable of criticism and improvement."[40] Insofar

---

[37]Alfred North Whitehead, *Process and Reality: An Essay in Cosmology,* ed. David R. Griffin and Donald W. Sherburne (New York: [Macmillan, 1929] Free Press, 1978), xi–xv.

[38]Ibid., xiv.

[39]Ibid.

[40]Ibid. Whitehead continued to reflect on existing cosmologies and to aim toward constructing a more adequate cosmology. A major section of his last published work was entitled "Cosmological." See Whitehead, *Adventures of Ideas* (New York: [Macmillan, 1933] Free Press, 1961), 103–72. The educational relevance of Whitehead's cosmology

as a scheme of ideas, or a theory of the universe, can be understood as a story, Whitehead was himself engaged in a story of the universe.

At least some process thinkers have seen it so. Brian Swimme, a physicist and process thinker in the spirit of Teilhard Chardin, is persuasive in discussing the importance of a story of the universe. He calls for cosmic storytellers to do what modern science could not do and to do what has been lost in modern Western culture, the tradition of telling cosmic stories.[41] The cosmic story begins with the molten rocks from which everything has come, the rocks who are our grandmothers and grandfathers.[42] The storyteller acknowledges: "This entire universe sprang into existence from a single numinous speck. Our origin is mystery; our destiny is intimate community with all that is."[43] Swimme has great hopes for the power of that cosmic story. He sees it as "the central political and economic act of our time" with the power of inaugurating "a new era of human and planetary health."[44] He sees the cosmic story as launching a new beginning.[45]

This foray into Brian Swimme's cosmic storytelling is not irrelevant to major streams in process theology. David Griffin holds out hope for process theology to offer a synoptic vision of the world, and Lewis Ford deals with God's persuasive movement in relation to biblical and evolutionary accounts of the universe.[46] I will attempt in this chapter to explain Whitehead's own scheme of ideas in relation to narrativity, and I will review some themes in process theology that are particularly relevant to a narrative method in education.

---

has been explored by Joe Burnett and others, but the possibilities have certainly not been exhausted. See particularly Joe R. Burnett, "The Educational Philosophy of Alfred North Whitehead" (Ann Arbor, Mich.: University Microfilms, 1958), Ph.D. Dissertation, New York University, 155–87.

[41]Brian T. Swimme, "The Cosmic Creation Story," in *The Reenchantment of Science: Postmodern Proposals*, David Ray Griffin, ed. (Albany: State University of New York Press, 1988), 47–56. The essay is also found in Swimme, "The Resurgence of Cosmic Storytellers," *Teilhard Perspective* 22 (July 1989), 5–9.

[42]Swimme, "Cosmic Creation Story," 54.

[43]Ibid., 55–56.

[44]Ibid., 47, cf. 56.

[45]Ibid., 53.

[46]David Ray Griffin, "Liberation Theology and Postmodern Philosophy: A Response to Cornel West," in *Varieties of Postmodern Theology*, ed. David Ray Griffin, William A. Beardslee, and Joe Holland, (Albany: State University of New York Press, 1989), 129–48; Lewis S. Ford, *The Lure of God: A Biblical Background for Process Theism* (Philadelphia: Fortress Press, 1978). In his essay, Griffin argues with Cornel West that process philosophy might be more promising in offering a synoptic vision than postanalytic neopragmatism.

One compelling theme in Whitehead's philosophy is that *aesthetics is important to all human activity*. Whitehead chooses this theme to close *Science in the Modern World*. In the last chapter he turns to education, regretting the ways in which modern education is compartmentalized and focused on analysis and abstraction. He expresses his regret that professional training is one-sided and his hope that education might stimulate aesthetic growth.[47] He says: "What is wanted is an appreciation of the infinite variety of vivid values achieved by an organism in its proper environment. When you understand all about the sun and all about the atmosphere and all about the rotation of the earth, you may still miss the radiance of the sunset. There is no substitute for the direct perception of the concrete achievement of a thing in its actuality."[48]

In response to the need for vivid values and concrete perceptions, Whitehead finds possibilities in art. He believes that aesthetic education is needed to "draw out habits of aesthetic apprehension."[49] Art in the more specialized sense is a kind of aesthetic education, but art in the general sense is a habit of apprehending an organism in fullness, or "the habit of enjoying vivid values."[50] Art, then, is necessary to human life. It provides "fertilization of the soul" by arranging the environment "to provide for the soul vivid but transient values."[51] Though the values are transient, they contribute to the permanent richness of the soul, which flourishes in the experience of newness.[52] The art represents the interaction between nature and human creativity, thus heightening a sense of humanity, contributing to intense feeling, and serving the curative function of revealing truth about the nature of things.[53]

This accent on aesthetics was not new for Whitehead in his later years. In 1917 he presented an address as part of a prize distribution at the Borough Polytechnic Institute in Southwark. In his address "A Polytechnic in Wartime," he spoke to the aesthetic dimension of education. He encouraged aesthetics not only in conventional forms, but

[47]Alfred North Whitehead, *Science and the Modern World* (New York: [Macmillan, 1925] Free Press, 1967), 199.
[48]Ibid.
[49]Ibid.
[50]Ibid., 200.
[51]Ibid., 202.
[52]Ibid.
[53]Whitehead, *Adventures of Ideas*, 270–72.

also in carving and modeling, dance, music, literature, decorative arts, bookbinding, and dressmaking. He said, "This list, incomplete as it is, tells us two great truths—you cannot separate art and recreation, and you cannot separate art and business."[54] In other words, aesthetics is a part of everything.

If this is true, what do we need to do in education? Certainly we need to be more like Zorba, absorbing and giving through all of our senses. Certainly we need fullness of experience. We need arts and crafts in public schools, not as fluff but as fundamentals. And we need arts and crafts in religious communities, not to fill time but to contribute to full spiritual growth.

A second theme in Whitehead's thought is that *the world is a world of concreteness.* This theme runs contrary to worldviews based in abstractions. In *Science and the Modern World,* Whitehead argues strongly against the value of pure abstraction because it leads to thinking detached from concrete reality and it leads to narrow specialization. He articulates the ways in which this focus on abstraction and specialization often dominates professional education and the work that professionals do. He speaks eloquently to the dangers in this kind of specialization:

> It produces minds in a groove. Each profession makes progress, but it is progress in its own groove. Now to be mentally in a groove is to live in contemplating a given set of abstractions. The groove prevents straying across country, and the abstraction abstracts from something to which no further attention is paid. But there is no groove of abstractions which is adequate for the comprehension of human life. Thus in the modern world, the celibacy of the medieval learned class has been replaced by a celibacy of the intellect which is divorced from the concrete contemplation of the complete facts.[55]

Whitehead makes his educational critique very specific. He points to the inadequacies in educational methods that focus on intellectual analysis and acquiring "formularized information"; he believes that

---

[54]Alfred North Whitehead, "A Polytechnic in Wartime," *The Organisation of Thought: Educational and Scientific* (Westport, Conn.: Greenwood Press, [1917] 1975), 65. The aesthetic emphasis in Whitehead's thought is highlighted by Robert Brumbaugh. See especially Brumbaugh, "Whitehead's Educational Theory: Two Supplementary Notes to *The Aims of Education," Educational Theory* 16 (July 1966): 210–15.
[55]Whitehead, *Science and the Modern World,* 197.

educators who use these methods "neglect to strengthen habits of concrete appreciation of the individual facts in their full interplay of emergent values."[56] Whitehead hopes instead for a more balanced development, one that leads to wisdom. Such a balanced development does include analysis and abstractions, but it also includes much opportunity for students to do things and to experience concrete apprehensions. Whitehead says, "In the Garden of Eden Adam saw the animals before he named them: in the traditional system children named the animals before they saw them."[57]

As we ponder narrative method, we can see ways in which narrative itself may introduce concreteness and value. Even in fairy tales, talking stones and larger-than-life animals call attention to the powers and interactions of the concrete world. Such stories can enhance apprehension of the world as it is. This may sound absurd since most of us do not hear stones talk, but in an organic worldview, everything is understood to be living to some degree. Talking stones, therefore, may reflect the world more adequately than inert, silent ones; in a world where the earth is silent, the living trees that see but do not speak may be our witnesses to the richness of the creation.[58] In any case, narratives allow for such a blending of concreteness and value, which is called forth but not developed in Whitehead's philosophy.

Whitehead himself makes indirect associations between narratives and concreteness when he writes on education. For example, he believes that history is important to our perception of movements in civilization, and even technology needs to be seen within an historical matrix.[59] The story of history requires a large picture of the flow of epochs as well as some concrete particularities.[60]

Literature is itself a concrete reflection of a particular civilization. Whitehead's proposal regarding classical literature is compatible with narrative method:

> The treatment of the history of the past must not start with generalized statements, but with concrete examples exhibiting the slow succession

---

[56]Ibid., 198.

[57]Ibid.

[58]Annie Dillard elaborates on an image of silence and speaks of her own experience of palo santo trees that see so much and say nothing. See Annie Dillard, *Teaching a Stone to Talk* (San Francisco: Harper & Row, 1982), 74–76.

[59]Whitehead, *Science and the Modern World*, 198.

[60]Alfred North Whitehead, *The Aims of Education* (New York: Free Press [1929] 1957), 72–75. The attempt to reflect on thought and movements in an historical flow is common to all of Whitehead's writing.

of period to period, and of mode of life to mode of life, and of race to race. The same concreteness of treatment must apply when we come to the literary civilizations of the eastern Mediterranean. When you come to think of it, the whole claim for the importance of classics rests on the basis that there is no substitute for first-hand knowledge.[61]

Stories, then, can be seen as reflections of concrete reality, or they can be seen as concrete realities in themselves, parts of a particular civilization. In either case, they are important to the development of human beings.

What does this mean for education? It means that stories themselves are concrete, and the characters of story become part of our concrete reality. One person's story inspires others to tell theirs. As we hear more and more stories, we also become more conscious of the concrete details in our own stories. The experience of reading a book and seeing our own lives more vividly through the book is common. The experience of laughing or crying in a movie is an experience of laughing or crying about ourselves. We can see more concretely and more vividly in a story-filled world.

A third Whiteheadian theme provides considerable support for a narrative method, namely, the idea that *a society is bound by a stream of meaning that gives it order.* For Will Beardslee this stream of meaning is an important feature of narrative. He believes that stories can help orient persons into a larger, overarching frame of meaning. He says: "One of the basic functions of stories is to place us in a larger world. . . . We see our own little story as part of a big story. This is one of the principal ways in which we find our identity, discover who we are."[62]

Such stories contribute much to our meaning-making. For Beardslee these overarching stories are resources rather than rigid structures, especially when they are seen as self-transforming and open.[63] The Gospels are such overarching and open religious narratives; unlike many archaic narratives, the Gospels reflect a dynamic balance between repetition of origins and openness toward the future.[64] Such religious stories re-present a stream of meaning and draw us into it.

---

[61]Ibid., 74.

[62]William A. Beardslee, "Vital Ruins: Biblical Narrative and the Story Frameworks of Our Lives," *Southern Humanities Review*, 24 (Spring 1990): 102, cf. 108, 112–15.

[63]William A. Beardslee, "Stories in the Postmodern World," in *Sacred Interconnections*, David R. Griffin, ed. (Albany: State University of New York Press, 1990), 20–22.

[64]William A. Beardslee, "Narrative Form in the New Testament and Process Theology," *Encounter* 36 (Autumn 1976): 309–10.

Such narratives are very fitting in organic education and in Whitehead's philosophy of organism. Such narratives reflect an interconnected world in which events are woven into nexus, and over time, into societies and societies of societies.[65] A human being, for example, is a complex society, and a faith community or culture is an even more complex society. For Whitehead the relationships in these complex societies are seen as expressions of value: "The Universe achieves its values by reason of its coordination into societies of societies, and in societies of societies of societies."[66] Nathaniel Lawrence sees this interconnected social fabric of Whitehead's philosophy of organism as the base for his beliefs about education.[67] The educable self reflects these natural social relationships. The question that naturally arises is What can education do to enhance the relationships and the process of order and value?

From where does this strand of personal order, or stream of meaning, come, and how do we assess the value of the order? We can assume that all orderings are not equally good, so how can these judgments be made? The ordering comes from the creative advance itself as one actual occasion is prehended and received into a succeeding occasion. When the process of transmission becomes conscious, the possibilities for exercising judgments are enhanced, and this is when narratives can be very important.

Narratives can raise our consciousness of how societies *are* ordered, and they can stir our imagination regarding how societies *could* be ordered. One function of narratives is to call attention to how societies are ordered and what values shape the order. According to Will Beardslee: "Stories are the great bearers of value in our culture. . . . Our finding ourselves in a story is a principal way of affirming the values that we believe in."[68] From this point, judgments can be made regarding the adequacy of the values embodied in the order. Naturally,

---

[65]When a society of societies is bound together by a common element, the result is a corpuscular society, or personal order. A human being or ethnic group or geographical community all reflect such personal order, differing in size and complexity.

[66]Whitehead, *Adventures of Ideas*, 206. Whitehead defines nexus and society in terms of mutual immanence, in which two or more occasions are interwoven. In the case of the society, the relationship is genetic because actual occasions contribute to the shaping of future occasions, thus providing a continuity and order (ibid., 201–6).

[67]Nathaniel Lawrence, "Nature and the Educable Self in Whitehead," *Educational Theory*, 15 (July 1965): 205–16.

[68]Beardslee, "Vital Ruins," 102.

narratives can also introduce new values by subverting the existing
order or introducing new ways of ordering and coordinating the societies.

Here Whiteheadian contributions to narrative method again become evident. Within a process perspective, no one way of ordering
the world is ever sufficient. We need orienting stories and disorienting
ones, conjunctive and disjunctive, formative and transformative.
Beardslee is quite helpful in drawing out the distinctive contribution
of process thought. He acknowledges with Dominic Crossan the importance of disorienting stories, like the parables of Jesus, especially
in face of dominant stories that are too neat ("too good to be true")
or exclusivistic.[69] Beardslee, however, argues that "the sounder pattern
is the alternation between orienting and disorienting story."[70] In short,
Beardslee values the importance of stories that shatter the existing
order, but shattering is not all there is. He argues that "we must
challenge the assumption that the alternative to rigid, constrictive
existing form is simply disruption."[71]

Beardslee urges instead that we see ourselves and our stories com-
plexly. This requires more than a simple dialectic between formative
and disruptive stories; Beardslee critiques Dominic Crossan and Fer-
nando Belo for bringing only one perspective, a dialectical one, to
narrative interpretation. Narratives have a propositional quality so
that they will be read in different ways by different readers at different
times.[72]

Furthermore, process thinking would add another dimension to
Crossan's basic idea of the establishment and subversion of world
through story. Story would act not only to establish and subvert
human perception, but also to order and reorder the concrete entities
of the world. Stories can affect the world directly, as well as through
human perception.

Narratives function in the world as symbols. Through symbols,
individuals experience feelings, ideas, and recollections, gaining access to meanings not easily elicited otherwise, such as religious emotions.[73] Even a single word like *forest* can be a symbol; it gives access

---

[69]Ibid., 106.
[70]Ibid., 113; cf. "Narrative Form," 313; "Changing Methods in the Study of Narrative
in the New Testament," unpublished manuscript, Claremont, Calif., 1986, 16–18, 21.
[71]Beardslee, "Stories in the Postmodern World," 18.
[72]Beardslee, "Changing Methods," 17–20.
[73]Whitehead, *Process and Reality*, 180–83.

to the experience of recollection when the experience of an actual forest may not be possible.[74] Certainly, narratives are evocative symbols that shape and challenge and reshape the world.

Narratives give access to meanings that might be inaccessible otherwise, or very difficult to experience directly. Few of us will have an opportunity to travel like Zorba, but most of us have traveled with Zorba, or with Celie in Alice Walker's *The Color Purple*, or with some other literary figure. These characters and their stories contribute to the stream of meaning that gives order to our world and poses the possibility of a new, more adequate world.

A fourth theme conjoining with narrative method is that *value is placed on interest and novelty in contributing to the richness of life*. One of Whitehead's famous epithets is "But in the real world it is more important that a proposition be interesting than that it be true. The importance of truth is that it adds interest."[75] One of the values of narrative communication is that it is interesting, and its claims to speaking the truth are more metaphorical and approximate than absolute. For this reason, narratives can add considerably to interest. Furthermore, narratives can also add novelty by introducing fresh descriptions of the world, new perspectives or new visions.

On the subject of novelty, Whitehead has been very clear. He believes that novelty is necessary for rhythm and for life. The process of concrescence itself involves uniting the given past with the novelty of the present.[76] Uniting novelty with what has always been can potentially contribute to the creative advance of the world. In *Science and the Modern World*, Whitehead says, "There are two principles inherent in the very nature of things, . . . the spirit of change, and the spirit of conservation. There can be nothing real without both."[77]

What is the challenge for educators? It means that education should never be dull. Educators need to learn to discern the novel and the interesting in their midst and to pass it on. And they need to help students discern the novel and interesting as well. Merging the past

---

[74]Ibid., 183.

[75]Ibid., 259.

[76]Ibid., 179–80. Whitehead discusses this in terms of the supplemental phase of presentational immediacy, which follows and is united with the responsive phase of causal efficacy.

[77]Whitehead, *Science and the Modern World*, 201.

heritage with the novelty of the present can contribute to emerging wisdom. This is the rhythm of education.

A fifth Whiteheadian theme is relevant to narrative method; that is, *events in reality are complex and interrelated*. Given that complexity and interrelatedness, narrative becomes an apt mode of communication. Stories can embrace considerable complexity and weave characters and events together in a way that communicates relationships more fully than most categorical and conceptual language can do. In fact, much conceptual language has promoted a disconnected view of the universe in which every entity is seen in isolation from every other entity. This way of thinking is actually dangerous, according to Whitehead, because it carries people away from the world of values and promotes the privatization of experience and, hence, of morals.[78] According to Whitehead, "The two evils are: one, the ignoration of the true relation of each organism to its environment; and the other, the habit of ignoring the intrinsic worth of the environment. . . ."[79] These habits of disconnected thinking only feed the problems of specialized training of professionals discussed earlier.

For Whitehead, interconnectedness does not obliterate differences and individuality into vague unity. In fact, every detail is important in relation to the whole. The quality of great art is that "the very details of its compositions live supremely in their own right."[80] At the same time, great art serves the harmony of the whole, contributing to the whole and receiving from the aesthetic quality of the whole.[81] In relation to narratives, we could say that each character and event are details that can reveal some important aspect of reality and touch deep feelings in the hearer or reader. At the same time, each character and event receive and contribute to the whole, and the story is more than the sum of its parts. Certainly, narrative method guided by this idea would include narratives vivid in detail but integrated and whole.

Furthermore, narrative method would include many different stories. Will Beardslee insists that multiple stories should be preserved so as not to lose the unique significance of each one. The stories of different religious traditions, for example, should not be swallowed

---

[78]Ibid., 195–96.
[79]Ibid., 196.
[80]Whitehead, *Adventures of Ideas*, 282.
[81]Ibid.

up in each other; otherwise, the richness of the different traditions will be lost.[82] The world itself is too complex for one story that denies all others. In response to this postmodern dilemma, Beardslee states, "The new vision arising in the postmodern world is perhaps above all a vision that can take account of our new awareness of pluralism and the problematic nature of the center."[83] Beardslee returns to this vision again and again, and he describes the challenge for people to live within their own traditions, while interacting and being influenced mutually by many others:

> But in the world as it is, one single story is no longer sufficient to give us direction. Whatever the orienting story is with which we identify, it has to be woven into others, and how we do that and still find a way of expressing a genuine loyalty to our faith, or to our country, is what we need to discover. To learn to live in our organizing stories as part of a rich and complex fabric of interwoven, interdependent stories, is one of the tasks of storytelling today.[84]

Narratives also have an unusual capacity to link past, present, and future, revealing the connections across time. If we agree with White-head that "the very essence of real actuality" is process,[85] then we need forms of communication that reveal the flow of time. History is more like a flowing river than a dark cave that we enter and fear we will never leave. We need forms of communication that reveal the spirit of change and the spirit of conservation, both of which are "inherent in the very nature of things."[86] In my book *Education for Continuity and Change,* I developed the idea that education is a process fostering both continuity and change.[87] Narrative education can be fruitful in this regard because of the potential in narratives to re-present the processive flow of reality across time and to heighten awareness of both continuity and change.

This flow of process continues on, but it does have endings. It is a flow in which events pass and death occurs. Stories communicate

---

[82]Beardslee, "Vital Ruins," 113.
[83]William A. Beardslee, "Christ in the Postmodern Age: Reflections Inspired by Jean-François Lyotard," in *Varieties of Postmodern Theology,* 64.
[84]Beardslee, "Stories in the Postmodern World," 5.
[85]Whitehead, *Adventures of Ideas,* 274.
[86]Whitehead, *Science and the Modern World,* 201.
[87]Mary Elizabeth Moore, *Education for Continuity and Change: A New Model of Christian Religious Education* (Nashville: Abingdon Press, 1983).

this transience of life as well as the flow. Stories open us to movements that are part of the enduring nature of time, but they also open us to tragedy and loss. In so doing, stories not only expand our lives, but also they set limits. We come to know ourselves in a world where death and loss are real; we can only face such a world if we face its tragedy along with its victory.

A sixth relevant theme in Whitehead is *that reality transcends our conscious perception of it.* Given the largeness of reality and the relative nature of human perception, education needs to point beyond what is empirically measurable and to invoke a sense of awe and wonder. Narratives are important to that process because they do not claim to portray reality in a straightforward way. By stirring imagination, they serve as reminders of the beyond.

If reality reaches beyond what we can see and touch, then story does not have purely descriptive functions. Though narratives are often used to describe reality and to correspond as closely as possible with the reality being described, narratives can also point to a new vision of reality, or they can point beyond the known to the unknown. In fact, no narrative is ever limited to one perspective anyway; a story always carries a surplus of meaning. Narrative corresponds to reality in some sense, but it also points beyond. As an art, it performs a valuable psychological function of pointing to the larger world beyond consciousness. It releases the soul from static values and offers vivid, though transient, values.[88] The result is vivid experience.

Furthermore, art is artificial and finite, representing the juncture of appearances in reality and human creativity. When these come together in art, the result is a heightened sense both of the conscious appearance of reality and of human creativity. We cannot talk about simple cause-and-effect relationships in art, nor one-to-one correspondence between art and nature. Whitehead says, "The work of art is a message from the Unseen. It unlooses depths of feeling from behind the frontier where precision of consciousness fails."[89] The narrative that is art, then, has this ominous power to reveal conscious reality and also to point beyond it. In so doing, it stirs awe and wonder in the presence of the universe.

---

[88]Whitehead, *Science and the Modern World,* 202.
[89]Whitehead, *Adventures of Ideas,* 271.

One last theme in Whitehead is that *historical communities may be related with the cosmic community*. Beginning with the more obvious part of that theme, Whitehead is clear that literature has a role in expressing the mentality of a culture. For this reason, literature is an important avenue for understanding a culture. For Whitehead, the study of literature becomes a way of discerning a particular culture and the broad flow of human affairs.[90] This is why the study of literature is given value in his educational philosophy, and why he also takes interest in how that study is done. For example, the scale and pace of the storytelling need to be tailored to the purpose of storytelling and to the story itself.[91] Thus, a range of hermeneutical tools is needed in accordance with the nature of the story and the purpose in reading and interpreting the story. Certainly, a narrative educational method would need to employ a range of hermeneutical approaches.

Furthermore, the study of history, according to Whitehead, is the study of the sweep of civilizations, a study that helps us to understand the intricacies of a particular civilization and its relation to others. He himself proceeds by framing intellectual and social questions historically, such as drawing connections between Greek thought and the practice of slavery. A narrative educational method would also need to include such historical consciousness.

Others since Whitehead have recognized the relevance of narratives for concrete action in the world. According to Beardslee, liberation theologians often base their theologies in biblical narratives; he explains, "Praxis needs a narrative world."[92] The liberative power of narrative is great.

Whitehead himself is not just interested in relating to communities of the past; he is also interested in the cosmic community of the present and future. In fact, according to Robert Brumbaugh, process philosophy reminds us that we are part of a cosmic community, and the effort to put forth a cosmology is an effort to put forth a vision of such a community. In fact, the search to express cosmic vision is the origin and inspiration of religions.[93] An important function of narrative

---

[90]Whitehead, *The Aims of Education*, 66–71, 74.
[91]Ibid., 70–71.
[92]Beardslee, "Changing Methods," 2.
[93]Robert S. Brumbaugh, *Whitehead, Process Philosophy, and Education* (Albany: State University of New York Press, 1982), 122–24.

is to put forth cosmic vision and invite people to participate in cosmic community. For Whitehead, imagination can help people anticipate the future, and anticipating unrealized possibilities can arouse the realization of these possibilities.[94] Narrative can expand the range of our imagination and our courage to act in new directions toward new possibilities.

NARRATIVE METHOD RE-FORMED
BY PROCESS THEOLOGY

The question now is what kind of narrative method is needed to teach organically. Some suggestions have been mentioned above, but a few concluding comments will be made to launch discussion. Certainly, a narrative approach to teaching would be important from the perspective of process theology, largely because story communicates in ways compatible with how students learn. Story communicates in wholes, rather than in isolated bits. In story, students can discern the flow of time and the interactions among characters and events. If stories are to function in this way, they must be full stories, developed with vivid characters and events woven into a whole. Stories that have one point, or moral lesson, have limited value in narrative education. The richer the story, the more it can contribute to the narrative approach.

If story functions as a symbol reflecting the interrelated world and fostering our relationship with the world, then we need to select stories that reflect many dimensions of the world. We need stories of animals, plants, fantasies, humans, historical and contemporary cultures, and divinity. We need a wealth of stories, and many different kinds to reflect the fullness of reality.

But description is not the only function of story; we also need stories that point to mystery. We need stories chosen because of the largeness of their vision, rather than because of the accuracy of their parts.

We also need stories that represent different perspectives, different forms of consciousness. We need stories from Native American perspective, women's perspective, South African perspective, and Wall

---

[94]Whitehead, *Adventures of Ideas*, 278–79.

Street perspective. We need this variety to help people cross over into other forms of consciousness and to see the world from the perspectives of others. This is important to living in a pluralistic world and to the self-development that we call education.

Narrative method is more than storytelling. A narrative method re-formed by process theology would integrate metaphysical and conceptual thinking with narrative and metaphorical thinking. In fact, metaphysics would actually be drawn from narratives as a source, and new narratives would be formed in response to new concepts in metaphysics. Further, each would critique the other. The dialogical relationship would be important if mutual enrichment and correction are expected.

Finally, if we are to take seriously an organic approach to narrative teaching, we will tell stories from different eras of history and different parts of the world, but we will also tell stories happening in our midst. We will see ourselves as living in the middle of story, so we will seek to tell, interpret, and participate more fully in that living story. We will ask other people to tell *their* stories, to draw stories from their own imaginations, and to make decisions about how they want to script the next chapter of their stories.

Teachers who use a narrative method are people who hear stories, gather stories, and tell stories. They are alert to what is happening around them; they see and hear and give birth to stories. They bear the heritage of generations and appreciate the stories forming in their midst.

PROCESS THEOLOGY RE-FORMED
BY NARRATIVE METHOD

Process theology has much to offer a narrative method, but the conversation moves both ways. The most obvious contribution of narrative method is to challenge process theologians regarding their theological methods. *The challenge for process theologians is to be more story-formed in approaching theology.* I noted earlier that Alfred North Whitehead described his work as a cosmology, but he tended to develop the theory aspects of cosmology more than the story aspects. One danger in this has been articulated by Robert Roth, who expresses concern that Whitehead's philosophy is so tied to the theories of modern physics that the critical revisions of postmodern physics could foster the collapse of process philosophy and theology.[95] Certainly, process theologians have been more active in generating and developing theory than in telling and interpreting story. On the other hand, some movement to story is already taking place in process theology where process thinkers like Brian Swimme are telling the cosmic story *in order* to move beyond the limits of modern science.[96] The process theologian who has worked most actively with story is William Beardslee; indeed, he does move toward a more organic theology—both biblical and philosophical, both formative and transformative. To move toward a more story-formed approach to theology can open many possibilities for process theology to be more organic.

Another important revision is that *process theology could appeal more to the imaginative and intuitive capacities of persons.* However much process philosophers and theologians have lauded the importance of aesthetics, little attention has been given to the imagination as a source of theological insight and critique, or to intuitions as a valued contributor in theological reflection. Perhaps the aesthetic quality so valued in art and life can actually be a valuable tool in stimulating creativity and insight in theology. Perhaps, even, the tools of imagination are as important as the tools of analysis; imaginative tools can complement the long-revered analytic tools in much-needed ways. One vivid example is the way Elisabeth Schüssler Fiorenza combines feminist analysis with imagination to reconstruct a feminist reading of the Bible.[97] Likewise, both systematic theologian David Tracy and religious educator Maria Harris have made imagination a major theme

---

[95]Roth, *Theater of God*, 31–32. Roth believes that story theology can do what philosophical schemes cannot do—allow for the changing sciences and for the mystery that eludes the sciences (see p. 32). Roth's other critique of Whitehead's doctrine of God (see pp. 32–33) seems easier to answer in Whitehead's own perspective, but space will not be devoted here to that discussion.

[96]Swimme, "The Cosmic Creation Story," 48–52. The question is whether Swimme is actually making story subservient to the findings of modern science by approaching story as a " 'world interpretation'—a likely account of the development and nature and value of things in this world" (ibid., 48). His language suggests otherwise. Swimme describes the Cosmic Story in relation to the Great Mystery. Scientific laws are simply part of the drama, drawing people into the story (ibid., 50–51).

[97]Elisabeth Schüssler Fiorenza, *In Memory of Her: A Feminist Theological Reconstruction of Christian Origins* (New York: Crossroad, 1983); Fiorenza, *Bread Not Stone: The Challenge of Feminist Biblical Interpretation* (Boston: Beacon Press, 1984).

in their theological methods.[98] Through imagination people are able to reach insights not accessible through other means.

As process theology becomes more story-formed, *narrative will be taken seriously as a source of truth and as a critique of present systems of thought*. This insight has been taken seriously by Korean Minjung theologians for whom stories of the people, the *minjung*, and stories of Jesus are primary sources of theological insight. They are aware that a theological system can never replace story. Likewise, Cornel West has expressed the ability of story to convey a culture's view of reality and, therefore, to critique the culture and its systems of thought.[99] Narrative becomes a powerful way to reflect, bear, and critique culture. For that reason, it is extraordinarily important in Christian theology as a way of bearing Christian culture and, also, as a way to carry the many particular cultures within Christianity. In this way, narrative is a way of transmitting Christian traditions so that the traditions may be open to view and critique. Narrative is also a way to bring conflicting theological traditions into active dialogue so that each may be taken seriously.

Two process theologians have recognized the way in which narratives reveal truth and open paths for social critique. Bernard Meland is persuasive in putting forth the significance of myth in revealing the depths of human culture and avoiding the problems of rationalism.[100] Catherine Keller has demonstrated the way in which the study of mythic stories and images can uncover patriarchal and misogynist foundations of culture, thus opening the way for cultural critique.[101] Both offer clues for a more story-formed approach to theology, particularly in seeking to understand and critique culture. Both Meland and Keller point the way to new possibilities.

A third possibility that emerges when narrative method is taken seriously by process theologians is that *theology itself will be expressed*

---

[98]David Tracy, *The Analogical Imagination: Christian Theology and the Culture of Pluralism* (New York: Crossroad, 1981); Harris, *Teaching and Religious Imagination*.

[99]West, "Politics of American Neo-Pragmatism"; "Historicist Turn in Philosophy of Religion"; "Dispensing with Metaphysics in Religious Thought," 53–56.

[100]Bernard E. Meland, "Analogy and Myth in Postliberal Theology," in *Process Philosophy and Christian Thought*, Delwin Brown, Ralph E. James, Jr., and Gene Reeves, eds. (Indianapolis: Bobbs-Merrill, 1971), 116–27, esp. 124–27.

[101]Catherine Keller, *From a Broken Web: Separation, Sexism, and Self* (Boston: Beacon Press, 1986).

more in story. The cosmology will be more than a theory of the universe; it will also be a story of the universe.[102] This would be helpful just for the sake of clear communication, but it is helpful for an even more important reason. Stories are able to express aspects of reality not communicable through direct discourse. Indirect communication, as discussed earlier in relation to Søren Kierkegaard and Minjung theologians, is a powerful way of describing the human condition.

Thus far, most of the theological storytelling by process theologians is direct communication within a story context. Two vivid examples are John Cobb's *Praying for Jennifer* and Robert Brizee's *Where in the World Is God?*[103] Both approach stories as the framework within which theological questions are asked, but the answers are given as direct communication from a process-theological perspective, especially in *Praying for Jennifer*. This in itself is a valuable way of expressing theology through story, adding texture and avoiding easy answers; what is being called for here, however, moves another step. Swimme's cosmic creation story also expresses theology in story, but as I said earlier, his attempt is to parallel the scientific description of creation— a significant but not exhaustive form of theological storytelling.[104] A multitude of stories is needed, told in a multitude of ways and yielding interpretation in depth. This will serve not only to illustrate and set a context for process theology but also, surely, it will yield fresh insight and critique—new questions *and* new answers.

One last possibility needs to be named here; *story-formed theology calls on the power of story to form and transform persons*. I discussed earlier the view of Dominic Crossan that stories can establish or subvert world. To say this is to recognize that stories are powerful and that

---

[102]This move has been made by Swimme in his cosmic creation story. His story, however, is intended to reflect the evolution of the universe rather than to play imaginatively with the unknown and mysterious, or to express the particular cultural stories of particular communities of people. See Swimme, "The Cosmic Creation Story."

[103]John B. Cobb, Jr., *Praying for Jennifer: An Exploration of Intercessory Prayer in Story Form* (Nashville: The Upper Room, 1985); Robert Brizee, *Where in the World Is God?* (Nashville: The Upper Room, 1987).

[104]In fact, Swimme describes his own creation story as a "common cosmic story," which is panhuman in the way it crosses cultures or "gathers every human group into its meanings" (Swimme, "The Cosmic Creation Story," 52). He recognizes cultural variations, but he is stressing the commonality. This is, indeed, a powerful function of story, but it is only one of many possibilities highlighted in this chapter. Through more particularized cultural stories, the fantasies, the stories and events of a people, and the central stories of a religious tradition can be taken much more seriously in expressing theology.

they have a life that goes beyond the storyteller's dramatic ability or the reader's interpretive ability. In fact, as Sallie McFague has reminded her readers, the reader of a story does not even have great control over the story. McFague has focused on parables, and she reasserts the point of the new hermeneutic that "we do not interpret the parable, but the parable interprets us."[105] To say this is to recognize that stories have power. Because stories can, and have, formed us, they require critique. Because they have the power to transform us, we need to choose stories that are creative, redemptive, and liberative.

To ponder the stories at the roots of our religious traditions is essential for theology, and to ponder the stories that point to new hopes for the earth is also essential. For Judaism and Christianity, these stories will include the Scriptures first of all, and the Scriptures themselves bear stories of eschatological hope. For general education, these stories will include the classics, broadly understood to include traditional stories of the whole world. Certainly, process theologians could be much more active in studying the stories of the world and in reflecting and communicating in narrative style. Many stories could be gathered, and many stories reflected on with the best of our critical and imaginative tools. In so doing, the power of story to form and transform persons would be unleashed and respected. The power of stories would be set loose to tell truth.

---

[105]McFague, *Speaking in Parables*, 71.

6
LIBERATIVE
TEACHING

Conscientizing Method

Theology and teaching need to be integrative and incarnational. But they also need to be liberative, especially in a world torn apart by racial and economic injustice, religious intolerance, and oppression of the powerful over the powerless. Liberative theology is a theology that makes a difference in the way people live in the world. It is a life-affirming theology that supports the reform of oppressive social structures. Liberative teaching is essential to organic education, freeing persons and societies to live more fully.

As in earlier chapters, certain passions underlie my writing on liberation. I am troubled with how easily I—as a white, middle-class, elaborately educated woman—am so easily blind to the struggles of persons whose race, class, or educational journeys are different from mine. I am troubled with how easily attempts at liberative education within my own communities become expressions of false generosity to people we do not really know, or exercises in raising the status of our own oppressions above others. My passion is to engage in liberative education that is truly liberative—opening our eyes to those realities that we have denied, opening our ears to those voices who wish to name their own realities, and opening our hearts to receive others and to enter partnership with them in their struggles for liberation.

In designing courses, I consistently give major effort to choosing books and presenting materials that represent diverse life experiences and points of view—to include diversity of religious tradition, gender, culture, ethnic community, and geographical location. Time after time, I reach the middle of a course only to recognize some major gap in my inclusiveness. I learn, course after course, that I always have more to learn. Similarly, I have worked ardently within my own institutions to address critical issues of liberation and to involve persons whose voices have been silenced. With each accomplishment, we open ourselves to hear new expressions of anger and alienation from silenced voices who carry years of accumulated frustration. These stories represent my own participation in false generosity and in efforts that are too little too late. But even more important, they represent the enormous challenge of liberative education. Education can only support liberation if it is comprehensive and enduring, if we are willing to learn at every turning so that we can continue on the journey toward liberation with new wisdom and renewed courage.

One of the most important developments in educational method in this century is the method described by Paulo Freire as conscientization. Through conscientizing methods people name oppressions and re-form social reality. They reach into the social structure and lead out to reform. The Latin *ducere* from which the word *education* is derived suggests an understanding of education as leading out into a more just social reality, a better world. The concerns are with transformation. The methods begin by looking for oppressive social structures—anything that destroys life—and they move toward reform of those structures in order to create, support, and preserve life.

The method is based on a strong valuing of freedom and a conviction that social transformation is possible. The possibilities of freedom and change are assumed in the worldview of process theology, and they are mandated in the worldview of liberation theologies. Process theology is claimed throughout this book to be an organic perspective on theology, but it is often taken to be an *alternative* to liberation theology. It is even viewed with suspicion by some liberation theologians. In reality, the perspectives of process theologians have often attracted feminist and Latin American liberation theologians because of many inherent commonalities.

Again my passions enter the picture. Process theology, if it is to be liberative, will need to change. Most seriously, the tendency in process thought to place cosmic theories above concrete particularities needs to be reconsidered. Such a tendency represents a hierarchical bent in which cosmic theories and theorists are valued over concrete descriptions and practitioners. Further, the tendency in process thought to attend largely to patterns of thought and worldview will need to be complemented more vigorously with analyses of the life experiences that shape these thoughts. Process theology is not by itself adequate to the challenges of liberation; neither are the diverse liberation theologies to which we now appeal. No one theology is full and complete, but each in dialogue with others is more adequate than it would otherwise be.

If we are to be fully organic about theology, even our dialogue across theological systems is important to liberation. The pitting of one system against another is not likely to move us in that direction. The commonalities and differences are indeed significant, but these theological systems do not represent totally different realities or locations on the landscape. These various systems live together in a land where people often move freely among theological systems, usually experiencing more power and authenticity in some than in others. To bridge between theology and liberative teaching, then, requires a complex of crossings—a network of bridges and boats moving from various theological landings. Each crossing leaves from a certain landing and serves a particular set of purposes; together, they form an effective network to sustain the movement of life. Most people will travel by more than one crossing, and their lives will be shaped by their travels along different paths and with different partners.

The tragedy is when all crossings are closed, or when debates about which crossing is best obscure the value of the various crossings. The dynamic of this metaphor is evident in Budapest, a beautiful city astride the Danube River. The life of Budapest and its place as a major center of life in Central Europe depend on the crossings between the two former cities of Buda and Pest. The merging of Buda and Pest into one city and the city's growing leadership as an important center in the world began with building bridges and creating alternative approaches for crossing between the two parts of the city. As life became more complex and the city expanded, more crossings were needed. So essential were the bridges that they were often targets of war, and Budapest has had its life stymied and damaged by the loss of its crossings. The rebuilding of the bridges has represented liberation and new life.

Crossings themselves are liberating, as links between realities. Likewise, liberation and new life in teaching depend on multiple crossings. As I explore conscientizing methods in this chapter, I will seek to build a bridge between process theology and conscientization. Traveling the bridge, I will seek a conscientizing method transformed by process theology and a process theology transformed by visions of liberation.

I am myself so deeply informed by feminist liberation and process theologies that I cannot even separate the strands; the crossings are interconnected. Likewise, I have been significantly informed by Latin American, Asian, and African-American theological movements. The varieties within each of these movements and the differences among them are exceedingly important, but they will be less important to this chapter than the possibilities in these movements, taken together, to envision a more organic theology and a more liberative approach to teaching.

CONSCIENTIZING METHOD

Conscientizing method is born out of a social context, so the birth of the term needs to be seen in its own context. Paulo Freire's vision of education is itself highly contextual, rooted first in his native Brazil and, later, in Africa's Guinea-Bissau shortly after it gained independence from Portugal. In both places, Freire was an educator, working primarily in literacy education. In both places, he dealt with the effects of colonialism and movements toward the liberation of oppressed classes. In such contexts, Freire was moved to reconceptualize education as a political and humanizing act. In the context of Guinea-Bissau, he described the act of teaching: "The educator is a politician and an artist who must use the science of techniques but must never become a cold, neutral technician."[1]

Freire began his liberative work while trying to enhance the quality of life among workers in Brazil in the 1950s. As a professor and educator, he became involved in attempts to communicate healthy

---

[1]Paulo Freire, *Pedagogy in Process: The Letters to Guinea-Bissau*, trans. Carman St. John Hunter (New York: Seabury Press, 1978), 28–29.

child-rearing practices to the peasants. Freire tells of his experience one evening when he presented a lecture on child rearing to a group of parents.[2] He was especially eager to communicate the problems with spanking as a form of discipline, and he wanted to encourage a more "dialogical" relationship between parents and children.

When Freire had finished speaking, a man in the audience stood and asked Freire how many children he had. When the man learned that Freire had five children, he began to describe Freire's life. He described Freire as living in a freestanding house that was probably not huge, but very comfortable. Probably the house had a kitchen with some equipment, a living area, and enough bedrooms for him and his wife to have one and for the girls and boys to have separate rooms. The man went on to say that Freire probably had a good teaching position with a comfortable income and secure future. Freire nodded. The man had described his family and life-style almost exactly.

Then the man went on. He said that he wanted to describe his own life to Freire. His family lived together in one room. He got up at four o'clock every morning to go to work in the manufactory, skipping breakfast. His children had only meager portions of breakfast. The man said that when he came home from work each day, his children were tired and cranky because they were hungry. He and his wife were tired and hungry too. He said that the family ate a small meal and then went to bed for the night. Sometimes he had to spank his children to get them to settle down so that he could go to sleep. He explained that if the children did not sleep, he could not sleep; and if he did not sleep, he could not work; and if he did not work, they would not eat. The man concluded by saying, " 'I would like, Doctor Paulo, to know whether in our situation you would be very dialogical.' "[3]

Freire learned that this peasant man possessed a wisdom from his experience that went beyond Freire's own wisdom. He learned that standard intellectual knowledge was not adequate for resolving issues

---

[2]Paulo Freire, address to Religious Education Association, Anaheim, Calif., November 1982; Freire's story is also recorded in Alice Frazer Evans, Robert A. Evans, and William B. Kennedy, *Pedagogy for the Non-Poor* (Maryknoll, N.Y.: Orbis Books, 1987), 227–29.
[3]Ibid., 228.

when people's lives do not conform to standard experience. He also learned that education needs to change radically, and that the changes will be inspired by the very people whom we think we are teaching.

This simple story is not so simple, especially in light of the experiences of peasants around the world who are debased by intellectuals and persons in power. But the story is even less simple if viewed from the standpoint of growing global awareness of child abuse and the problems that emerge when a culture approves of harsh physical and psychological punishments. The work of Alice Miller in her native Germany indicates an elaborate set of cultural supports for such abusiveness; harsh punishments are justified as being for the children's "own good."[4] The issues of child rearing exist in a complex web, and they cannot be resolved simplistically. At the same time, they cannot even be addressed if the peasant man who taught Freire is excluded from the dialogue.

Further, Freire learned that when a person makes a radical change of perspective in one area, the person is more ready to change other perspectives as well. His own experience with the peasant man in Brazil led him to an ideological shift regarding the wisdom of the peasants. He shifted from an assumption that knowledge is born in universities to an assumption that people, especially oppressed people, have a knowledge born in their social reality.

Once Freire had come to that insight, he found himself more open to other ideological shifts. For example, when his book *Education for Critical Consciousness* was published in English, it was full of male language for human beings. He soon received a letter from an irate woman in the United States who was shocked that he would discuss pedagogy and oppression in a book written entirely in sexist language. The very night he received this letter, he told his sons that from now on, the men in the family were going to do the dishes. Freire received many other letters on the same issue; however, the first letter was sufficient to help him see the issue because he had already seen the reality of oppression. Freire does not argue that consciousness of one oppression leads automatically to consciousness of others, nor that full consciousness arises in one simple step. He simply argues that

---

[4]Alice Miller, *For Your Own Good: Hidden Cruelty in Child-Rearing and the Roots of Violence*, trans. Hildegarde and Hunter Hannum (New York: Farrar, Straus & Giroux, 1984).

when a person sees one oppression, that person may be increasingly open to seeing other forms of oppression as well.

Basic Assumptions of Conscientization

Several basic assumptions of conscientization should be named as background for what follows. In these assumptions lies a worldview regarding social systems and how they function to oppress or liberate. The first assumption is that *education either perpetuates the present social system or brings about transformation*. It cannot be neutral. This point is made vividly by Richard Shaull in introducing Freire's *Pedagogy of the Oppressed*:

> There is no such thing as a *neutral* educational process. Education either functions as an instrument which is used to facilitate the integration of the younger generation into the logic of the present system and bring about conformity to it, *or* it becomes "the practice of freedom," the means by which men and women deal critically and creatively with reality and discover how to participate in the transformation of the world.[5]

This is a frightening assumption if taken seriously because it reminds us that the stakes in education are very high. Education is never innocuous, and whether or not we attend to it or value it, we will, in fact, shape the world by the ways we engage in it. We will maintain the shape of the status quo or transform the shape into a new social reality.

A second assumption is that *humanization is the human vocation, but dehumanization is a real option*.[6] Humanization is a calling, and we choose whether we will participate in humanizing the world or in dehumanizing it. Those who choose the latter steal the humanity of others and, in the process, dehumanize themselves as well. Though this is a real option, it is a "*distortion* of the vocation of becoming more fully human."[7] Given this assumption, we can already see why critical

---

[5]Richard Shaull, "Foreword," in Paulo Freire, *Pedagogy of the Oppressed*, trans. Myra Bergman Ramos (New York: Herder & Herder, 1970), 15; cf. Paulo Freire and Ira Shor, *A Pedagogy for Liberation: Dialogues on Transforming Education* (London: Macmillan & Co., 1987).

[6]Freire, *Pedagogy of the Oppressed*, 28.

[7]Ibid.

reflection on our own actions is essential if we are to be conscious of our own participation in humanizing and dehumanizing activities.

A third assumption is that *oppressors are not capable of liberating the oppressed; the task of the oppressed is to liberate both themselves and their oppressors.*[8] Any attempt by the oppressors to liberate the oppressed will be experienced by the oppressed as "false generosity." A certain suspicion attends any effort by persons in power to give up their power for others. Questions naturally arise whether their efforts are in their own self-interest or whether the efforts are only empty gestures. In fact, Freire believes that false generosity will even become part of the problem because oppressors will perpetuate the unjust social system to remain in a position to be generous. On the other hand, he challenges the oppressed to free both themselves and their oppressors: "Only power that springs from the weakness of the oppressed will be sufficiently strong to free both."[9]

Another assumption is that *education needs a "pedagogy of the oppressed."*[10] Sometimes Freire describes this education as the practice of freedom.[11] Such a pedagogy is created *with* oppressed individuals and peoples, and it is aimed at humanization. Oppressed persons are subjects in the process, not objects. Such a pedagogy is grounded in critical reflection on oppression and its causes, and the oppressed must be a part of these reflections or the conclusions will be distorted and the people dehumanized. Freire insists on this point: "Attempting to liberate the oppressed without their reflective participation in the act of liberation is to treat them as objects which must be saved from a burning building. . . ."[12]

Two other assumptions are closely related. *A pedagogy of the oppressed leads to action.* It is concerned not only with absorbing knowledge but also, more importantly, with identifying social realities and responding through liberating action. In addition, *the action itself is subject to continuing reexamination and revision.*[13] In other words, the action-reflection process does not end, but continues to cycle. All action is subject to critical reflection, and all critical reflection leads back into

[8]Ibid., 28–29.
[9]Ibid., 28.
[10]Ibid., 33.
[11]Paulo Freire, *Education for Critical Consciousness* (New York: Seabury Press, 1973).
[12]Freire, *Pedagogy of the Oppressed*, 52, cf. 53.
[13]Ibid., 33.

action. Because pedagogies are continually made and remade, the commitment involved is great. According to Freire, "Those who authentically commit themselves to the people must re-examine themselves constantly."[14] They will be converted to the people. In simple terms, teachers who invest themselves in a pedagogy of the oppressed will never have all of the answers themselves. They will always be so involved with learners in the educational process that they will continue to be changed themselves, and they will continually engage with others in re-forming the pedagogical process.

Pedagogy

The conscientization method cannot be singular, given the assumptions discussed above. Freire's approach to literacy education in Guinea-Bissau was not the same as in Brazil. Furthermore, neither approach was his alone, even though he articulated the pedagogy in print. In relation to the contexts and in partnership with others in those contexts, the pedagogy of the oppressed takes shape.

Given this rejoinder, I can artificially identify two basic stages of pedagogy—consciousness-raising and work for transformation. In the one stage, pedagogy serves to "unveil the world of oppression," and in the other, it serves to transform that world.[15] Conscientization is quite different from "banking" education, in which the teacher stores information in students.[16] Freire sees banking education as problematic because it "attempts to control thinking and action, leads men [sic] to adjust to the world, and inhibits their creative power."[17] On the contrary, conscientizing education might best be described as cooperative problem posing. Learners are encouraged to identify the problems in their social context and, then, to seek liberating social actions. The central educational act is action-reflection, and this is done by the teacher and learners together.

The method Freire developed with Brazilian peasants proceeded by steps. The first step was *to name the world*. More precisely, this was a time to listen to the generative words that the peasants most often

---

[14]Ibid., 47.
[15]Ibid., 40.
[16]Ibid., 58–59.
[17]Ibid., 64.

used to describe their world. The next element was *to discern the meaning in those words,* especially what the words revealed about the social structure and the peasants' relationship to it. This naturally led to a third step: *to define the problems in the social structures.* On the basis of the analysis, the peasants engaged in the final step: *to formulate strategies of action and to act.* The last step began the cycle again because the peasants reflected on their actions, thus beginning to listen and reflect anew on their situation.

The liberative power of this pedagogy comes from its close relation to action as the beginning and ending point and, also, from its continuing engagement in critical reflection. The process is not guaranteed to lead toward liberative action, but the dynamic of critical reflection is a continuing test of people's actions and their fruits. Furthermore, the pedagogy is so fully participatory that the people as a whole—not simply those people who are in power—are reflecting on those actions.

Three religious educators who have been particularly concerned with liberative teaching are Thomas Groome, Maria Harris, and Daniel Schipani. I will briefly present their methods here to show how liberative methods can take form in North and Central American religious contexts. Thomas Groome has taken the work of Paulo Freire very seriously, as well as the work of critical theorists in general, and he has offered a clear liberation method to religious education. For Groome, education is a process of reflection on shared praxis. His emphasis, as with Freire, is critical reflection on practice, which leads back into reformed practice. This kind of reflection is done in community; hence, it is shared.

Groome's method proceeds through five movements that coincide in many ways with Freire's movements in literacy education. In the first movement, participants describe their own or society's praxis, followed in the second movement by identifying the stories and visions that underlie that praxis. In the third movement, the community reflects on the Christian story and vision, followed by a dialogical reflection between their own praxis and the Christian story/vision in the fourth movement. The concluding movement makes decisions for renewed praxis. In this last movement, the dialectic leads to the reformation of action.[18]

---

[18]These movements are expressed in somewhat different language in Groome's

Groome has given considerable attention to developing this shared praxis method and, also, to identifying qualitative dimensions of the teaching act. For example, he has developed the ideas that to educate for justice is to educate justly and that the heart of religious education is the heart of the religious educator.[19] In both cases, Groome attends to the qualities that make the process of education compatible with the goals. He, as Freire, recognizes the importance of the qualities of the teacher and the teaching act.

Maria Harris has also approached the issue of liberative education, drawing significantly from feminist theory. She, also, has given attention to the qualities of the teacher and of the teaching act.[20] And she, also, has posed a method described in steps. Harris draws an analogy with the steps of a dance, making clear that the steps do not follow a linear order even though they often lead into one another. She describes the steps of silence, political awareness, mourning, bonding, and birthing.[21] For Harris, the steps include not only the element of critical reflection but also the elements of listening, grieving, and celebrating. These steps are highly consistent with her own concerns with women's liberation and with the intuitive and affective dimensions of knowing. She, therefore, gives much more attention to the aesthetic dimensions of teaching than do Freire or Groome.

One other educator has given attention to conscientization in an explicitly Christian context. This is Daniel Schipani who has taught in Puerto Rico as well as in the United States. Schipani has given particular attention to the content of liberation within Christianity,

---

various writings, but the basic purpose and flow of the movements remain the same. See Thomas H. Groome, *Christian Religious Education* (San Francisco: Harper & Row, 1980), 207–23; Groome, "A Religious Educator's Response," in *The Education of the Practical Theologian*, ed. Don S. Browning, David Polk, and Ian S. Evison (Atlanta: Scholars Press, 1989), 77–91.

[19]Thomas H. Groome, "Education for Justice by Educating Justly," in *Education for Peace and Justice*, ed. Padraic O'Hare (San Francisco: Harper & Row, 1983), 69–82; Groome, "The Spirituality of the Religious Educator," *Religious Education*, 83 (Winter 1988): 9–20.

[20]Harris has taken teaching to be her primary focus, and for her the person of the teacher and the dynamics of the teaching act are both important. See particularly Maria Harris, *Teaching and Religious Imagination* (San Francisco: Harper & Row, 1987); Harris, "Teaching: Forming and Transforming Grace," in *Congregations: Their Power to Form and Transform*, C. Ellis Nelson, ed. (Atlanta: John Knox Press, 1988), 238–63; Harris, *Women and Teaching* (New York: Paulist Press, 1988).

[21]Harris, *Teaching and Religious Imagination*, 97–116. Harris names the steps somewhat differently elsewhere. See *Women and Teaching* for a description of silence, remembering, ritual mourning, artistry, and birthing.

namely, the gospel of the kingdom of God by which the church should be oriented, conceived, and evaluated.[22] Appropriating this gospel becomes the purpose of Christian education, which he elaborates to include following Jesus Christ, promoting social transformation for the increase of freedom, knowing and loving God, and becoming more human.[23]

For all of these educators—Paulo Freire, Thomas Groome, Maria Harris, and Daniel Schipani—certain themes persist. All seek a liberative approach to education, freeing human beings to be more fully human. All are concerned with the person of the teacher and the qualitative relationship between teachers and learners. Furthermore, they all insist that the teaching relationship and the methods of education reflect the goals of the educational process. We cannot engage in humanizing education with a banking approach to education; we cannot engage in justice education if we do not educate justly; and we cannot free the human intuition and imagination if we do not teach with intuition and imagination. These four educators, with others, have laid forth a challenge for liberative teaching that would recreate our present educational systems in schools and religious communities.

PROCESS THEOLOGY AND CONSCIENTIZATION

A sense of urgency arises from process theology regarding the importance of liberative education. Since the educational methods of conscientization emerge philosophically from critical theory, then many reflections from a process perspective may, as yet, be unspoken. They are, however, relevant to the tasks of liberative theology and education. The passion within process theology to understand organic relationships and to care for all of life is vital to liberation.

Within a process perspective, *persons are understood to be both determined and free; thus, all beings are partially self-determined.* If this is true,

---

[22]Daniel S. Schipani, *Conscientization and Creativity: Paulo Freire and Christian Education* (Lanham, Md.: University Press of America, 1984), 104.
[23]Ibid., 128–31.

then educational methods need to foster more thoughtful self-determination by helping people become more conscious of their environment and more active in shaping it. Conscientization methods are significant because they enhance people's consciousness of their environment and its impact. From a process perspective, this consciousness is urgent because people are free to shape their world. They are free to become agents of humanization.

A process liberation perspective would also highlight another aspect of determination and freedom, that is, the effects of the past on the present situation and the freedom people have to make new decisions in regard to their past.[24] In other words, people are not bound to follow the patterns of the past; nor are they fully determined to allow the feelings they have about their past, whether negative or positive, to shape their present actions. They may, in fact, appropriate their personal or cultural past in a radically new and transformed way. The heritage of patriarchal social structures, for example, can be as oppressive as the currently existing patterns of patriarchal domination. The heritage influences and supports the present practices, and the present practices provide the interpretive lens through which the past is seen and described. Education can free people to critique, reject, or revise the heritage so that its relation to the present can be seen both as determined and free.

Another feature of process philosophy is important here, namely, the idea that *concern for the future is a natural characteristic of all occasions.* This does not mean that concern for the future is always a conscious or even a dominant influence on the decision of a becoming occasion. It is simply a natural quality and, as such, it might even be "enlarged and strengthened."[25] In other words, the futuristic impulse can be enhanced in an educative environment. What Alfred North Whitehead describes as creative self-expression is the aim to express oneself and influence the future environment. Teachers and leaders can appeal to this concern for the future in their practice of conscientization.

---

[24]Kathleen Gershman and Donald Oliver identify this freedom with creativity and call it "the secret of learning." Creativity moves learners beyond the limits of tradition and beyond teacher-led precision into a self-impelled movement in learning. The result can be a "happy blend of conservatism and creativity." See Kathleen Gershman and Donald W. Oliver, "Towards a Process Pedagogy," *Process Studies* 16 (Fall 1987): 195–96, cf. 191–97.

[25]John B. Cobb, Jr., and David Ray Griffin, *Process Theology: An Introductory Exposition* (Philadelphia: Westminster Press, 1976), 27.

At the same time that beings are concerned with the future, they are affected by all that is past. *Beings are affected by the entire past experience of their culture, including the beliefs that help shape their character and action.*[26] The history of a society needs, then, to be taken seriously in education, and the beliefs of that society need to be subject to the critical reflection that conscientization makes possible. Cultural patterns often emerge in the context of historical events and decisions, but they persist long after those events and decisions have been critiqued or revoked. One clear example of this is the persistence of racism in the United States, a racism so deeply buried in the psyche of the country that it vigorously resists change. All of the events and decisions that were part of that practice of slavery combined with an elaborate belief system to make slavery possible. The historical practices and events have left a heritage of racism that is not easily eliminated, even with good intentions.[27]

Other ideas at the center of process theology have to do with how God relates to the world. Important to liberation is the belief that *God is an active force in the creation of justice;* God is not simply the creator of the idea of justice nor the motivator for people to act justly, but God also acts to create justice. Such a belief mitigates against simplistic notions that people can band together in a few liberative acts and justice will naturally follow. The complexity and persistence of problems in the social order are far too great to yield to simple solutions. Hope comes from the idea that God is on the side of justice and that God will work to effect justice in the world; at the same time, human efforts for justice can also make a difference.

One of the debates within liberation theologies is between feminist and Latin American liberation theologians regarding the power of God to effect liberation. Christian feminist theologians often speak of the limitedness of God, carrying forth an idea common to Jewish thought. In contrast, Latin American theologians often proclaim that

---

[26]Alfred North Whitehead, *Religion in the Making* (New York: Meridian Books, [1926, 1954] 1960), 15.

[27]Lillian Smith has reflected powerfully on the persistence of racist patterns of thinking that overwhelm the efforts of well-meaning individuals who wish to counter them and transform the racist mentality. One mark of the validity of her argument is the fact that her book, written originally in 1949, is now demonstrating a resurgence and has been reprinted. The racist patterns that she observed in 1949 are not dead. See Lillian Smith, *Killers of the Dream*, rev. ed. (New York: W. W. Norton, [1949] 1978).

God will finally be victorious for justice, bringing the reign of God to its fullness. One poignant expression of the limits of God is found in Isabel Carter Heyward's *The Redemption of God*. The very title suggests her concern that God needs our help in redeeming the world because God cannot effect redemption alone.[28] She interacts with Elie Wiesel and his own questioning of God's omnipotence. She affirms with Wiesel that God relies on the goodness of human love and the willingness of humanity to work for justice.[29] On the other hand, Latin American and African-American liberation theologians often accentuate God's liberating power and God's ceaseless work to empower human liberation and lead into the reign of God.[30]

The contribution of process theology to this debate is the affirmation that God is passionately working for justice, but that human participation in those efforts is vital because God does not have all of the power in the world. The very existence of human freedom suggests that human beings themselves have some of the power, and they can use that power for liberation or for destruction.

Within religious communities, then, education might inspire the sense of co-creating with God in the liberation of the world. This inspiration can come from participating in the liberating praxis described by Paulo Freire and, also, participating in meditation and prayer to God, who inspires, guides, and supports all educative acts for justice. The sense of God's participation is evident in the liberative work of Martin Luther King, Jr., Mother Teresa, and Dorothy Day, all of whom have included prayer and worship as part of their life routines. The challenge of this discussion is to work for justice as if our efforts will make all of the difference and to pray for justice as if nothing that we do will be enough.

A related element of process theology is the idea that *God's initial aim pulls creation in the direction of acting justly, though the subjective aim*

---

[28]Isabel Carter Heyward, *The Redemption of God: A Theology of Mutual Relation* (Lanham, Md.: University Press of America, 1982).

[29]Ibid., 89–100, 179–83.

[30]The difference is more a matter of emphasis because none of the liberationists ignore the integral relationship between God's work and human work. The difference is, however, real. See, for example, Gustavo Gutiérrez, *We Drink from Our Own Wells: The Spiritual Journey of a People*, trans. Matthew J. O'Connell (London: SCM Press, 1984); James Cone, *God of the Oppressed* (New York: Seabury Press, 1975), esp. 163–94; José Miguez Bonino, *Doing Theology in a Revolutionary Situation* (Philadelphia: Fortress Press, 1975).

of each being may not actualize God's pull toward justice at every moment.
God motivates by persuasion rather than coercion; therefore, God
does not control human responses in a determinative way. On the
other hand, people may become more responsive to God's initial aim
as they become more conscious of God's persuasive pulls. Conscientization can arouse people's awareness and responsiveness to God's
initial aim.

The human passion for justice itself arises from God's aims for
creation. For Jewish communities, the revelation of God's justice is
revealed in the Torah. Within Christianity the life, death, and resurrection of Jesus Christ is understood as decisive witness to God's
justice; even the ability of individuals to be touched and persuaded
by the Christ event is testimony that God's persuasion is always at
work.[31] For Muslim communities, revelation of the justice of Allah is
found in the Qur'an. In any of these traditions viewed through a
process understanding, the freedom to make choices and act resides
within the human community, and conscientizing education empow-
ers learners in their ability to decide for justice.

The accent on persuasion makes conscientization all the more important as a way of naming and transforming oppressive realities.
The dynamics of persuasion imply not only harmony but also conflict
and struggle. The struggle of persuasion is undergirded by nonvio-
lence and inspired by "God as Holy Advocate, calling us and empowering us to advocacy for justice and peace."[32]

Another process notion that has already received some development is the idea that *God offers liberation to the whole of creation and to
every part of it.* Charles Birch and John Cobb have developed this theme
in *Liberation of Life.* In that book they articulate the concern that God
directs toward sustaining and preserving the life of every part of
creation.[33] Earlier in this book I noted that all actualities experience
some amount of enjoyment, and God acts to enhance that enjoyment.
Further, God wants the enjoyment of one entity to enhance the enjoyment of others.[34] This suggests that conscientization needs to encourage liberative praxis that will enhance the enjoyment, or full life,

[31]Marjorie Hewitt Suchocki, *God, Christ, Church: A Practical Guide to Process Theology*
(New York: Crossroad, 1982), 116–18.
[32]Lois Gehr Livezey, "Women, Power, and Politics: Feminist Theology in Process
Perspective," *Process Studies* 17 (Summer 1988): 76; cf. 67–77, esp. 73, 75.
[33]Charles Birch and John B. Cobb, Jr., *The Liberation of Life: From the Cell to the
Community* (Cambridge: Cambridge University Press, 1981).
[34]Cobb and Griffin, *Process Theology,* 56–57.

of others, including other nations, other racial groups, and other parts of God's creation.

Conscientization may seem incompatible to the process vision of harmony, but this is deceiving. The purpose of conscientization is to reform the social structures so that they will be less oppressive and more humanizing. Conscientization challenges process theologians to engage in structural analysis in order to critique and re-form society. Such a challenge should be well received by these theologians whose ethical vision includes care for the whole of creation and the hope to contribute enjoyment to every becoming occasion. Trivial harmony is not the process ideal; neither are happy, patchy social agreements that do not re-form basic problems. Harmony is a vision of wholeness in which every particular part is valued. To maximize harmony is to convert opposition into contrast so that differences are held together and not destroyed. Differences in race, gender, or nationality are not denied; neither are they forced into homogeneity or destructive power relationships. Conflicts are re-formed in ways that create the maximum enjoyment for all people and all of creation.

With this idea of God's relation to creation comes the idea that *a social order is only of value insofar as it enhances the enjoyment of its members.*[35] According to Whitehead, "God's purpose in the creative advance is the evocation of intensities. The evocation of societies is purely subsidiary to this absolute end."[36] This perspective reinforces the idea in conscientization that social structures are subsidiary to the value of human life. When they interfere with the quality or intensity of life, they must be changed. In fact, from a process perspective, the structures are subsidiary to the value of all creation; thus, social structures that allow or even support the destruction of rain forests in Africa or air quality in the United States need to be critiqued and reformed.

Critical reflection on theological systems and views of the world is needed because these views have themselves led to oppression, such as the oppression that emerges from dualistic patterns of thinking and relating. Dualisms exist between human and nonhuman, mind and body, male and female. Such dualisms often foster destructive patterns in which one part of

---

[35]Ibid., 60.

[36]Alfred North Whitehead, *Process and Reality: An Essay in Cosmology*, ed. David R. Griffin and Donald W. Sherburne (New York: [Macmillan, 1929] Free Press, 1978), 105.

the dualism is valued over the other. Even movements of liberation are often concerned with only one part of a dualism, such as the liberation of humans with no concern for the nonhuman, or the liberation of the mind as if it were disconnected from the body, or the liberation of men with no concern for the liberation of women.

One of the most dramatic historical cases of dualistic thinking has to do with race. Susan B. Anthony and Elizabeth Cady Stanton, noted for their liberative leadership in the women's suffrage movement in the United States, were sometimes flagrant in their racist attitudes, or what could be called dualistic thinking about black and white. African-American women are not eager to identify with white women who worked so hard to get the vote for white women in the United States. Anthony and Stanton were single-minded in working for women's suffrage, but openly racist in doing so.

Given the prevalence of dualistic thinking in the modern world, critical reflection on such dualisms needs to be part of liberative praxis. Much attention has been given to this problem by feminist theologians, notably Rosemary Radford Ruether, for whom the reform of these destructive ideas is essential to liberation and, also, to Jewish-Christian relations.[37] Process theologians have focused considerably on the critique of just such ideas, and their work complements the work of others. Persons as disparate as John Cobb, Sheila Davaney, Schubert Ogden, and Marjorie Suchocki have questioned common-sense ways of thinking and have posed alternative views. This kind of theoretical critique is vital to liberation.

One vivid consequence of dualistic thinking is the strong bias against women in most theological systems. Church leaders have often attended to visible problems of church practice, such as the denial of ordination to women, without questioning the theological systems that have supported these practices. Even though many Christian churches now do ordain women, many problems of oppression toward women persist in these very churches. In fact, the problems are quite similar to problems in those churches that have kept their doors closed to women's ordination. Changing the practices and ordaining women have not ended patriarchy. Many beliefs continue to

---

[37]See particularly Rosemary Radford Ruether, *To Change the World: Christology and Cultural Criticism* (New York: Crossroad, 1986), 31–43.

support oppressive attitudes and practices, and these need to be critiqued alongside the practices themselves.

CONSCIENTIZATION RE-FORMED
BY PROCESS THEOLOGY

Reflecting on conscientization and process theology reveals common emphases. On both ends of the bridge, the purposes and processes of education are envisioned in similar ways. I will explore some of these similarities and some of the ways in which conscientization might be extended and re-formed in light of process theology.

Purpose of Education

Because the visions of reality have much in common on the two ends of the bridge, the purposes of education in conscientization find much support in process theology. The first purpose held in common is *to lead people to know the world and to participate in it*. A second purpose is *to lead people into encounter with the world, subject to subject*. This encounter begins with listening, especially listening to the poor and oppressed, whose voices may be the hardest to hear. The focus on listening is not based in a naive optimism that every voice is equally true but, rather, on an assumption that more evil is usually done by not respecting truth in the voices of others than by taking those voices too seriously. A third purpose of education is *to lead people toward social consciousness so that they will know themselves as social beings connected with other beings in social systems*. Such social awareness includes an awareness of how the action of one people affects other people, one nation affects other nations, one person affects other persons. One other common purpose is a natural outgrowth of the others, that is, *to lead people to envision how their decisions in this moment will contribute to the future*. Individuals and communities are encouraged to see themselves as actors whose actions in the world will influence the future shape of the world. For this reason, their decisions are of crucial importance to that future.

Re-formed by process theology, conscientization would continue to move toward these goals, but each would be expanded. The first purpose revised would be *to lead people to know and participate in the whole world, including all peoples and the nonhuman natural world.* Addressing oppressions in the individual's own situation would expand to include oppressions where culture meets culture, tradition meets tradition, and nation meets nation. Outdoor education would also be important. Freire and his colleagues actually moved in that direction with educational reforms in Guinea-Bissau during the 1970s. They took urban children into rural areas where they lived in camps.[38] Here the children continued their regular studies and also worked on farms, learning from the peasants as they worked. The children also taught the peasants, but Freire acknowledged that the children probably learned more from the workers than the other way around.[39] From a process perspective, this mode of learning is extraordinarily promising because the learners are interacting with people and an entire environment that they would not ordinarily know; they are also participating with all of their senses and with many forms of work. Some of the disconnections between study and work are overcome.

From a process perspective, the natural elements of the environment would be accented even more than Freire and his colleagues envisioned. Learners might be encouraged to participate in a broad range of outdoor activities in which they could listen to the plants and the earth and interact with them in a variety of ways. In other words, people could be encouraged to learn from the natural environment as well as from the workers in that environment.

This is akin to one Native American tradition of teaching children by taking them into a remote area to listen to the rocks and winds and sun. The child remains alone all day in this school. At the end of the day, the child returns home. At such a school as this, the conscientization is very different from the conscientization of Paulo Freire, but it is an urgent awakening of consciousness to the earth and to the human community's participation with it. This form of consciousness can lead to reformed action, just as consciousness of human social systems can lead to action for reform of those systems. Perhaps communing with the earth will arouse ecological consciousness and lead us to act differently toward the earth so that the earth might survive.

---

[38]Freire, *Pedagogy in Process*, 20–22.
[39]Ibid., 22.

Continuing the re-formation, the second purpose is *to lead people into encounter with the world, subject to subject; this includes listening to one another and to the physical world—its groans and needs—and to those excluded from social participation for any reason, including reasons other than economic oppression.* These persons may be children, women, the aged, gay and lesbian people, or individuals with disabilities. Encountering the world also includes listening to those people who are more oppressor than oppressed, for even their voices are heard very little at a deep level. Even their oppressive acts come in part from their own internal cries and prejudices that lead them to meet their own needs by using others. Those internal cries and prejudices need to be heard. Although these people are not able, according to Freire, to free the economically oppressed, they may well be able to free themselves, insofar as they are oppressed by other forces. This may, in turn, contribute to eliminating their oppression of others.

White women who participate in the oppression of African Americans, especially African-American women, provide a clear example of people who are both oppressor and oppressed. This pattern has been identified most clearly by African-American women who have suffered oppression in this system.[40] The very fact that naming the pattern was done by those who suffered most from it supports Freire's argument that only the oppressed can free both themselves and their oppressor. At the same time, the naming of the issues by black women opens the possibility that white women will name their own issues and oppressions and will see how they have participated in oppressing others.

For white women who are also southern, the dilemma is particularly profound. Being southern is cause for derision in many circles, and being white means that they have been collaborators in racism, at least by receiving privileges not available to their black sisters and brothers. Furthermore, by being women they have been limited in the choices they could make regarding vocation, life-style, and manner. In identifying the limits placed on them in their culture and the

---

[40]See, for example, Delores Williams, "The Color of Feminism: Or Speaking the Black Woman's Tongue," *Journal of Religious Thought* 43 (Spring–Summer 1986): 42–58; Williams, "Women's Oppression and Lifeline Politics in Black Women's Religious Narratives," *Journal of Feminist Studies in Religion* 1–2 (1985–1986): 59–71; Jacquelyn Grant, *White Women's Christ and Black Women's Jesus* (Atlanta: Scholars Press, 1989), esp. 195–230.

stereotypes imposed on them, they may become more conscious of their own relation to the social system and the ways by which that system has seriously limited the quality of their lives. If they can be given opportunity to reflect critically on how such social systems function, they may find the power to remake the system and participate more as reformers than as oppressors.

Educationally, such a shift requires a real encounter with the world, subject to subject. This can be done in part through the obvious means of interaction among people, but it can also be done through the media, through literature, and through listening to political voices of oppressed persons who identify the problems. Direct person-to-person interaction can bring forth human qualities of compassion and understanding, and it can allow individuals to reflect honestly together on their different social situations. On the other hand, it can also be threatening and can foster further alienation. Printed and other media resources can introduce individuals and issues in a less threatening way and can allow them opportunity to reflect on their own reactions outside of the presence of those people who would be most affected by those reactions. Part of education is seeking different kinds of opportunities for people to interact with other people and issues, including opportunities to interact person to person and opportunities to read and view media that foster encounters with another person or community in a real way.

Part of the teaching act is introducing students to these resources and encouraging them to discover and identify with others. Also important is encouraging students to listen and respond self-critically; without self-critical reflection, the resources may offer only empty information. Another part of the teaching act is to offer students experiences of the art, music, folklore, and history of a culture so that the encounter is broad and deep.

Culturally grounded education is essential if we are to know people in relation to their culture. According to Donald Oliver and Kathleen Gershman, process education is existentially oriented, aimed not toward transcending culture, but toward apprehending the fullness of immediacy.[41] Transformation is important, but not transcendence

---

[41]Oliver and Gershman see the process orientation as more existential and less apocalyptic than the liberation orientation. They do see considerable correspondence, however, in that both are concerned with "creative trauma" and transformation. Donald W. Oliver and Kathleen Waldron Gershman, *Education, Modernity, and Fractured Meaning: Toward a Process Theory of Teaching and Learning* (Albany: State University of New York Press, 1989), 229, cf. 218–29.

in the sense of moving beyond culture. The other alternative is not very promising. Encountering persons apart from their culture is an extreme of abstraction and individualism; it fosters a tendency, often unconscious, to judge others through our own cultural lenses. In this case, the encounter is superficial, partial, and misleading. A person may be judged as "nice" or "not-so-nice," but the judgment is based on our own cultural standards, which means that our encounter with the other culture is minimized, our self-criticalness about our own culture is pushed to the background, and our ability to meet other people subject to subject is limited.

From a process theological perspective, the third purpose also needs to be expanded. The third purpose is *to lead people to social consciousness so that they will know themselves as social beings connected with others in a web of social relationships, including all elements of the world as part of the social matrix.* Social consciousness is important if individuals are to know themselves within a matrix of social relationships. This is essential to liberative teaching, but most especially now when wars rage and when racism, classism, sexism, and heterosexism persist. Writing about critical pedagogy, Maxine Greene says: "We need to teach in such a way as to arouse passion now and then; we need a new camaraderie, a new en masse. These are dark and shadowed times, and we need to live them, standing before one another, open to the world."[42] Such standing before one another and opening to the world would be a major feature of process liberative education.

Further, from a process view, the social system does not include only people and political structures; geography, climate, the ozone layer, and many other elements are part of the social web influencing the quality of life.[43] A popularized version of Chief Seattle's protest speech during a land dispute with the U.S. government provides an eloquent statement of the connections among every part of the earth: " 'Teach your children what we have taught our children—that the earth is our mother. Whatever befalls the earth, befalls the sons of the earth. All things are connected like the blood which unites one

---

[42]Maxine Greene, "In Search of Critical Pedagogy," *Harvard Educational Review* 56 (November 1986), 441, cf. 427–41.

[43]The relation between ecology and process education is noted explicitly by Oliver and Gershman, *Education, Modernity, and Fractured Meaning*, 229–34.

family. Man is merely a strand in the web of life. Whatever he does to the web, he does to himself.' "[44]

Chief Seattle's imagery of children, mother, blood, and web suggests an organic view of the universe and a social awareness that includes everything.

This theme has appeared in earlier chapters. In discussing re-formed case study, gestalt, and phenomenological methods, I noted that elements of the entire environment need to be included in teaching. In repeating the theme again here, I am accenting conscientization and the role that the entire earth plays in the social system. With such consciousness, we realize that critical reflection includes all of the earth in the social structures to be critiqued. We reflect on the influence of a hurricane or acid rain, and we reflect on the influence of desertification in the Southern Hemisphere. These are subjects for reflection not only because of their influence on human beings but also because of the earth itself.

The last revision of purpose flows from the others: *to lead people to envision how their decisions in this moment will contribute to the future of the whole planet.* Key to re-formulating conscientization is acknowledging that all of the earth is affected by what we do and do not learn, and what we do and do not do. Also, the immediate future is not the whole story; our decisions need to take account of the long future.

The past continues to affect the future for generations. Nathaniel Hawthorne wrestled with his heritage as a descendant of a judge in the Salem witch trials. More than 150 years after these infamous trials, he wrote *The House of Seven Gables*, a book that wrestled with inherited evil and ended with a new beginning. In a similar way, the residents of New England are now wrestling with the heritage of acid rain that has been swept from the Midwest, residue of industrial pollution released into the skies several years ago. The sense of being interconnected in a web across generations and across hundreds of miles is critical if we are to make responsible decisions today.

Pedogogy

Educationally, all of these purposes accent the need for persons to reflect critically on their situation and to participate in transformation.

---

[44]Chief Seattle made a speech between 1853 and 1855 in connection with the Port Elliott Treaty, but the exact words of that speech are not known. The words quoted here were actually written by screenwriter Ted Perry for the film *Home*. See *Environmental Ethics* 11, 196.

To these reflections process theology adds the need to analyze many aspects of any situation, recognizing how complex every situation is and how interrelated are the many dynamics that come together.

Freire's steps in literacy education might be extended to greater complexity. First, in naming the world, *learners need not only to name the world as they experience it but also to hear how others experience and name it. They need to name not only the aspects of a situation that are obvious to them but also the aspects that might be invisible.* Revolutions are not caused by one or two precipitating incidents; neither are airplane crashes or oil spills caused by one simple flaw in the system. Revolutions are fed by inequities, oppression, ambitions, ideological differences, and human needs of all kinds. Airplane crashes are caused by labor practices, consumer desires, weather conditions, profit motives, and human error of all kinds. All of these are elements in a situation, and if we are to name the world, we need to take all of these factors into consideration. If we do not, we tend to pose one simplistic description of the world against another.

The second step is to discern meaning in the words people use to name the situation, trying to understand what the situation reveals about the social structures. Learners need to be encouraged *to discern the meanings in the many different perspectives and to discern what each perspective reveals about the vast social structures that include every dimension of the planet.* This requires an ability to move back and forth between particular perspectives and a larger, global picture.

To think that people can actually discern all possible meanings is ridiculously naive, but to avoid the effort is still more naive. Various interpretations are needed for a fuller picture of the social structures. A student captured this spirit of inclusiveness in a few lines of poetry:

If pigs could fly . . .
You would hear the trees cough from all the smog
And then we'd want to clear the air
For no one could sleep at all
With all the trees coughing all night long.[45]

Though we may never be able to hear the coughing of the trees, the effort to listen can help us discern something of the anguish that trees experience in the midst of pollution.

---

[45]Julie Roberts-Fronk, "If Pigs Could Fly . . . ," a redemption metaphor presented in Education and Issues of Faith class, School of Theology at Claremont, June 12, 1987.

The third step is to define the problems in the social structures. The challenge from a process perspective is *to define the problems in a way that is sufficiently complex to take account of the many interrelated aspects of a situation and the ever-changing nature of the social structures.* In other words, the analysis needs to take account of the many perspectives discussed above, to allow for complexity, and to recognize the tentativeness of any definition of the problems. Tentativeness is especially important because no one can possibly know and include every aspect of a problem in analysis and, also, situations do actually change.

Feminist theology is a clear revelation of this point because feminist theology includes many different perspectives and different ways of defining problems. Three perspectives are commonly identified in relation to Christianity—Christian, revisionist, and radical feminist theologies. All of these define the problems of women from very different perspectives on women's relation to the Christian tradition. These terms themselves are limited, however, because they have generally referred to Christian feminist theology done by white, middle-class, Euro-American feminists—and not even those persons fit comfortably into the categories. An explosion of feminist dialogue has led to the realization that feminism is quite different in different religious traditions and within each tradition. Not only that, feminism is quite different across races, social classes, and nationalities. The differences are so great that the word *feminism* even proves inadequate as a defining term, and many African-American women prefer to call themselves *womanists.*

Various people define the problems of the world in various ways, and no one way can be claimed as total or final. Each way of defining problems in the social structure is partial and tentative, drawing from perspectives available to the individuals engaged in defining. Each way is important to the whole, however, and much can be learned from sharing across communities.

Educationally, this serves as a reminder that individuals need to engage in education together. Freire did not create an educational plan for Guinea-Bissau in his World Council of Churches office in Geneva; rather, he entered into a partnership with the people living in Guinea-Bissau.[46] In a similar way, we need to join with others in

---

[46]Freire, *Pedagogy in Process,* 8–9.

defining problems. Education needs to become a forum for teachers and learners to work together in defining problems and to draw on multiple resources in literature, media, and art in the effort to understand the issues. Multiple voices are needed, as well as negotiation among those voices. Finally, we need to redefine the problems continually, supporting the critical reflection and revision so characteristic of conscientization.

The final steps in Freire's conscientization are to formulate strategies of action and to act. Here again, the challenge offered by process theology is *to formulate and participate in multiple strategies of action as a response to the multiple factors in any situation.* If only one definition of the problems and one strategy of action are put forth, the likely result is inadequate response to the problems. Also, some persons will be excluded from the solutions and their oppression will be perpetuated.

Again if we look to feminist theology, the problems in singular analyses become apparent. The strategies of action put forth by white feminists in the United States often encourage a kind of independence from men that is incompatible with the images of liberation among many black womanists or feminists. Also, women who identify themselves with one perspective of feminist analysis often reject or ignore women whose perspective is different. These patterns perpetuate the objectification of persons, the oversimplification of issues, and the oppression of one group by another. Furthermore, strategies for liberation suffer.

What we need is a chorus of voices working together, or at least in dialogue. What we need is pedagogy modeled after the work of Ada Maria Isasi-Diaz and Yolanda Tarango in which they hear and interpret voices of many Hispanic women in many different situations.[47] As we listen to many voices, we can draw out plans for action. The strategies and actions will not fit together into one neat package, nor will they always be compatible, but they will address different aspects of the issues and will inform and often complement one another.

The teacher's role in such a pedagogy is to inspire, stand with, and offer resources to students as they seek to name the world, define

---

[47]Ada Maria Isasi-Diaz and Yolanda Tarango, *Hispanic Women: Prophetic Voice in the Church* (San Francisco: Harper & Row, 1988).

problems, make decisions, and engage in action. This is not an easy form of teaching, and it requires a spirit of humility and courage. The teacher has responsibility to seek after wisdom; to share with learners, being honest and explicit about teaching methods and commitments; to respect students, even when their methods and commitments are quite different; to engage with students in action and reflection; and to incarnate the best of life that has been, for the sake of life to come.

PROCESS THEOLOGY RE-FORMED
BY CONSCIENTIZATION

The primary critique that conscientization methodology offers to process theology is that it too often does not go far enough in critical reflection on the social structures and on the oppression therein. Having been born in philosophical reflection, process theologians have most often analyzed systems of thought and the influence of those systems on the world; they have also given considerable attention to issues in reality, including nuclear, environmental, economic, animal rights, and personal loss issues. Attention to the social structures themselves and to contextual analyses has been less thoroughly included in the reflections. The danger here is that, without self-conscious reflection on the social structures, the theological analyses may actually perpetuate oppressive structures or may become disembodied from concrete social realities.

Such a critique as the one proposed is much too simple and overly generalized; however, two emphases do recommend themselves. One is *the need to include social analysis in the beginning and throughout theological analysis,* and the other is *the need to test the adequacy of theological constructions in terms of how they affect human lives and the earth.*

These recommendations move in the direction in which some process theologians have already moved. Marjorie Suchocki and David Griffin have considered the existence and interpretations of evil in the world, and Delwin Brown has analyzed the role of theology in relation to concrete liberation.[48] Some process theologians have attended to the demands of liberation and the ethical judgments it

[48]Marjorie Suchocki, *The End of Evil* (Albany: State University of New York Press, 1988); David Ray Griffin, *God, Power and Evil: A Process Theodicy* (Philadelphia: Westminster Press, 1976), esp. 275–313; Delwin Brown, *To Set at Liberty: Christian Faith and Human Freedom* (Maryknoll, N.Y.: Orbis Books, 1981).

requires. Jay McDaniel has given attention to a biocentric ethic that fosters the liberation of all life, including land and animals as well as human beings.[49] In fact, concern for the concrete issues of the world seems to be a prominent feature in the work of most process theologians. John Cobb has attended especially to issues of ecology and economic systems, and David Griffin has attended to the threat of nuclear destruction.[50] In addition, others have observed the actual process of theological reflection in relation to liberation. Schubert Ogden has given considerable attention to this, dealing primarily with questions of appropriateness and understandability.[51]

What then is needed? The need is a matter of emphasis. The question is whether emphasis will be placed on evaluating the adequacy of ideas in relation to the world in general, or on evaluating the particular ways in which those ideas emerge from and affect their particular contexts and the oppression within those contexts.

Sharon Welch would argue that the problem goes even beyond emphasis; she notes the difference between a theology focused on ontology and the liberating attributes of God, and a theology focused on liberation actualized in history. She specifically identifies process theology with the former, reflecting on how the primordial and consequent natures of God are discussed in relation to God's liberating activity.[52] She sees this as vastly different from a focus on the way language does or does not lead to liberation, concluding that "the truth of God-language and of all theological claims is measured not

[49]Jay B. McDaniel, *Of God and Pelicans: A Theology of Reverence for Life* (Louisville: Westminster/John Knox, 1989), 51–84.

[50]See, for example, Birch and Cobb, *Liberation of Life*; John B. Cobb, Jr., "Postmodern Social Policy," in *Spirituality and Society: Postmodern Visions*, David Ray Griffin, ed. (Albany: State University of New York Press, 1988), 99–106; Herman E. Daly and John B. Cobb, Jr., *For the Common Good* (Boston: Beacon Press, 1989); David Ray Griffin, "Peace and the Postmodern Paradigm" in *Spirituality and Society*, 143–54; Griffin, "Imperialism, Nuclearism, and Postmodern Theism," *God and Religion in the Postmodern World: Essays in Postmodern Theology* (Albany: State University of New York Press, 1989), 127–45.

[51]Schubert Ogden, *Faith and Freedom: Toward a Theology of Liberation* (Nashville: Abingdon Press, 1979); cf. rev. ed., 1989. Ogden continues to clarify his own perspective on appropriateness and understandability as he dialogues with critics of *Faith and Freedom*. See particularly Ogden, "Response to Dorothee Soelle," in *The Challenge of Liberation Theology: A First World Response*, ed. Brian Mahan and L. Dale Richesin (Maryknoll, N.Y.: Orbis Books, 1981), 17–20; cf. Ogden, "The Concept of a Theology of Liberation: Must a Christian Theology Today Be So Conceived?" ibid., 127–40.

[52]Sharon D. Welch, *Communities of Resistance and Solidarity: A Feminist Theology of Liberation* (Maryknoll, N.Y.: Orbis Books, 1985), 6–7.

by their correspondence to something eternal but by the fulfillment
of its claims in history, by the actual creation of communities of peace,
justice, and equality."[53] This leads Welch, as others, to give "primacy
to the particular," showing more concern for particular realities than
for universal truths.[54]

Working with similar themes, Rebecca Chopp interacts with Latin
American liberation theologians and notes the radical way in which
liberation theology offers a new paradigm for theology, especially with
its focus on suffering, transformation (rather than understanding),
and praxis (a praxis of solidarity with the poor).[55] Liberation theology
is necessarily a situated theology in which analysis of the particular
sociopolitical situation is essential. All interpretation relates to a particular situation and yields liberative action for that situation. Further,
priority is given in theological reflection to those who suffer—to the
poor and oppressed.

In light of the issues raised by Welch and Chopp, the proposals
for reforming process theology become exceedingly important: the
need to include social analysis in all theological analysis, and the need
to test theological language and images by their effects on human
lives and the earth. Efforts made thus far by process theologians
continue to accentuate the issue of worldview, truth, and belief. The
primacy of particularity is less evident. The worldview accent is evident in David Griffin's postmodern theology in which he proposes
a postmodern worldview as a source of action.[56] He argues that attention to questions of worldview and truth is actually required by
the particularities of North Atlantic countries. He recognizes the problems of false universalism in modern theology that has been written
by white, middle-class, North Atlantic men, but he cautions against
a reverse form of false universalism. Griffin states, "A postmodern
theology, especially one written for Americans, must deal with the
question of truth and justified belief. And, because in a post-author-
itarian age the claim to truth can only be made in terms of consistency
and adequacy to the facts of experience, postmodern theology must

---

[53]Ibid., 7.

[54]Ibid., 75–84.

[55]Rebecca S. Chopp, *The Praxis of Suffering: An Interpretation of Liberation and Political Theologies* (Maryknoll, N.Y.: Orbis Books, 1986), 150–52. Some development is given in relation to Gustavo Gutiérrez (pp. 57–62) and José Miguez Bonino (pp. 83–91).

[56]Griffin, *Spirituality and Society*, 1–24.

be *more*, not less, coherent and systematic than modern thought."[57] However we evaluate Griffin's argument regarding the significance of worldview for sociopolitical particularities, the issues raised by Welch and Chopp continue to play in the background.

The issues are probably most apparent in analyzing Schubert Ogden's work. In his concern for extending the discussions of liberation theology, he introduces two criteria for judging any theological position. The criteria are the appropriateness of the witness in light of the apostolic norm and its understandability to human existence in light of common experience and reason.[58] Much discussion has taken place regarding the adequacy of Ogden's criteria and approach to liberation theology.[59] The effort here is more modest; it is to point to some problems in this approach in relation to issues raised in the quest for liberation.

The criterion of appropriateness to the apostolic norm runs into the danger of limiting the scope of God's activity to Jesus Christ and the apostolic witness. The real danger is that theologians might become exclusivist regarding Jesus Christ, thus deploring other religious communities, and they may lose sight of God as revealed in everything, a critical emphasis in the theological reflections of many Asian theologians and women. Furthermore, theologians will likely demean or ignore the voices of children, women, slaves, and other outsiders who were rarely included in the apostolic witnesses. The apostolic witness can too easily become a control on orthodoxy that further subjugates oppressed people.

The criterion of understandability is an important criterion, and Delwin Brown has made a lucid defense of the importance of thinking thoroughly and systematically about God from the vantage point of the poor themselves.[60] Even with this caveat, however, Ogden's criterion of understandability does not go far enough in testing theological constructs by human experience. Johann Baptist Metz argues

[57]David Ray Griffin, "Postmodern Theology as Liberation Theology: A Response to Harvey Cox," in *Varieties of Postmodern Theology*, David Ray Griffin, William A. Beardslee, and Joe Holland, eds. (Albany: State University of New York Press, 1989), 90.

[58]Schubert Ogden, *Faith and Freedom*, 115–22.

[59]Two review essays summarize the discussions: Anselm K. Min, "How Not to Do a Theology of Liberation: A Critique of Schubert Ogden," *Journal of the American Academy of Religion* 57 (Spring 1989): 83–102; Mark Lloyd Taylor, "The Boundless Love of God and the Bounds of Critical Reflection," ibid., 103–47.

[60]Delwin Brown, "Thinking About the God of the Poor: Questions for Liberation Theology from Process Thought," *Journal of the American Academy of Religion* 57 (Summer 1989): 267–81.

that theology needs to be wary of comprehending and understanding too much, especially in face of tragedy and in search of liberation. He deals particularly with Auschwitz and the unavoidable demands it places on Christianity. He says, "To confront Auschwitz is in no way to comprehend it."[61] Furthermore, even statements of meaning must be measured by whether that meaning lived in Auschwitz and not outside or above it.[62] To face real human tragedy is to move beyond a world of understanding into a world of contradiction. Theological meanings are real only when they face the contradictions; theological affirmations must be measured by how much meaning they carry for the most oppressed and victimized in the world.

Similarly, Elisabeth Schüssler Fiorenza argues that biblical interpretation needs to be measured by its correspondence to women's experience (a criterion very similar to Ogden's criterion of understandability), but she adds that the interpretation also needs to be measured by its effects on women.[63] If the effect is oppression, then something is wrong with the interpretation or with the text itself. That judgment goes beyond understandability and extends into asking very contextual questions about liberation.

Within process theology are seeds for moving in these new directions. John Cobb urges that a process political theology be contextual, but even more that it be open to the contradictions that emerge from diverse communities, including, for example, feminist communities and diverse religious traditions. He calls for a "radical openness," or a "readiness to encounter the simply unexpected."[64] Such a direction would lead away from theological absolutes, even in relation to the goals of liberation. The implications of Cobb's plea go far beyond his own work on a process political theology, calling for a radical contextualization of theology. Theology would be done and liberation effected within very particular contexts, but the analysis of particular contexts would be done in relation to the broader contexts of culture,

---

[61]Johann Baptist Metz, *The Emergent Church: The Future of Christianity in a Postbourgeois World*, trans. Peter Mann (New York: Crossroad, 1986), 19.

[62]Ibid. Metz's wariness about understanding is expressed in relation to other contexts as well (see pp. 112–13).

[63]Elisabeth Schüssler Fiorenza, *In Memory of Her: A Feminist Theological Reconstruction of Christian Origins* (New York: Crossroad, 1983); Fiorenza, *Bread Not Stone: The Challenge of Feminist Biblical Interpretation* (Boston: Beacon Press, 1984).

[64]John B. Cobb, Jr., *Process Theology as Political Theology* (Philadelphia: Westminster Press, 1982), 61–62, cf. 44–64.

religion, gender, and sociopolitical realities within which the particulars reside.

From the point of view of conscientization, the contextual questions must be prominent at the beginning, middle, and end of theological reflection. The adequacy of any method or idea must be judged by how it functions toward liberation in a particular context. The challenge to process theologians is to be even more thorough in performing social analysis and in judging the effects of theological systems, including their own, within particular contexts.

7
THE ART OF TEACHING
FROM THE HEART

The Heart of the Matter

How do I end a book written on the bridge between process theology and educational method—a book intended to inspire more organic perspectives on theology and education? To be organic is to be alive, and for theology and education to be organic, they must be filled with liveliness. In these last reflections, then, I will attend to the qualities that evoke life in teachers and learners and in acts of teaching and doing theology. Theology is lifeless if engaged without passion, and educational method is no more than technology if engaged without compassion. To say that the source of life is God is to recognize the source of our teaching in God's Spirit. The art of teaching is fueled by the passions inspired in us through the working of the Spirit. That inspiration is the center of this chapter.

Once four-year-old Mathews Jon Metyko was enjoying a family reunion. He had run all morning and all afternoon, so about ten o'clock that night, everyone was amazed to see him still running. His cousin looked at him and asked, "Do you still have energy?" The little boy quickly answered, "Yes!" The boy's mother chuckled and asked him if he knew what energy was; he replied, "Sure!" "What is it?" she queried. "Something" was his answer. When pressed again, he said, "It is something that runs through you and makes you go run, run, run; then, it slowly runs out of you and you fall down and close your eyes." To this he added, "It goes through your heart." His mother was getting very curious by this time, so she asked, "What is your heart?" The little boy answered, "It is a muscle—a great *BIG* muscle; it has to hold all of your blood and energy and brain."

Young Mathews has basically said all that I want to say in this concluding chapter. He has given a wonderful description of the heart. It pumps energy all through the body, steadily pumping, keeping the energy flowing as we need it. The one place that the four-year-old boy seems to have made a mistake is in thinking that the energy runs out and we fall down and close our eyes. On the other hand, he does have a point. When we sleep, the heart does continue to pump energy, but in somewhat slower motion. The heart pumps blood in rhythms of exhilaration and rest. And, when finally the heart does stop pumping and cannot be revived, we die.

Mathews's description of the system is fascinating because he speaks of real energy coursing through the body. It is motivated by a really big muscle called the heart, and it affects how we move and rest. The four-year-old boy avoided defining the heart solely as a thing; instead, he defined it in relation to energy and in relation to the whole body. It is a motivating and coordinating force.

Teaching, too, involves sending forth energy. The teacher who teaches from the heart does not create the energy, but works in harmony with the source that keeps energy flowing through the whole body. Also, teaching involves rhythms—responding to and contributing to the rhythms of the body.

Herein lies the heart of this entire book—the passion for organic theology and organic teaching for the sake of a healthy "body." The passion itself derives from God, the source of passion and of life. The particular theological precepts and the particular educational methods are important, but only in relation to the whole. Hence, the energy that binds the whole and the heart that pumps the energy are the heart of the matter.

THE HEART AS METAPHOR

The heart is a rich metaphor to describe what is at the center of the human body. A metaphor is an analogy used to compare one thing with another, often describing a complex or abstract reality by comparing it with a more simple or common physical reality. In view of the mystery of human life, the heart offers an apt metaphor for describing what a person is. The heart has often been used as a metaphor for human affections. But here I will probe the metaphor further, hoping to uncover meanings that go beyond affection.

The heart is part of a large circuit, but not an easily discernible circuit. Not until 1628 did William Harvey discover that blood moves constantly in a circle. The circulation system serves two basic purposes—to fuel the body and to remove waste. The role of the heart is to move the blood through that system. With its four chambers, the heart performs multiple functions all at one time. The freshly oxygenated blood enters the left side of the heart from the lungs, to be pumped out into the whole system of the body. At the same time, deoxygenated blood enters the right side of the heart and is sent out into the lungs for replenishing. All of this happens in one heartbeat.

The heart itself is regulated by a pacemaker that controls the rhythmic pumping of the heart muscle. In addition, heart valves control the blood flow among the chambers of the heart and into the aorta and pulmonary artery. Once blood leaves the heart to be distributed in the body, a number of other parts come into play. The arteries carry the blood to smaller arterioles, which carry the blood to the very small capillaries, which carry the blood to every nook and cranny of the body. The blood flows to every cell, and the cells absorb the oxygen and nutrients they need while giving off waste and carbon dioxide. The blood then returns to the heart via the capillaries, venules, veins, and the inferior and superior venae cavae. The heart receives this tired blood and sends it promptly to the lungs for a fresh supply of oxygen. Altogether the heart pumps blood through a network of vessels sixty thousand miles long.

This crude biology lesson points to the vital functioning of the heart, as well as to the enormous and complex system of which the heart is part. The heart cannot and does not function unilaterally, but in harmony with an intricate system of organs and regulatory mechanisms, vessels, and cells. The brief description here does not touch even half of the complexity; the brain, kidneys, and many other organs are intimately connected with the working of the heart. When we turn to the heart for a metaphor, then, we cannot be simplistic and deal with it as a separate entity apart from the brain or from any other part of the body. The heart is related to the entire body, continuously giving and receiving.

When we turn to teaching from the heart, we see immediately that it is done in relation to all of the other organs in the educational system; when one organ is not functioning, the most brilliant teaching will be impaired. Teaching from the heart has to do with sending forth energy to every part of the body, not just the largest or most prestigious or smartest parts, but to all parts. And teaching from the heart has to do with receiving depleted energy, not to hold onto it or judge it bad, but to send it out again for renewal.

Another aspect of the heart is important here; the heart is affected by the decisions made for the body as a whole, such as decisions relating to diet, exercise, and the monitoring of stress. The health of the whole body affects the heart, and the health of the heart is vital for the functioning of even the minutest part of the body.

Teaching from the heart is similarly connected to the wholeness of the body. Teaching from the heart is teaching from a source that needs the rest of the body to exist. One educational administrator recently said to me, "I really miss teaching because that is how I learn and stay fresh." He recognized that interacting with a learning community (the body) is vital to his health.

I recently had an experience that made me very aware of this interactive influence. I gave six keynote addresses in six days to a large audience of experts. What seemed like fun to prepare in advance became frightening to deliver, especially the first night when everyone was tired from traveling and I was intimidated by this unknown group of people. With the first address behind me, I began to meet people face to face and relax. I was learning much from them, and by the middle of the week I was actually having fun. By the time I reached the sixth day, however, my fear quotient had risen again. I was de-livering my sixth address, and that was challenge enough. But the audience was *listening* to its sixth, and that was really frightening. I probably would have collapsed into my fears and tiredness, but the participants kept sharing with me over meals and along the walkways. Their energy nourished mine. We all survived and, yes, we learned together. Every teacher can tell hundreds of such stories; even so, the awareness of how much the teacher depends on the learners is often underplayed when institutions make decisions about education.

One last play on the metaphor of the heart is important to teaching. Testing and evaluation of the heart are done by blood tests, measures of blood pressure and pulse rates, X rays, and electrocardiograms.

No test, taken alone, is adequate to assess the condition of the heart and circulatory system. In fact, all of the tests, taken together, still leave unanswered questions. The evaluation at best is partial.

This arouses some interesting ideas about educational measurement. Teaching from the heart is beyond measure. The measures that are available reflect the condition of the educational heart and circulatory system, but they can never give a full and adequate picture anymore than X rays and blood tests can give a full and adequate picture of a physical human heart. A person teaching from the heart will care about the quality of life in the circulatory system and will be affected if any part of that system goes awry; therefore, educational measurement will be needed. Educational evaluation will likely include observations of actual teaching and measures of student learning, but none of these measures can ever give a full and adequate picture of the health of the system. The system is always beyond measure.

The educational system cannot be adequately described in terms of the purely mechanistic systems of computers and technology, nor in family-system theories that derive from the mechanistic systems by analogy. The system is not based in cause and effect, but in a complex interaction of many events interwoven in the whole. These various events include growing teachers and students, learning interactions, cultural dynamics, and environmental movements. These various events do influence one another, but they cannot be separated into simple cause-and-effect components and laws.

Neither can the various aspects of educational events be separated for measurement except by way of abstraction. We need to remember that the measures can only focus on one or two parts of a complex whole. Sometimes these focused evaluations are useful in identifying the strengths and weaknesses in a school program or the aptitudes of students, but too often they are limiting. Howard Gardner has identified multiple intelligences and elaborated on seven forms.[1] Only two of these are measured in most standardized testing (the linguistic and logico-mathematical). Not only are other forms of intelligence ignored in most testing and marginalized in school programs, but

---

[1]Howard Gardner, *Frames of Mind: The Theory of Multiple Intelligences* (New York: Basic Books, 1985). The intelligences he discusses are linguistic, musical, logico-mathematical, spatial, bodily-kinesthetic, intrapersonal (sense of self), and interpersonal.

also the limited focus on two intelligences is even a source of discrimination against some racial-ethnic groups.[2]

In relation to faith formation, a student's ability to recite a Bible
verse is also an abstraction from the total learning situation. The
memory work may play a part, small or large, in the forming of faith,
but its role will always be more complex than we can measure. A
teacher's ability to communicate many ideas to learners or to teach
them how to interpret biblical texts may also play a small or large role
in forming faith or teaching biblical interpretation. Occasionally, however, we hear testimonies from students to the positive influence of
a particular teacher, even though the teacher's method and content
were sorely lacking. Such stories testify to the dynamic of teaching
that goes beyond the normal measures.

Teaching from the heart is teaching that affects every student, not
in a controlling way because the heart only sends out nutrients and
energy, but in a nourishing way. Perhaps the most helpful measure
of teaching from the heart is the extent to which the lives of students
and societies are nourished and transformed.

THE HEART AS BIBLICAL SYMBOL

The metaphor of heart is not new to human language, nor is it new
to associations with teaching. The central confession of faith for the
early Hebrews, as well as the central mandate for teaching, is found
in the Shema, Deuteronomy 6:4-9. The very word Shema means
"hear." The text begins, " 'Hear, O Israel: The Lord our God is one
Lord; and you shall love the Lord your God with all your heart, and
with all your soul, and with all your might' " (Deut. 6:4-5). The language of love already suggests the primary attitude expected toward
God—a love that comes in response to the pronouncement that the
Lord our God is one Lord. The command to love God with all our
heart and soul is a recurring expression in Deuteronomy. In fact, it
appears at least four other times (Deut. 10:12; 11:13; 13:3; 30:6). The

---

[2]Janice E. Hale-Benson, *Black Children: Their Roots, Culture and Learning Styles* (Bal-
timore: Johns Hopkins University Press, 1986), esp. xi–xiv, 21–44. See also Hale-Benson,
"Psychosocial Experiences," in *Working with Black Youth*, ed. Charles R. Foster and Grant
S. Shockley (Nashville: Abingdon Press, 1989), 30–54, esp. 42–45.

heart and soul are associated frequently in Deuteronomy with seeking God and following God's commands (Deut. 4:29; 26:16; 30:2,10). Clearly, the heart and soul are associated with being faithful to God with the whole of the self.

The heart is an important image in the biblical witness; it functions as a metaphor, describing by analogy what human beings are like. Within the biblical understanding, the heart is even more than a metaphor, however. It is also a symbol in that it points beyond itself and participates in the reality to which it points. In fact, Karl Rahner and Herbert Vorgrimler call the heart a primordial symbol.[3]

In early Hebrew thought, the heart was understood to be the seat of the mind and will, as well as the emotions. Within this perspective, the four-year-old boy in my story was correct in saying that the heart contains the blood and energy and brain. The heart, *leb*, was not literalized as an organ in Hebrew biblical language so much as it was taken to be a representation of the thinking and willing and feeling of the human being. In fact, the "heart" was even associated at times with organs other than the heart. Alongside the heart was the soul, *nephesh*, representing the source of vitality; together they represented the whole being. The addition of *might* to heart and soul in the *Shema* adds an additional element of strength for good measure.

In short, the heart in Hebrew is the center that coordinates a person's life, and it is the source of physical, intellectual, emotional, and volitional energies. It is both a coordinator and motivator—the dynamic principle undergirding human life. As such, it is often seen as the primary avenue for communicating with God. Within the heart, the character of a person is shaped, and within the heart, God is at work. God communicates with the heart, and religious experience and moral conduct are rooted there.

This does not mean that the heart is beyond reproach because the heart can be evil and can shape the human character in evil ways (Gen. 8:21; Prov. 6:18; Jer. 3:17; 17:9) or become hardened (Zech. 7:12) or turn away from God (1 Kgs. 11:2; Job 36:13). This does mean, however, that the heart is extremely important to the relationship with God and to the whole being of a person. What is needed is a

---

[3]Karl Rahner and Herbert Vorgrimler, *Theological Dictionary*, ed. Cornelius Ernst, O.P., trans. Richard Strachan (New York: Seabury Press, [1965] 1973), 199.

true and upright heart (1 Kgs. 8:61; Pss. 32:11; 119:80), a penitent heart (2 Kgs. 22:19), and a clean heart (Ps. 51:10).

The heart itself can be renewed (Ezek. 18:31) or guided and taught (Ezra 7:10; Prov. 23:19). In Ezra, for example, we read, "For Ezra had set his heart to study the law of the Lord, and to do it, and to teach his statutes and ordinances in Israel" (Ezra 7:10). Here, as in Deuteronomy 6, the posture of the heart is associated with the being of the person and what the person will teach.

The Hebrew notion of heart is quite complex, and even more development is needed to discern the richness of the image. Another idea particularly relevant here is that the heart is the seat of the intellect. In the Hebrew language, thinking is associated with the heart so that the Hebrew word *leb* is often translated into English as *mind* (1 Kgs. 10:24; Prov. 23:19). This same idea carries into New Testament writing, as do the others I have presented. One example is Mary's response in Luke 2:19 to the birth of her child and to all of the events surrounding the birth. Luke tells us, "But Mary kept all these things, pondering them in her heart."

One last comment is important here regarding the relation between a person's heart and God. The relationship is portrayed in the Hebrew Bible as very dynamic and interactive. Through the heart, a person speaks to God, seeking after God's face (Ps. 27:8), and through the heart, a person trusts God (Ps. 28:7). As noted earlier, the heart can turn to God and follow God's commands (Deut. 30:8-14). The heart has ability and will to reach out to God and to obey God's lead. At the same time, God knows the secrets of the heart (Ps. 44:21) and may reach out to the heart to test it (Ps. 17:3), harden it (Exod. 4:21), open it to the people (Ezra 6:22), put fear into it (Jer. 32:40), or grant it understanding (1 Kgs. 3:9; Neh. 2:12). God is thereby very active, fashioning the hearts of all the inhabitants of the earth (Ps. 33:14-15).

These actions reflect not only an awesome power of God, but also a hope that God can renew people's hearts (Ps. 51:10; Ezek. 36:26) and write the law on them (Jer. 31:33). Such promises as these are made in the context of God's covenant; in fact, both the Ezekiel and Jeremiah texts are accompanied by the promise to the people that God will be their God and they will be God's people. God's actions toward the heart are actions toward the motivating and coordinating center of persons, and these actions are communicated as a covenantal bonding. God is acting not for the sake of displaying power, but for the sake of relationship.

These Hebrew Bible images of heart are especially important to understanding the art of teaching from the heart because the heart embraces the fullness of human life. The image of heart is extended in the New Testament with the same themes. The Synoptic Gospels all include the command to love God with all one's heart, soul, mind, and strength (strength being omitted in Matthew—Matt. 22:34-40; Mark 12:28-34; Luke 10:25-28). They all join this injunction with the injunction to love one's neighbor as oneself (deriving from Lev. 19:18), and Mark and Luke explicitly draw the connection between these injunctions and eternal life or the kingdom of God. For the Gospel writers to convey the same fullness as the confession in Deuteronomy 6:4-5, however, the word *mind* was added to heart, soul, and strength. The Greek word *heart* did not embrace mind in the same way that the Hebrew word did; hence, the Synoptic statements are made equivalent to the Deuteronomic Shema by adding the word *mind*. The encounter with the Greek language had already laid groundwork for a bifurcation between heart and mind, feeling and thinking, that plagues us still.

Actually the bifurcation was not a simple shift because the Greek word used in Mark for mind was *dianoia*, or "coherence." Thomas Trotter suggests that the meaning might be interpreted as " 'Love God by the way you put things together.' "[4] He proposes that Jesus, in the face of his questioners, must have caught their attention by reciting the familiar Shema, but he took the liberty to add to it. Because the word *dianoia* refers to poetic as well as rational knowing and to knowing that pulls events and concepts together, Trotter sees the addition of *dianonia* as "the appropriate response to folk who had grown unimaginative in sensing both the scripture and the power of God."[5] As Trotter makes a strong case for loving God with one's mind, I want to make a case for loving God with one's heart, recognizing that the language of both mind and heart is rich, expansive language that is belittled and disempowered if we allow either word to be thrown into

---

[4]F. Thomas Trotter, *Loving God with One's Mind* (Nashville: Board of Higher Education and Ministry, United Methodist Church, 1987), 24.

[5]Ibid., 64.

a narrow category, or if we allow the two words to be pitted against one another.

The extent to which the bifurcation between heart and mind has pervaded Western thinking can be seen in the statement someone made to me after reading the title of this chapter in an earlier draft. This person, a friend who knows me well and knows process thought well, said that he was intrigued with my topic. He said that he had an idea for a respondent who would offer another view. I perked up because this sounded interesting. He then said, "This woman would offer an interesting response on bringing the heart and mind *together* in education." I understood what my friend was saying, but I laughed aloud because I had never dreamed of separating them in the first place.

Why do people so easily assume that teaching from the heart has nothing to do with the mind? Why have we allowed the metaphors of heart and mind to become so separate? Even if the metaphors are elaborated on in relation to the biological organs of heart and brain, the heart pumps blood to keep the brain alive, and the brain sends signals to regulate the heart. Furthermore, just as the heart pumps blood throughout the entire body, every part of the body participates in some degree of mental activity. The brain is filled through and through with blood from the heart, and the heart is filled through and through with mental activity.

One other example of the bifurcation is seen in the work of Parker Palmer who has probably done as much as any other educator to overcome the split. He has done this, however, by posing two separate realities that need to be brought together:

> Many of us live one-eyed lives. We rely largely on the eye of the mind to form our image of reality. But today more and more of us are opening the other eye, the eye of the heart, looking for realities to which the mind's eye is blind. Either eye alone is not enough. We need "whole-sight," a vision of the world in which mind and heart unite "as my two eyes make one in sight." . . .
>
> With the mind's eye we see a world of fact and reason. It is a cold and mechanical place, but we have built our lives there because it seemed predictable and safe. . . . So we open the eye of the heart and see another sight: a world warmed and transformed by the power of love, a vision of community beyond the mind's capacity to see. . . . How shall we bring together these two lines of sight?[6]

---

[6]Parker J. Palmer, *To Know as We Are Known: A Spirituality of Education* (San Francisco: Harper & Row, 1983), xi.

For Palmer a new perspective comes from bringing together his vocation of spiritual life with his avocation of education, or the quest for knowledge. He believes that the former relies on the eye of the heart and the latter, on the eye of the mind. He himself believes that the heart's vision can include the mind, though the mind's vision does not include the heart. He is seeking what he calls "wholesight."[7]

Palmer's aims and proposals coincide in some remarkable ways with what I am proposing here. The one dilemma in his work, however, is that the heart and mind metaphors are described in dichotomous language so that the wholeness is seen as something that people have to construct; the inherent wholeness is not recognized. As long as the bifurcation is assumed, the inherent relatedness of what people have called mind and heart will be ignored. The danger is compartmentalization and further distortions in teaching; the danger is that educators will ignore the affective influence of students' learning cognitive data, or the cognitive information explosion that can occur in the context of affective learning experiences.

The educational challenge that comes from this exploration of teaching from the heart is to recognize the largeness and richness of the heart symbol. No matter what teaching method a teacher uses, and how skillfully the method is employed, teaching will be empty without the great big muscle that pumps energy throughout the whole body.

REVEALING STORIES

What, then, is the art of teaching from the heart? Answering this question will not be easy. Since people can usually say, "Well, I know it when I see it," I will present some stories of teaching from the heart as a way of beginning to describe the art.

A theological professor described the interests of theological students in his school: "Students today want the professor along with the subject matter; they do not want courses with subject matter alone. My courses are popular because I give *myself* with the subject."

Another theological professor in biblical studies described her experience in teaching controversial biblical texts such as Paul's household codes: "Wives, be subject to your husbands, as to the Lord. . . .

---

[7]Ibid., xi–xii.

Children, obey your parents in the Lord. . . . Slaves, be obedient to those who are your earthly masters . . ." (Eph. 5:21—6:9). Inevitably, the discussion of these texts stirs debates about the relationship between women and men, parents and children, slaves and master. Students raise issues about sexual abuse, violence against women and children, economic abuse, and other oppressions experienced by women, children, and slaves. The professor said that she had learned to respect the strong feelings evoked in students by these texts, and she had learned to leave room in the discussions for these feelings to be expressed.

These two stories point to the art of teaching from the heart. In the first testimony, the art has to do with sharing oneself, and in the second, the art has to do with getting to the heart of critical issues. The first teacher expressed his willingness to be human with his students, and the second described her willingness to allow students to wrestle with difficult texts in an atmosphere of encouragement and support.

A REVEALING WORLDVIEW

These stories not only introduce the art of teaching from the heart, but also they introduce the framework of a worldview—an organic worldview that heightens the art and heart of teaching. Like the five methods presented in this book, teaching from the heart is deeply informed by process theology and by the practice of education. None of the methods discussed in this book are likely to bear fruit without teaching with all our heart; at the same time, each of the methods holds promise to inspire and support such teaching. Here I will consider five aspects of the undergirding worldview and then explore a series of guidelines for teaching from the heart.

The first aspect of this organic worldview is that *God is the empowering center of life—the spirit moving and creating in the universe, inspiring and requiring our love.* God is not only the source of life and the ever-present Redeemer and Creator of new life, but also God is *our* God.[8]

---

[8]Charles Hartshorne, *A Natural Theology for Our Time* (LaSalle, Ill.: Open Court Publishing Co., 1967), 131–37. Hartshorne is here emphasizing the God-human relationship, but the biblical affirmation of God's relation to the lilies of the field pushes

God is more than the philosophical ideas about God; God relates personally with creation and evokes love in us.

The very possibility that creation could love and be whole derives from God. According to Charles Hartshorne, the idea of cosmic wholeness is a religious conception, emerging from the wholeness and integrity of God.[9] The oneness of God in Judaism, Christianity, and Islam corresponds to God's call to human beings to be whole in our response to God—to love God with all our heart and mind and soul and strength. For Hartshorne this love is the embodiment of worship in the three religious traditions. He interprets it to mean: "Simply every response, every aspect, must be a way of loving God."[10]

Teaching from the heart, then, is loving God with all that is in us. And to this we must add loving our neighbor as ourselves. God loves every aspect of creation; thus, all creation is holy. Our love of God is linked inextricably to love of creation. Teaching from the heart is, most importantly, loving God and neighbor.

A second critical insight in this organic worldview is that *knowledge is energy; the heart of the matter is not matter at all, but energy.* To probe the heart of the matter in education is to explore movement. We know in advance that the heart of the matter can never be fixed, finalized, and objectified. Even though the past is complete—and in that sense, objective data—its retrieval and interaction with the present are still fluid. The effect of this view is humbling because it debunks any expectation that we will find *the* answer and be able to hold onto it. The effect is also motivating because it arouses expectations that we will make discoveries. What is more, the effect is consoling, leaving us with a sense that we do know something, but we will always find more to learn.

If knowledge is energy, then all teaching will generate energy, whether teaching is done through case studies or conscientization. Even an oral exam can be a time of self-discovery, learning from others and sitting together in awe of what is known and what is not known.

---

the idea even more fully and wonderfully. All creatures can express that God is our God. Actually, this latter view is more compatible with the organic worldview of process theology as it has developed, for God is seen as relating at every moment with every event of creation.

[9]Ibid., 7–8.
[10]Ibid., 8.

If knowledge is understood as energy, then exploring knowledge together in any form will naturally generate more energy.

The third insight of an organic worldview is that *the world comes together in every moment of experience*. Just as one heartbeat does many things all at once, receiving blood in and sending blood out, so every event of experience includes both a receiving from the world of everything that has gone before and a sending out into the world of something new or refreshed. In the process of concrescence, an actual entity includes all other actual entities within itself. This is what Alfred North Whitehead describes as the "solidarity of the world."[11]

Appropriately the word *solidarity* now has clear political connotations. The political idea of solidarity with workers or with victims is enhanced by a worldview in which everything is seen as related to everything else. Such a worldview reminds us that the actions of people are so intertwined that if one group does not choose to participate in a positive solidarity with others, it may participate in a solidarity destructive of others in ways it never expected or intended.

If this is the case, the politics of teaching from the heart means that study needs to include politics, such as considering political reasons why God has come to be defined and described in certain ways and also contemporary political issues that continue to affect the community's definitions of God. Issues of inclusive language in hymns and racism in church politics are not, therefore, auxiliary issues, but part of the solidarity of the world and relevant to basic doctrinal and conceptual discussions.

A fourth insight in an organic view of the world is that *living is an art; hence, teaching is an art*. The way the world comes together in every moment of experience is artistic. No master plan exists that programs the construction of every new moment in experience, but each emerges as an aesthetic event. God participates in and guides the process, but each emerging occasion decides what it will be. God contributes an initial aim to the emerging subject, and the subject constitutes itself through its own subjective aim.[12]

---

[11]Alfred North Whitehead, *Process and Reality: An Essay in Cosmology*, ed. David R. Griffin and Donald W. Sherburne (New York: [Macmillan, 1929] Free Press, 1978), 7.

[12]Ibid., 244. Whitehead describes this process of concrescence as one in which God has influence, but freedom remains with the emerging subject to respond in its own decisive way: "The immediacy of the concrescent subject is constituted by its living aim at its own self-constitution. Thus the initial stage of the aim is rooted in the nature of God, and its completion depends on the self-causation of the subject-superject."

Aesthetic appreciation is actually the second phase of concrescence in which the many feelings of the emerging event are transformed into one.[13] Concrescence involves the integration of conceptual feelings with pure physical feelings, or the integration of imagination and physical experience. The two together constitute the becoming occasion. Concrescence is also a coming together of "inheritance and novel effect," that is, the givenness of the past with the novelty of the moment.[14] Aesthetic experience is the experience of the contrast.[15]

If the very process of reality is aesthetic, then, surely, teaching is aesthetic. In fact, Whitehead himself understood education in this way. From his earliest to his latest writings, this was a major theme. In his explicit writings on education written in the early 1900s, he defined education thus: "Education is the guidance of the individual towards a comprehension of the art of life."[16] In another address on technical education and its relation to science and literature, he claimed: "In its essence a liberal education is an education for thought and for aesthetic appreciation."[17]

Even in his later writing, Whitehead turned again to his hopes for education to stimulate aesthetic growth.[18] He believed that such an education was needed to "draw out habits of aesthetic apprehension" or to stir "an appreciation of the infinite variety of vivid values."[19] That, in fact, is how he defined art—the "habit of enjoying vivid values."[20]

Art itself is an important activity to stir aesthetic appreciation. It stimulates an interaction between nature and human creativity, heightening a sense of humanity and intense feeling.[21] The arts are important to all human endeavors, from recreation to business.

---

[13]Ibid., 212–14.

[14]Ibid., 279. See a much fuller discussion of the interaction of past, present, and future in education in Mary Elizabeth Moore, *Education for Continuity and Change: A New Model of Christian Religious Education* (Nashville: Abingdon Press, 1983).

[15]Whitehead, *Process and Reality,* 279–80.

[16]Alfred North Whitehead, *The Aims of Education* (New York: Free Press, [1929] 1957), 39.

[17]Ibid., 46.

[18]Alfred North Whitehead, *Science and the Modern World* (New York: [Macmillan, 1925] Free Press, 1953), 199.

[19]Ibid.

[20]Ibid., 200.

[21]Alfred North Whitehead, *Adventures of Ideas* (New York: [Macmillan, 1933] Free Press, 1961), 270–72.

The fifth insight in this organic worldview is that *learning is a rhythmic process of discovery*. Whitehead opposed the rigid empiricism of Francis Bacon, and he proposed an alternative approach to learning: "The true method of discovery is like the flight of an aeroplane. It starts from the ground of particular observation; it makes a flight in the thin air of imaginative generalization; and it again lands for renewed observation rendered acute by rational interpretation."[22] This is really a description of praxis knowing. Reflection is grounded in particular observations, taking off from one set of observations and landing back in the land of renewed observations. And the reflection is both imaginative and rational. Both creative muddling, as one student called it, and rigorous application of critical reflection and logic are called into play.

THE ART OF TEACHING FROM
THE HEART

In a way this whole chapter is playful and exploratory, but some very engaging possibilities do emerge to guide our teaching. Perhaps the art of teaching from the heart is really an act of reverence, that is, feeling awe again and again and again (*re-vering*). We will spend the remainder of our time considering reverent teaching.

In chapter 1 I acknowledged that for Whitehead education is at its heart religious:

> The essence of education is that it be religious. . . . A religious education is an education which inculcates duty and reverence. Duty arises from our potential control over the course of events. Where attainable knowledge could have changed the issue, ignorance has the guilt of vice. And the foundation of reverence is this perception, that the present holds within itself the complete sum of existence, backwards and forwards, that whole amplitude of time, which is eternity.[23]

Education is by nature religious; it calls forth the art of revering.

Teaching is, first, *revering God—giving reverence to the spirit and source of life*. Here I speak self-consciously to those who teach in religious

---

[22]Whitehead, *Process and Reality*, 5.
[23]Whitehead, *The Aims of Education*, 14.

communities—those for whom God is the source of all reverence. In a real sense, teachers in public arenas and in nontheistic religious communities will also find themselves revering a central source of meaning as they teach from the heart. The central meaning will be named in many different ways, but the power will be strong in their teaching. Here, however, I will address myself directly to those who teach in theistic religious communities, particularly in Jewish, Christian, Muslim, and many Unitarian Universalist communities. In these communities, teaching cannot be understood apart from God. God is the spirit and source of life, therefore, the beginning and ending of our teaching.

To revere God is to receive and pass on the gifts of God; this is an act of traditioning, or participating in a living tradition.[24] To revere God is to see ourselves living with God. We participate in a living tradition in which God has acted, is acting now, and will draw us toward a future that is God's new creation. The tradition is not a thing to be passed on. Tradition is God alive in the world, a living reality that flows through time and bids us to be co-creators with the living God. Teaching that reveres God is teaching that supports our relationship with God and inspires us to respond to God's call in our lives.

Teaching from the heart is also *revering the other—other persons, other cultures, other parts of the environment.* The theme has been repeated again and again throughout this book. In chapter 2, I spoke of revering the particularities of a concrete case; in chapter 3, revering the many as they come together into unity; in chapter 4, revering the subjectivity of the other; in chapter 5, revering the narratives that weave together our lives and the life of the earth; and in chapter 6, revering the oppressed and the poor and the dynamics of liberation. The art of revering can take place in hundreds of different ways, but it is an art to practice. It involves appreciating the teachers and learners, the texts, and the ideas and feelings that are part of the educational process. It involves what Thomas Groome describes as passion for the people: "a deep passion and caring for the well-being of those we

---

[24]Moore, *Education for Continuity and Change.* This book puts forth a traditioning model of Christian religious education.

would presume to educate."[25] To re-vere is to recognize the sacredness of the educational drama and its participants.

One teacher in my experience who practices the art of revering is John Cobb. Very important to him is re-vering the voice of a person whose work is being discussed, a pattern discussed in chapter 4 on phenomenological method. When a student makes a class presentation on someone's thought, Cobb will call the student to task if she or he begins to give opinions about the person too soon. He asks, "First, what did *that* person say?" He insists that students respect the subjectivity of the other first. Then, they are welcome to interact with their own opinions.

For Paulo Freire, the reverence for the other demands that an educator be in tune with the social realities of the people. Freire dedicated his *Pedagogy in Process* to Amilcar Cabral, an educator "who learned from his people."[26] He quotes Cabral:

> I may have an opinion about many things,
>   about the way
> to organize the struggle; the way to organize the
>   Party; . . .
> I cannot, however, pretend to organize a Party or a
>   struggle on
> the basis of my own ideas. I have to do this
>   starting
> from the reality of the country.[27]

Freire, in fact, learned that education was different in Brazil and Chile and Guinea-Bissau, so his own teaching had to be shaped by what he learned of the social context in which he taught or consulted.[28]

Another remarkable teacher was Mary Tully, a religious educator who is lauded by her students, but who rarely finds her way into anthologies of great religious educators. Maria Harris studied Tully's teaching as a model. One of the recurring insights that Harris reports

---

[25]Thomas H. Groome, "The Spirituality of the Religious Educator," *Religious Education* 83 (Winter 1988): 15. In this essay Groome describes the heart of religious education as the heart of the religious educator. This metaphor calls forth passion, generosity, love, and commitment (see pp. 9–20).

[26]As quoted in Paulo Freire, *Pedagogy in Process: The Letters to Guinea-Bissau*, trans. Carman St. John Hunter (New York: Seabury Press, 1978), frontispage.

[27]Ibid.

[28]Ibid., 9–10.

is the way Tully invited students to interact with an object such as clay. The emphasis was not on molding the clay, but on letting the clay "speak" and on being involved with the material. As students interacted with the clay, a form would begin to emerge.[29] This is revering the subjectivity of the clay. Tully also used to spend hours arranging a teaching environment for her classes, taking care to consider what kind of environment and materials would be fitting to her students at the time.[30] Thus, she revered the subjectivity of the students as well.

Such reverence for the other is a way of appreciating the value of the other. This is the work of an artist—the work of one who perceives and appreciates the beauty in creation. However hidden, distorted, or degraded that beauty might be, the art of teaching is the art of seeing beauty and calling it forth. Gordon Jackson has similar words to say about pastoral care. He sees every client as "a soul seeking beauty."[31] Thus, "the art of caring is the art of helping a soul become a thing of beauty."[32] Teaching, like pastoral care, is a calling to revere the other, including not only other persons, but also other cultures and other parts of the environment.

In addition to revering God and the other, *teaching from the heart is also revering oneself.* I acknowledged in chapter 1 that education has to do with self-development,[33] recognizing the value and initiative of each individual learner. Teaching from the heart can never be defined as something that someone does to someone else; true teaching is an act in which teachers revere students and encourage them to revere themselves. Teachers also revere themselves and encourage students to revere them as well.

The hope is that teachers and learners will come together with respect for their mutual subjectivity and for the considerable importance of the decisions they must make. Teaching that does not enhance the sense of subjectivity and the importance of decision making on

---

[29]Maria Harris, *Teaching and Religious Imagination* (San Francisco: Harper & Row, 1987), 34, 122, 128. Tully often spoke of being "faithful to the object as a point of departure" (see p. 128).

[30]Ibid., 121.

[31]Gordon E. Jackson, *Pastoral Care and Process Theology* (Lanham, Md.: University Press of America, 1981), 101.

[32]Ibid.

[33]Whitehead asserts, "Valuable intellectual development is self-development." See *The Aims of Education,* 1.

the part of all participants will objectify, control, and manipulate. Whether the teacher controls in an authoritarian way or in a co-dependent effort to "help" the learners, the control can undermine the personhood of the learners and the ability of the learners to revere themselves.

The art of revering oneself does not simply emerge from happy, respectful relationships in a classroom or youth group, however. We cannot encourage people to revere themselves if the social structures of our institutions and society are not re-formed to include and em-power persons across race, gender, social class, age, and sexual pref-erence.[34] As long as the social structures stereotype and degrade and exclude certain persons, the socialization processes will pressure those persons *not* to revere themselves. The art of teaching from the heart, then, has to do with cultivating respectful interpersonal relations and with transforming social structures to enhance the liberation and par-ticipation and empowerment of all.

If teaching includes revering God and the other and oneself, then naturally *teaching from the heart is re-vering relationships*—relationships among teachers and students, people and subject matter, thinking and feeling, theoretical concepts and practices, play and work, imag-ination and logic. The physical heart links the body together, or feeds the relationships among the various body parts, such as the relation-ship between the lungs and every cell of the body. Teaching from the heart links the many dimensions of the learning community in order for the parts to work together.

The heart pumps blood steadily no matter what the body is doing. The heart responds not just to emergencies, but also to the routine relationships of the body. Teaching from the heart does include the dramatic teaching that is responsive to teachable moments when a person is faced with sudden illness or death or disillusionment or, even, unexpected joy. But teaching from the heart also includes the steady teaching of ordinary times, responding to the ordinary needs of the ordinary body.

---

[34]This theme has been discussed especially in critical pedagogy. A helpful discussion of critical education theories and their relation to social change is found in Kathleen Weiler, *Women Teaching for Change: Gender, Class and Power* (South Hadley, Mass.: Bergin & Garvey, 1988), 4–25. Weiler deals extensively with the roles of resistance and counter-hegemony (developing collective opposition to oppressive structures) in the transfor-mation of society (ibid., 27–56).

The pumping heart responds to particular situations or relationships of the body. When a bone is broken, the heart responds; when a person hears beautiful music or sees the happy play of children, the heart responds. Teaching from the heart responds to the particular relationships of the moment. It responds to political situations as demonstrated by Paulo Freire, to the materials of the environment as shown by Mary Tully, and to texts and their authors as done by John Cobb.

One vivid example of responding to a text is found in the biblical scholarship of Phyllis Trible. Trible, a literary critic, does elaborate grammatical analyses of biblical texts. When she presents an analysis, she crafts her own language to reflect the language of the text. She spends months on a single passage.[35] This approach to writing and lecturing suggests much about teaching with reverence for relationships, in this case, relationships between readers and texts.

In my own teaching I have found that if I approach written texts with methods similar to the methods of the authors, I make fresh discoveries. For example, C. S. Song uses narrative interpretation to begin his theological reflections. If a class studying C. S. Song's theology approaches his work by first telling and interpreting his narratives, then his own theological interpretations can be seen in a fuller light. Similarly, a class can reflect on a living text of political conflict using methods of interpretation similar to those used by the parties involved. To begin with critical social analysis will uncover new insights into the situation and into the perspectives of the respective parties.

The heart responds to all of these relationships and, what is more, it responds to the cries of the body, sometimes by sending extra supplies of nourishment and sometimes with the holy anger of a rapid heartbeat. The situation of Chief Seattle is a story of holy anger. Sometime between 1853 and 1855 Chief Seattle made a speech in relation to the Port Elliott Treaty (1855). This was a treaty of land settlement, but not one without pain for Chief Seattle's people. The cry from his heart on that day was " 'Your God loves your people

---

[35]Phyllis Trible, *Texts of Terror: Literary-Feminist Readings of Biblical Narratives* (Philadelphia: Fortress Press, 1984). See pp. 11–12 for an example of her grammatical analysis and presentation.

and hates mine. . . . The white man's God cannot love his red children.' "³⁶ Chief Seattle was teaching with holy anger. Teaching from
the heart is not always a mild and mellow relationship.

But teaching from the heart does involve a relationship filled
through and through with compassion. Phyllis Trible dedicated her
book *Texts of Terror* to Mary Tully because of Tully's "compassion for
the sufferings of human beings."³⁷ Likewise, Paulo Freire is known
for his spirit of compassion. Jonathan Kozol has commented on the
seeming incongruity between Freire's gentle and affectionate personality and his revolutionary education theories that lead to such con-
flict.³⁸ Freire himself gives one answer to this incongruity in *Pedagogy
in Process*. Quoting Che Guervara, Freire says, " 'Let me say, with the
risk of appearing ridiculous, that the true revolutionary is guided by
strong feelings of love.' "³⁹

A fifth maxim, or guideline, for education is that *teaching from the
heart is re-vering the vocation of teaching*—the vocation to nourish the
body and receive and replenish the depleted blood. The vocation,
however, cannot be idealized because the dangers are as real as the
possibilities. Freire has made his point with great clarity that teaching
will either support or subvert the status quo; what we do in teaching
will never be neutral.⁴⁰

The physical heart always interacts with a system. Whitehead reminds us that we must have respect for both the greatness and evil
in any system. He goes on to say, "There is a greatness in the lives
of those who build religious systems, a greatness in action, in idea
and in self-subordination, embodied in instance after instance through
centuries of growth." But on the other hand, Whitehead says, "There
is greatness in the rebels who destroy such systems; they are the titans

---

³⁶*Environmental Ethics* 11, 196. The words quoted here are a translation of Chief
Seattle's actual speech, and the accuracy of the translation is not known. This language
was changed by Ted Perry, a screenwriter, for a film called *Home*. Perry's version has
come to be much better known, even though the meaning is considerably changed:
" 'Our God is the same God. . . . He is the God of man, and His compassion is equal
for the red man and the white' " (ibid.). The very change in language and popularization
of the change reflect how uncomfortably we sometimes receive holy anger.
³⁷Trible, *Texts of Terror*, xiv.
³⁸Jonathan Kozol, "Foreword," in Freire, *Pedagogy in Process*, 3–4.
³⁹Ibid., 4, cf. 2–4; cf. *Venceremos, The Speeches and Writings of Che Guervara*, ed. John
Gerassi (New York: Macmillan, 1969), 398.
⁴⁰Paulo Freire, *Pedagogy of the Oppressed*, trans. Myra Bergman Ramos (New York:
Herder & Herder, 1970).

who storm heaven, armed with passionate sincerity."[41] In short, Whitehead recognized possibilities and dangers side by side. To explore knowledge is to face both. In his words, "Philosophy may not neglect the multifariousness of the world—the fairies dance, and Christ is nailed to the cross."[42] The vocation of teaching is carried out in these very systems of practice and thought amid the possibilities and the dangers. It is a frightening vocation.

But to revere the vocation of teaching is to approach it as a calling and an art. It is a calling to nourish and replenish the body. For the religious educator, this is a calling to nourish and replenish the community of faith. Maria Harris describes this as "fashioning a people."[43] Such a vocation requires the church or religious community itself to be an artist. Harris says, "If our vocation is the fashioning of a people— more specifically, if our work is fashioning—we need to work as poets and sculptors and creative artists, colleagues of the brooding, hovering, indwelling Spirit."[44] She sees curriculum planning as an artistic work in this sense, involving us in contemplation, engagement, form giving, emergence, and release.[45]

To revere the vocation of teaching, then, is to live in awe of our work—the calling of God's Spirit, the possibilities for nourishing and receiving and replenishing the community, the dangers of perpetuating oppression, and the artistry of our acts. To approach our work with such awe is to teach from the heart.

A sixth maxim is that *teaching from the heart is revering the process of education itself,* including the rhythms of the educational process. Teaching from the heart puts more emphasis on the process of education than on the end product. The act of teaching has to do with coordinating the inflow and outflow of energy so that the body will work. Just as the circulatory system has no real beginning or ending, the educational system is one in which energy is circulated and exchanged in order to support life. The circulatory system is highly organized; that is why it works so well. But it is a system in which we can expect the unexpected, and adaptations are required. Likewise,

[41]Whitehead, *Process and Reality,* 337–38.
[42]Ibid., 338.
[43]Maria Harris, *Fashion Me a People: Curriculum in the Church* (Louisville: Westminster/ John Knox, 1989).
[44]Ibid., 171.
[45]Ibid., 172–82.

teaching from the heart is highly coordinated with the rest of the system, but it is a kind of teaching in which persons come to expect the unexpected and respond to it.

This process of education has been highlighted by Robert Brumbaugh. He discusses the rhythms of education and also the idea that teaching "must give the student a feeling of being together with the teacher in a shared creative present time."[46] Teaching is an adventure, not unlike "the Socratic idea of philosophy as engaged adventure, with debate, search, interaction of characters, change of fortune."[47] To appreciate such an adventure, teachers and students must revere the process of education itself, or engage fully in the adventure that is learning.

One last aspect of teaching from the heart is re-vering the ordinary. Whitehead's cosmology lends itself to valuing every actual occasion, every throb of experience. His own careful attention to the process of concrescence suggests a reverence for every actual occasion and the fullness of its becoming. Whitehead saw a clear relation between the particular, ordinary parts of reality and the whole. In education, then, he thought both were important. A popular saying in English is that sometimes we cannot see the forest, or the wood, because of the trees. Whitehead was not concerned just with the forest *or* with the individual trees; he was concerned with both. His conclusion for education was that "the problem of education is to make the pupil see the wood by means of the trees."[48]

Seeing the wood by means of the trees is a fascinating idea, given the propensity of educators in religious communities and public education to seek after grand theories to explain and guide their work. The actual theories come and go as one fad fades into another, but the search for a grand theory persists. In this book I am not disparaging educators from utilizing grand theories; I *am* encouraging them not to depend on these theories for all-encompassing insight. What is needed is to take a close look at the ordinary. We have been looking at approaches to education that begin with particular cases or moments

---

[46]Robert S. Brumbaugh, *Whitehead, Process Philosophy, and Education* (Albany: State University of New York Press, 1982), 98.

[47]Ibid., 101. Brumbaugh develops the idea that this approach to philosophy is appropriate to education (ibid., 99–108).

[48]Whitehead, *The Aims of Education*, 6.

of experience or narratives rather than with grand theoretical frameworks, and these approaches are important if we are to see the wood by way of the trees.

The heuristic value of theories is that they offer frames of reference that can be suggestive for our work,[49] but they are also limiting insofar as we rely on them to do more than they are capable of doing. In fact, they can even be dangerous because they are inevitably constructed on limited data and limited perspectives on reality. Such theories are often biased toward dominant ethnic groups or social classes, or toward men.

Attention to the ordinary can have two important values in research. First, it can lead researchers to attend to ordinary realities that are often ignored in the construction of social theories, such as the life experiences of the lower classes, women in the private sphere, African-American children, and immigrant youth. In the case of gender and class discrimination, the awareness of existing research biases has led many feminist researchers to give particular attention to ordinary experience in order to take account of life experiences most ignored in existing studies and theories of social reality.[50] A broad body of research literature in theology and education is also growing from studies of cultural and ethnic groups that have been excluded from other studies.[51] In both cases researchers are attending to ordinary realities that have been mostly ignored in social psychology, education, and theology.

---

[49]Elliot W. Eisner, *The Educational Imagination: On the Design and Evaluation of School Programs* (New York: Macmillan, [1979] 1985), 177–79.

[50]Weiler, *Women Teaching for Change*, 60–66; cf. 60–100. See also works studying development in women: Carol Gilligan, *In a Different Voice: Psychological Theory and Women's Development* (Cambridge, Mass.: Harvard University Press, 1982); Mary Field Belenky, Blythe McVicker Clinchy, Nancy Rule Goldberger, and Jill Mattuck Tarule, *Women's Ways of Knowing: The Development of Self, Voice, and Mind* (New York: Basic Books, 1986); Carol Gilligan, Janie Victoria Ward, and Jill McLean Taylor, eds., with Betty Bardige, *Mapping the Moral Domain: A Contribution of Women's Thinking to Psychological Theory and Education* (Cambridge, Mass.: Center for the Study of Gender, Education and Human Development, Harvard University Graduate School of Education, 1988); Lois Weis, ed., *Class, Race and Gender in American Education* (Albany: State University of New York Press, 1988); Alison M. Jaggar and Susan R. Bordo, eds., *Gender/ Body/Knowledge: Feminist Reconstruction of Being and Knowing* (New Brunswick, N.J.: Rutgers University Press, 1989).

[51]To gain a sense of the broad range, consider: Hale-Benson, *Black Children*; Eva Young and Mariwalda Padilla, "Mujeres Unidas en Accion: A Popular Education Process," *Harvard Educational Review* 60 (Feb. 1990): 1–18; Leonardo Boff, O.F.M., *When Theology Listens to the Poor* (San Francisco: Harper & Row, 1988); Ada Maria Isasi-Diaz

A second value in researchers' attending to the ordinary is that the art of education can be observed. An art is an embodied reality that cannot be seen in general. It can be seen only as we develop our powers of perception to see and appreciate the ordinary. This is what Elliot Eisner calls educational criticism, akin to art criticism and connoisseurship: "Effective criticism, within the arts or in education, is not an act independent of the powers of perception. The ability to see, to perceive what is subtle, complex, and important, is its first necessary condition. . . . To be a connoisseur is to know how to look, to see, and to appreciate. Connoisseurship, generally defined, is the art of appreciation."[52] Such connoisseurship requires forms of educational evaluation that go beyond letter grades and standardized test scores, evaluation that captures the fullness of educational practice. Eisner, therefore, draws heavily on anthropological modes of describing, even using nontextual materials such as photography to provide "visual anthropology."[53] This kind of full description of educational practice is an artistic reporting of the educational process, much needed in both religious communities and schools if we are to revere the ordinary.

I have been speaking of educational research that attends to the ordinary; this is relevant to the art of teaching in many ways. It yields data and theories that teach the art of teaching, and it yields modes of evaluating the quality of education. Educational research of this kind can also sharpen our own perceptive abilities so that we might become more able to perceive and appreciate. This quality is vital to the practice of any art, including the art of teaching. One visitor to the artist Georgia O'Keefe observed this artistic attentiveness in O'Keefe: " 'Everything is done with full attention,' Carol marveled, even to the precise way O'Keefe folded a silk scarf or a linen handkerchief. 'She's not thinking of anything else. She's right there folding that napkin. . . . There's something about that woman. It isn't just

---

and Yolanda Tarango, *Hispanic Women: Prophetic Voice in the Church* (San Francisco: Harper & Row, 1988); Brian Holmes and Martin McLean, *The Curriculum: A Comparative Perspective* (London: Unwin Hyman, 1989); Donald Ng, ed., *Asian Pacific American Youth Ministry* (Valley Forge, Pa.: Judson Press, 1988); Sid Smith, *10 Super Sunday Schools in the Black Community* (Nashville: Broadman Press, 1986).

[52]Eisner, *The Educational Imagination*, 219.

[53]Ibid., 208–14. See examples of the anthropological studies, or educational criticism, in Eisner's work (ibid., 253–338).

charisma, and it isn't just personal. I think it's other levels of consciousness.' "[54] The art of attending to the ordinary actually enhances the art of teaching, which itself has to do with revering the ordinary.

In the ordinary folk humor of Robert Fulghum in *All I Really Need to Know I Learned in Kindergarten*, he offers what he calls "uncommon thoughts on common things."[55] This is a way of revering the ordinary. For example, he recalls one of the ordinary rules of kindergarten: "When you go out into the world, watch out for traffic, hold hands and stick together." He ruminates on this and decides that "it is still true no matter how old you are—when you go out into the world, it is best to hold hands and stick together."[56]

Fulghum also includes an essay on the ordinary "Stuff" that collects under beds, bookcases, and dressers. When he investigated the composition of such "Stuff," he learned that it is mostly from people (skin and hair) and meteorites that have disintegrated on entering the earth's atmosphere. He concludes that this ordinary "Stuff" is "mostly me and stardust."[57] And because plants grow in it so well, he gives it another name, "cosmic compost."[58] However flip these stories may sound, they convey a reverence for the ordinary.

One last story on revering the ordinary: Teaching at its best is a relationship, and a relationship at its best gives reverence to the ordinary. This is a poem that I wrote on the first anniversary of my father's death, and it speaks to the ordinary in relationships:

Others Told Me
Others told me what I could not do.
"These are your limits,"
They would say,
"Expect to achieve this,
But not this;
You are really very ordinary."
But you never told me what I could not do.
You expected me to dream dreams
And follow them across the rainbow,

---

[54]Laurie Lisle, *Portrait of an Artist: A Biography of Georgia O'Keefe* (New York: Washington Square, 1980), 429.

[55]Robert Fulghum, *All I Really Need to Know I Learned in Kindergarten* (New York: Villard Books, 1989).

[56]Ibid., 7.

[57]Ibid., 123.

[58]Ibid., 124.

But you never told me
What those dreams would be.
Sure enough, I have dreamed many dreams
And I have followed them
Along paths soft and rocky;
I discover new dreams every day,
And I have also discovered myself.
I really *am* very ordinary,
But I am *extraordinarily* ordinary
Because of you!

This is the gift of a teacher—to revere the ordinary so much that it becomes extraordinarily ordinary.

The art of teaching from the heart is all of these things and more. It is an art that defies description, but invites our participation. The theme of teaching from the heart was originally inspired in me by teachers who have been important in my life. I realize now that their own gifts of teaching from the heart are not gifts that stay in a box. They are gifts of energy that invite response. The energy makes us go run, run, run until we fall down and close our eyes.

INDEX

225

540336